THE CONTEMPLATIVE POETRY OF

Gerard Manley Hopkins

THE CONTEMPLATIVE POETRY OF
Gerard Manley Hopkins

THE
CONTEMPLATIVE
POETRY OF
Gerard Manley
Hopkins

❧

MARIA R. LICHTMANN

PRINCETON UNIVERSITY
PRESS

PR
4803
.H44
Z7116
1989

Publication of this book has been aided by a grant from
the Paul Mellon Fund of Princeton University Press

This book has been composed in Linotron Bembo

Clothbound editions of Princeton University Press
books are printed on acid-free paper, and binding
materials are chosen for strength and durability.
Paperbacks, although satisfactory for personal
collections, are not usually suitable for library
rebinding

Printed in the United States of America by
Princeton University Press
Princeton, New Jersey

Library of Congress Cataloging-in-Publication Data
Lichtmann, Maria R., 1945–
The contemplative poetry of Gerard Manley Hopkins /
Maria R. Lichtmann.
p.   cm.
Bibliography: p.
Includes index.
ISBN 0-691-07345-7 (alk. paper)
1. Hopkins, Gerard Manley, 1844–1889—Criticism and
interpretation. 2. Contemplation in literature. I. Title.
PR4803.H44Z7116 1989
821'.8—dc19   88-39915 CIP

TO THE MEMORY OF MY FATHER,
Carl Lichtmann

Contents

Acknowledgments

M Y INTEREST in the poetry of Gerard Manley Hopkins has grown from my initial bewilderment when I first encountered his poetry as an undergraduate to the much more exacting study required for a doctoral dissertation. As anyone knows who has read Hopkins, the wealth of insights uncovered in his poems, letters, and essays more than repays the hours spent in patient seeking. As poet and thinker, he continues to inspire and delight. Whatever merit this book possesses derives from his genius and from the many interpreters who have shared their insights over the years since Bridges' publication of his poems in 1918.

I would like to thank the professors—Hans Frei, James Kugel, Geoffrey Hartman, Louis Dupré—who worked with me at Yale University in various stages of this project while it was in dissertation form. I would especially like to thank my dissertation advisor, Peter Hawkins, who continually challenged me, as much by his own example as by admonition, to sharpen my prose style and to clarify my ideas.

This project might have remained in dissertation form were it not for the good graces of Father Paul Edwards, S.J., Director of Campion Hall, the Jesuit residence hall at Oxford University, where the unpublished manuscripts of notes and essays made while Hopkins was studying as an undergraduate at Oxford are kept. As a result of examining these notes, I was able to trace connections in Hopkins' thought and to amplify the major themes of parallelism and contemplation in his work. Although not available to the general readership, the unpublished notes are catalogued in Appendix F of *The Journals and Papers of Gerard Manley Hopkins*. All poetry quoted in this text is taken from the fourth edition of *The Poems of Gerard Hopkins*, ed. W. H. Gardner and N. H. Mackenzie (London: Oxford Univ. Press, 1967); reprinted by permission of Oxford University Press on behalf of the Society of Jesus.

Several of my colleagues at Appalachian State University, H. Lawrence Bond, Frans van der Bogert, and Richard Rupp, as well as my sister, Charlene Lichtmann, read this manuscript as it emerged from the chrysalis of the dissertation into its present form, and I am grateful for their comments. The Graduate School of Appalachian State University provided me with an invaluable editorial assistant, Catherine B. Emanuel, and with several typists.

Finally, I am deeply grateful to my daughter, who was nine when the dissertation was begun and is now sixteen, and whose wisdom and grace have in these intervening years far outstripped her mother's other offspring.

Introduction

*I*N THE YEARS since Robert Bridges' publication of the poetry of Gerard Manley Hopkins,[1] scholarship has grown immensely in its understanding of Hopkins' genius. Yet, scholars and students have continued to ask the questions, what major strategy informs Hopkins' oeuvre and how did his own reflections on poetry affect his writing of it? It is obvious both that form meant a great deal to him and that it was never mere form. To provide some answers to these questions I have concentrated on the interplay between form and spirit, between parallelism and contemplation, in Hopkins' poetics and poetry. I examine Hopkins' early essays on poetry and read his own poetry in light of those essays.

A student of Scripture all his life, Hopkins emulated Scripture's predominant form of parallelism as the major strategy of his poetics. For him, parallelism struck deep into the souls of readers and hearers, tapping into preconscious rhythms and bringing about a healing response, one he was to refer to as contemplation. By its very nature, parallelism communicated a kind of religious emotion he was to call "instress."

What I seek to discover is why Hopkins, hailed by many for his modernity, turned to an ancient, perhaps the most ancient,

[1] Robert Bridges, *The Poems of Gerard Manley Hopkins*, 1st ed. (London: Oxford Univ. Press, 1918).

poetic device to define poetry. Why did he choose parallelism as the fundamental principle and controlling device of poetry? The answers to this question will emerge from a study of parallelism in its formal and extraformal functions in Hopkins' poetics as reconstructed from his early essays. In Chapter 1 these essays on poetics are examined in their dialogue with and reaction against literary and aesthetic movements of the nineteenth century. Hopkins' choice of parallelism is viewed as a way of overcoming Romanticism. In Chapter 2 I analyze Part I of Hopkins' *The Wreck of the Deutschland* for its parallelisms of resemblance, and in Chapter 3 the sonnets for their parallelisms of antithesis. Chapter 4 establishes the use of parallelism for contemplation, construing the poetry as primarily contemplative rather than meditative. The book concludes, in Chapter 5, by exploring the subject and practice of contemplation in Hopkins' poetry.

The term "parallelism," as the *Oxford English Dictionary* shows, entered the English language only in the seventeenth century, in the contexts of geometry and astronomy. With the 1778 English translation of the Book of Isaiah by Bishop Robert Lowth, the former Professor of Poetry at Oxford, parallelism acquired its special and perhaps most persistent technical meaning of a correspondence, in sense or in form, of successive clauses in lines or half-lines of poetry. Because of its semantic correspondences, biblical interpreters often refer to parallelism as "thought-rhyme." Hopkins universalized this technical feature of Hebrew poetry by extending it to English poetry and exploiting its congruence between form and meaning. In the parallelism of Hebrew poetry, Hopkins found a way to unite verse's disparate effects so that sound correspondences of alliteration and rhyme work to create correspondences in word meanings. Those correspondences in turn create parallelism of thought in the reader's response to the poem. In Hopkins' unified poetics, parallelism in form engendered parallelisms in diction and in thought.

Because it embodies likeness in form as it communicates likeness in meaning, parallelism exemplifies the incarnational ideal of matter as spirit. As parallelism increases, and as sounds, words, and meanings approach unity while never fully achieving it, poetry becomes less meditative and more contemplative; with parallelism the poem moves away from multiplicity of things toward unity of spirit. Because it joins likeness with unlikeness, parallelism holds in tension what we will call the Heraclitean moment of multiplicity and entropy in the poems, at the same time as it works toward the unity we will call the Parmenidean element. Parallelism in its many forms becomes both the inscape or individuating design and the instress of Hopkins' poems. With its parallelistic inscape, Hopkins' poetics privileged the contemplative response in deliberate reaction to the Romantics' emphasis on reflection and imagination. In conformity with his poetics, Hopkins' poems, written with a kenosis of intellect in their parallelism and simple connectives, invite not meditation but contemplation.

My assumption in this study is that to a mind like Hopkins'—at once poetic, filled with sensuous appreciation of beauty; philosophical, capable of penetrating to that beauty's essence or form; and spiritual, aware that all beauty can be "charged with God"—the parallelism of Hebrew poetry was the perfect statement of the integrity of outward form and inner meaning. In effect parallelism was poetry's "inscape." For, if poetry is *versus*, return, then no other poetic device—not rhyme or alliteration or assonance—re-turns so much of the discourse of poetry as does parallelism. What alliteration and assonance do for phonemes, and what rhyme does for morphemes, parallelism does for syntax. As it tells our intellect of likeness, it embodies that likeness in auditory and visual correspondences, evoking precognitive, almost visceral, responses. Phonetic and semantic correspondences are not confined to a word, as in onomatopoeia, but are sustained over whole clauses or phrases. Because it mimics in form what it suggests in meaning, parallelistic form is, therefore, quintessentially poetic. Through its multivalent achievement of return, parallelism effects a *re-ligio*, a binding back, which is at the same time quintessentially religious.

1

"Exquisite Artifice": Parallelism in Hopkins' Poetics

*H*OPKINS CONTINUALLY turned to parallelism as his point of departure for discussing poetry.[1] As an undergraduate at Oxford (1863–1867), a teacher at John Henry Newman's Edgbaston Oratory (1867–1868), and a Jesuit teacher of rhetoric at the Roehampton Novitiate (1873–1874), he explicitly invoked parallelism in constructing his poetics. Sprung rhythm, the prosodic innovation Hopkins singled out in what Bridges titled the "Author's Preface,"[2] does not exhaust his poetics, as his essays and notes, written over a ten-year span, attest. In light of these essays, we must come to see chiming, alliteration, assonance, and sprung rhythm as aspects of a larger, more inclusive phenomenon, the phenomenon of parallelism.

Hopkins wrote his undergraduate essays in the Oxford of the 1860s, a climate predominantly Romantic in its views of art and religion. Wordsworth and Coleridge in poetry, New-

---

[1] See especially "On the Signs of Health and Decay in the Arts," "Poetic Diction," and "On the Origin of Beauty: A Platonic Dialogue," in *The Journals and Papers of Gerard Manley Hopkins*, ed. Humphry House (London: Oxford Univ. Press, 1959).

[2] In *The Poems of Gerard Manley Hopkins*, ed. W. H. Gardner and N. H. Mackenzie, 4th ed. (London: Oxford Univ. Press, 1967), pp. 45–49.

man in religion, had contributed to a synthesis whose chief values were subjectivity and emotion. Yet Hopkins, though barely twenty, rather than being swayed by the Romantic synthesis, sought to overcome its "atomism" and "suggestiveness" by a turn to form. Parallelism, the form he chose as generic, displayed for him both order and disorder, symmetry and asymmetry, sameness and difference. Hopkins first found parallelism in nature, as many of his journal entries witness.[3] Parallelism therefore described to him not only the spontaneity of the human heart, which the Romantics had found in the parallelistic language of the biblical prophets, but the very wildness and fecundity of a nature that *yet* rhymed. For Hopkins, parallelism mimed reality even more than it expressed the self.

PARALLELISM AS INSCAPE

The word "parallelism" appears in three of Hopkins' undergraduate essays[4] before his first recorded use of the much debated word peculiar to his vocabulary—*inscape*. Parallelism operates in these early essays in much the same way as inscape operates later on. That is, parallelism is the inscape of poetry, its distinguishing mark or pattern. With its tendency to repeat, parallelism works toward an ontological integration of the poem, making for unity with regard to both space and time. The key word here is *unity*, perhaps the first word of Hopkins' poetic creed, but one that remains largely unspoken within the poetic corpus. This fundamental need for unity we will identify as the "Parmenidean" element of Hopkins' poetics, concentrating on his Parmenides essay to supply this most inchoate moment. The Parmenidean element exists in tension with an entropic "Heraclitean" one. That is to say, Hopkins' original intuition of unity suffers breakdown at the hands of

---

[3] See *Journals*, pp. 53, 66, 138, 139, 143.
[4] See n. 1.

the disintegrating variety and individuality of reality. It is this Heraclitean element that accounts for the strong emphasis in Hopkins' works on antithesis, difference, and variety. Inscape in Hopkins' theory of poetry is thus a composite of polarities—of order and disorder, symmetry and asymmetry, absolutes and wildness—written into the very structure of poetry. Yet we must remember that neither the Parmenidean nor the Heraclitean element wins a final victory over the poem, nor is the tension between them resolved *in* the poem; they are left to collide until the reader's contemplative response restores the unity without denying the diversity.

Hopkins' intuitive need for unity is nowhere more explicitly worked out than in his essay on Parmenides, probably written in 1868 while he was teaching at Newman's Oratory.[5] Parmenides was the pre-Socratic philosopher who asserted that "Only Being is" and that "Being and thought are the same"; in so doing he made true being the equivalent of higher logic and reason. In his formula, ἔστι τὸ ἔιναι, "Being and thought are the same," we get a happy, if naive, statement of the coincidence of logos and reality, and of the power of human reason to penetrate reality. His statement, challenged by Plato, finally succumbed in the wake of Kantian agnosticism. Nevertheless, in spite of Kant, some such statement of faith or idealism is necessary if the poetic enterprise is not to founder in subjectivity. The poetic creed of the idealist become realist, and Hopkins was certainly such a realist, is that "I can know the world."

Parmenides' monistic philosophy of undifferentiation, however, intolerant of division, change, or contradiction, seems a curious philosophical counterpart to Hopkins' emphatically differentiated view of reality. Yet it is evident throughout Hopkins' essay that he is in sympathy with this basically mystical vision of the oneness of all. Commenting

---

[5] It has been settled among scholars that Hopkins did in fact return to teaching at the Oratory after Christmas 1868, and left at his Easter retreat.

on Parmenides' *things are* or *there is truth*, he says, "But indeed I have often felt when I have been in this mood and felt the depth of an instress or how fast the inscape holds a thing that nothing is so pregnant and straightforward to the truth as simple *yes* and *is*."[6] Nowhere is the coincidence between Being and thought more true, the truth of Being more apparent in language, or the conception of Being more idealized, shorn of its involvement in nonbeing or appearance, than in "simple *yes* and *is*."

Hopkins is inspired by Parmenides' affirmation of *what is* to make his first formulation of the peculiar notions "inscape" and "instress." Inscape, here described as a "stem of stress between us and things to bear us out and carry the mind over,"[7] an *ecs-stasis*, is his ontology of an outward form of inward beauty,[8] and instress is his epistemology. Both coincide in the poetic act of saying "simple *yes* and *is*." Hopkins, not submitting to the subjectivity either of Kant or of the Romantics, insists that in being borne out and carried over, in *ecs-stasis*, we can know. Moreover, what we know and acknowledge is Being. "The truth in thought," he says, "is Being, stress, and each word is one way of acknowledging Being and each sentence by its copula *is* (or its equivalent) the utterance and assertion of it" (*Journals*, p. 129). The phrase "utterance and assertion of [Being]" contains a rich ambiguity, one that results in a double reading: both we and Being are the utterers of Being. Breaking somewhat with Parmenides' hubristic view that the subject or knower can ascend to the possession of truth, Hopkins adds, "Perhaps it would be better referred to the object and Parmenides will say that the mind's grasp— νοεῖν, the foredrawing act— . . . is to be looked for in Being, the foredrawn, alone, not in the thing named blood or the blood we worded as being red." Being, anterior to the mind,

---

[6] *Journals*, p. 127.

[7] Ibid.

[8] See *Further Letters of Gerard Manley Hopkins*, ed. Claude Colleer Abbott, 2d ed. (London: Oxford Univ. Press, 1956), pp. 306–307.

is the true subject of knowing; we are grasped by Being in each act of knowing.

This reference to the object, Being, is fundamental to Hopkins' epistemology, to his poetics, and to his revision of Wordsworth's poetics, as we shall see in the second part of this chapter. As in Parmenides, the mind's grasp surpasses the naming of common language and the things of commonsense experience to get to Being itself. The direction Hopkins indicates is distinctly objective and other-centered. For him, as for the mystics, it is more true to say that Being first and foremost is knowing than to say that knowing, mounting the rungs of the ladder of logic, is Being. Thus, the mind's act is to be self-alienated, to be distanced from itself and foredrawn to Being, and the necessary condition for establishing Being's priority is a kenosis or self-emptying.

This priority of ontology over epistemology sharply differentiates Hopkins both from his Romantic predecessors and from the structuralists who now claim him. Without the stress that carries us over to Being, "not only universals would not be true but the copula would break down even in particular judgements" (*Journals*, p. 127). Hopkins is thus no nominalist or atomist: universals and the ability to relate them must remain. His Parmenidean belief in the unity of being and knowing closes the gap between universal and particular and between the ideal and the real. Without such unity, all would be atomistic, relative but unrelated. In other Oxford notes, he states that the common element in sophistry and philistinism "is the denying all objectivity to truth and to metaphysics. This denial destroys earnestness in life" (Unpublished Oxford Notes, D8; catalogued in *Journals*, Appendix F). Hopkins' own earnestness with reality prevented such a sophistic, solipsistic denial.

In another essay, "The Probable Future of Metaphysics," Hopkins points to the loss of unity as a "form of atomism" that hangs on the age when a philosophy of continuity such as Hegel's predominates (*Journals*, p. 120). He seems to be combating not only Hegel but the relativism introduced by Darwin only a few years earlier. Science, he says, would be "scopeless," that is, "atomic, not to be grasped and held together—without metaphysics." This scoping, or holding together, clearly a variant of inscape, is accomplished by the "simple *yes* and *is*," the copula that dares unity between things and the "yes" that affirms relation between ourselves and things.

Hopkins expresses the need for unity in art in his essay, "The Origin of Our Moral Ideas": "All thought," he says, "is of course an *effort at unity*" (*Journals*, p. 83; the underlinings were probably supplied by the essay's reader, Walter Pater). He continues, "In art it is essential to recognize and strive to realize on a more or less wide basis this unity in some shape or other." But art tolerates and realizes not only "unity, permanence of law, likeness, but also, with it, difference, variety, contrast: it is rhyme we like, not echo, and not unison but harmony" (*Journals*, p. 83). Rhyme in Hopkins' view encompasses contrast and is not a mere matter of sameness. "Healthy art," he tells us elsewhere, "is always breaking from [its first attained idealisms], forming new ones, and then again advancing" (Unpublished Oxford Essays, D1). Encountering the real, art's idealism must break down to be won anew within the real. Hopkins' insistence on unity and variety is a statement of what we have been calling the Parmenidean and Heraclitean elements of his poetics. He is willing to risk the submersion of his idealisms in the real, for only there do they become incarnated.

In the same essay, Hopkins draws a distinction between unity as an ideal in art and unity as an ideal in morality. Whereas art tolerates difference, in morality only the "highest consistency" is the highest excellence. The reason for morality's consistency is that "the desire of unity is prior to that of difference" (*Journals*, p. 83). Why, Hopkins asks, do we desire unity? "The first answer," he says, "would be that the ideal, the one, is our only means of recognizing successfully our being to ourselves, it unifies us, while vice destroys the sense of being by dissipating thought" (*Journals*, p. 83). The ideal, the one, wherever it is recovered, because it enables us to recognize our true being, leads to the unity of "know thyself." This ethic of self-unification becomes for Hopkins a major goal of his contemplative experience; in the contemplative act, scattered energies are drawn back to Being and to recovery of oneself in Being. Again, being becomes knowing, as in the contemplative tradition. The moral ideal of a oneness of self overcoming a divided, dissipated self is what Hopkins will call in a letter to Bridges that "chastity of mind" that Christ possessed.[9] Paradoxically, this chastened, unified self is the precondition for the discovery of otherness and difference.

Hopkins was not alone in seeing the need for unity arise in a person's life. At about the time he wrote this essay, Pater, his tutor at Oxford, was writing an essay called "Diaphaneité" in which he quotes the *Imitatio Christi's* "Sibi unitus et simplificatus esse" to illustrate that transparency of character that is "a kind of moral expressiveness."[10] For Pater, unity of self is self-simplification. Further, says Pater, the diaphanous spirit's simplicity is a condition of true seeing, because it "lets through unconsciously all that is really lifegiving in the established order of things." For Pater and Hopkins, the Parmenidean unity achieved in the self lets through and lets be the Heraclitean riot of life, a contemplative response to the world.

In Hopkins, although unity precedes difference as an ontological fact, it is also an activity at work unifying us wherever we discover it as the ideal. In essays written for his tutor, Pater, Hopkins says of Plato that "His aim in all he says about

---

[9] *The Letters of Gerard Manley Hopkins to Robert Bridges*, ed. Claude Colleer Abbott (London: Oxford Univ. Press, 1935), p. 174.

[10] Walter Pater, *Miscellaneous Studies* (London: Macmillan and Co., 1901), p. 249. Pater's statement that "It is just this sort of entire transparency of character that lets through unconsciously all that is really lifegiving in the established order of things" could be taken as prophetic of Hopkins' character and way of seeing the world.

education is to preserve unity in the distracting multiplicity of life" and that "every quickening of the sense of unity will act on morals" ("Plato's view of the connection of art and education," Unpublished Oxford Essays, D3). Hopkins' inscape, whether in nature or art, is unity of being, which, rather than being a static ideal, becomes alive and active, instressing us. Every poem, then, instresses us toward greater unity of being.

Hopkins focuses again on an originating unity in laying out the tenets of a "New Realism," a mixture of Platonism and Realism that he proposes to oppose a Hegelian philosophy of flux. Countering Hegel's principle that knowledge is a "history of growth and mounts from the part to the whole," the New Realism maintains that the Idea is given only "from the whole downwards to the parts" (*Journals*, p. 120). The consequences of such a patently idealist notion may seem remote from Hopkins' actual poetic practice. Clearly, his is not a poetry of abstract ideals aerially presiding over their particulars. But another reference to unity provides the clue to his actual practice. In notes written in Birmingham in 1868, just preceding the "Parmenides" essay, Hopkins writes of capturing the unity of the whole: "It is however true that in the successive arts . . . the whole's unity retires, is less important, serves rather for the framework of that of the parts" (*Journals*, p. 126).

What we have, then, as we shall see in Hopkins' actual poetry, is a reticent, retiring unity, one that has retired to the framework of the poem rather than being foregrounded in it. That "framework" is actually made up of Hopkins' original Parmenidean intuition of unity and the reader's contemplative recovery of that unity. According to these notes, the word has three moments: its prepossession, its definition, and its application; so too does the poem. And its "prepossession," that which flushes it with enthusiasm, is the same as its application, that which enables us to recognize our being, that which unifies us. Prepossession, Hopkins tells us, bears a "valuable analogy to the soul" (*Journals*, p. 125). Both the prepossession by the poet and the application by the reader (what Hopkins would come to call the poem's "bidding") are part of that framework of retiring unity. The poem is the actual definition and the passage from the poet's soul to the reader's.

Parallelism within the poem serves Hopkins' need for unity by providing pointers to it. In its capacity to create likeness, symmetry, and law, parallelism provides nodes of the absolute. An elaborate musical analogy expresses this belief that where likeness and harmony recur, there is the absolute:

> The new Realism will maintain that in musical strings the roots of chords, to use technical wording, are mathematically fixed and give a standard by which to fix all the notes of the appropriate scale: when points between these are sounded the ear is annoyed by a solecism, or to analyse deeper, the mind cannot grasp the notes of the scale and the intermediate sound in one conception; so also there are certain forms which have a great hold on the mind and are always reappearing and seem imperishable . . . and some pictures we may long look at and never grasp or hold together, while the composition of others strikes the mind with a conception of unity which is never dislodged: and these things are inexplicable on the theory of pure chromatism or continuity—the forms have in some sense or other an absolute existence. (*Journals*, p. 120)

Hopkins marshals both musical and visual analogies to support his belief in a realism with absolutes. It is characteristic of him to make what seems at first a mere sense-reaction ("the ear is annoyed by a solecism") into an intellectual experience as well ("the mind cannot grasp the notes of the scale"). Much of his notion of parallelism, with its joining of sound, grammar, and thought, operates on this correspondence between the sensuous and the spiritual. Those forms that have a great hold on the mind, striking it with the conception of unity, intimate the presence of the ideal amid the real. Hopkins' ear-

nestness with reality does not discount the ideal of unity. This
essay makes therefore a philosophical statement of what Hop-
kins discusses in his essays on poetics under the generic term
parallelism. His Platonic realism could be considered a kind of
Aristotelianism, where the forms, instead of having a merely
ideal, other-worldly existence, become the essences of things.
One difference from Aristotle, however, is that these forms
result from harmonic relations or proportions, in effect from
parallelisms.

In the discussion of parallelism that is at the center of three
undergraduate essays written at Oxford, Hopkins shows that
it serves not only the need for unity, the Parmenidean moment
of his poetics, but also the Heraclitean moment, the need for
multiplicity, variety, and contrast. Whereas the Parmenidean
side of Hopkins illustrates his attraction to the ideal of unity
in his "New Realism," the Heraclitean side illustrates his faith-
fulness to reality in its concreteness. A touchstone of the high-
est art, he told Bridges, is "the being in earnest with your sub-
ject—reality."[11] Moreover, the worst fault a thing can have is
unreality.[12] To another correspondent, Coventry Patmore,
Hopkins commented on the lack of reality in a poem given
him by the young man, William Butler Yeats: "it was a
strained and unworkable allegory about a young man and a
sphinx on a rock in the sea (how did they get there? what did
they eat? and so on: people think such criticisms very prosaic;
but commonsense is never out of place anywhere, neither on
Parnassus nor on Tabor nor on the Mount where Our Lord
preached)."[13] The historical-literal level, in Greek myth as well
as in the New Testament, cannot be excised for the allegori-
cal-symbolical meaning to rise victorious from it. Hopkins'
incarnational, sacramental aesthetic proclaims that the ex-

---

[11] *Letters to Bridges*, p. 225.

[12] Ibid., p. 216. Hopkins allowed, however, three kinds of departure from
truth: changes in history, fiction, and allegory.

[13] *Further Letters*, p. 374.

traordinary can be found only *in* the ordinary, the ideal in the real.

Although Hopkins did not devote an essay to the thought of the pre-Socratic philosopher, Heraclitus, he referred to him often in the Oxford notes, and explicit references to him within his poetry justify my emphasis. Remarks on Heraclitus, who seemed to exercise a fascination for Hopkins, can be found throughout the unpublished notes and essays from Oxford. In an essay raising the question "How far may a common tendency be traced in all pre-Socratic philosophy?" after briefly discussing the contributions of the Ionian and Eleatic schools, Hopkins devotes a lengthier section to Heraclitus: "But the logical assurance of the Eleatics itself was balanced by Heraclitus, whose teaching about flux is the reaction against the supremacy of principles established by reason, and substitutes for the immovable spherical one or whole of Xenophanes the sole unity of variety, the certainty of change" (Unpublished Oxford Essays, D6).

Perhaps Heraclitus' "reaction against the supremacy of principles established by reason," his countering the anthropocentrism of the Eleatics like Parmenides, accounts for Hopkins' fascination with him. Hopkins singles him out again in attesting: "Heraclitus, who felt beyond any of his predecessors the chaos, uncertainty, and illusion of all things, spoke nevertheless of a rhythm, something imposed by mind as an air on the notes of a flute" ("The Connection of Mythology and Philosophy," Unpublished Oxford Essays, D6). Hopkins' sympathy with Heraclitus is of course evident in his poetry. "That Nature is a Heraclitean Fire" offers an explicit poetic reference, but the cosmic bonfire also burns in "God's Grandeur," another testimony to the Heraclitean vision of the world as eternal fire. In his emphasis on the unique particularity of things (the *haecceitas* in Scotist terms), on antithesis, and on surprise, Hopkins is Heraclitean. As Heraclitus put it, men in earnest with reality must discard formal logic and mental models and "acquaint themselves with a great many particulars."[14] Hopkins was such a man.

Anyone familiar with Hopkins' journal can say that he does indeed acquaint himself with particulars and that it is knowledge by experience rather than by inference. The manifold of the world is taken seriously. His method, as he put it in a letter of 1863, is that of "passing through stage after stage, at last arriving at Nature's self."[15] But, of course, the problem for one stripping himself of universals to confront the particulars is not to be overwhelmed by their multitudinousness, or, in Hopkins' words, their "scopelessness" or "atomism."[16] Parmenides solved this problem by equating the one and the many. Even Heraclitus was able to perceive a logos in the ceaseless flow of the universe.

In fact, it is the case with Hopkins that patient attention to the particulars in nature does yield a sense of their inner law, what he calls their inscape. And, often, this inscape is expressed in terms of a parallelism. In his early diaries, he notes, "Shapes of frozen snow-drifts. Parallel ribs. Delightful curves" (*Journals*, p. 53), and "Clouds showing beautiful and rare curves like curds, comparable to barrows, arranged of course in parallels" (*Journals*, p. 66). Clouds are found to be "wonderfully symmetrical," traced in "fine horizontals" (ibid.) and in "two parallel spines" (*Journals*, p. 138). Waves are discerned as "Parallel straight lap-waves" (*Journals*, p. 139). Even faces in a crowd yield a "visible law," a sort of beauty that is "synonymous with finding order, anywhere" (ibid.). Not only external form but the keeping of the moral law is seen this way, as when he says, "supposing all mankind acted on the categorical imperative they w[oul]d all be acting,

---

[14] Heraclitus, Fragment 3, *The Presocratics*, ed. Philip Wheelwright (New York: Odyssey Press, 1966).

[15] *Further Letters*, p. 201.

[16] Geoffrey Hartman addresses this problem in his study of Hopkins in *The Unmediated Vision* (New York: Harcourt, Brace, and World, 1966), pp. 49–67.

as we might compare it, in parallels, and this w[oul]d give the look of acting by strict law" ("The Autonomy of the Will," Unpublished Oxford Essays, D10). Examples could be multiplied,[17] but by now it should be clear that it is parallelism that Hopkins sees whenever the laws of being disclose themselves within the manifold. His realism with a vengeance wins through to idealism on the other side. Insofar as it was possible, then, Hopkins effaced the ideal but found it again in the real.

With regard to the "anxiety of influence," while Hopkins' tendency was, as he said, "to admire and do otherwise,"[18] recent critics are beginning to appreciate the influence on him of one who in many ways formulated the aesthetics and sat in judgment over the art of the nineteenth century—John Ruskin. Like Pater, Ruskin taught Hopkins to see innocently or purely, as Hopkins himself stated in an undergraduate essay.[19] Ruskin could also have taught Hopkins to find pattern in leaves, clouds, and other phenomena of nature. Hopkins' notion of inscape resembles Ruskin's own explorations of definitive form in *Modern Painters*. Ruskin declared in the preface to the first volume of that five-volume study: "There is an ideal form of every herb, flower and tree, it is that form to which every individual of the species has a tendency to arrive, freed from the influence of accident or disease."[20] Only by long attention to the mass of various beauty, however, is "the con-

[17] For example, "Lawn shews half-circle curves of the scythe in parallel ranks," *Journals*, p. 143.

[18] *Letters to Bridges*, p. 291.

[19] "On the Signs of Health and Decay in the Arts," *Journals*, p. 77: the eye must be "trained to look severely at things apart from their associations, *innocently* or *purely* as painters say. . . ."

[20] John Ruskin, preface to 2d ed. *Modern Painters*, 5 vols. (London: Smith, Elder, and Co., 1873; originally published, 1843), 1:xxv. D'Arcy W. Thompson in his 1914 study, *On Growth and Form*, 2 vols. (London: Cambridge Univ. Press, 1952) and Peter Stevens in *Patterns in Nature* (Boston: Little, Brown, and Co., 1974) explore, like Ruskin, the ideal, and even mathematical, forms of living things.

ception of the constant character—the ideal form" fixed.[21] Ruskin's third volume of *Modern Painters* contains detailed drawings of leaf patterns, including the star-like arrangement of the horse chestnut leaf,[22] a leaf that forms the basis of Hopkins' discussion of parallelism and symmetry in his essay, "On the Origin of Beauty."

Beyond Ruskin's influence on Hopkins' conception of ideal form, however, is the more pervasive influence of Ruskin's entire theological aesthetics. Ruskin endeavored to show art's true beauty as a reflection of and participation in each of the divine attributes. For example, repose in art is the type of divine permanence, symmetry the type of divine justice, and unity that of divine comprehensiveness. In this last conception of a unity inclusive of variety rather than mere singleness or oneness,[23] Ruskin inspired Hopkins' pluralistic notions of unity. Ultimately, such notions derive from Plato who, in turn influenced by the Pythagoreans, spoke in the *Timaeus* of proportion as best adapted to effect union and of the body of the world as "harmonized by proportion."[24]

Accordingly, for Hopkins the way back to unity from Heraclitean flux is the discovery of proportion and harmony through comparison. Atomism, in a world of apparent entropy, is overcome by comparison.[25] In his 1864 essay, "On

[21] Ruskin, *Modern Painters*, 1:54.

[22] Ibid., 3:211.

[23] Ibid., 2:48–50.

[24] Plato, *Timaeus*, 31c, trans. Benjamin Jowett; *The Complete Dialogues of Plato*, ed. Edith Hamilton and Huntington Cairns (Princeton: Princeton Univ. Press, 1980), pp. 1163–1164. It is important to note that we are using the translation of Hopkins' tutor, Benjamin Jowett, and the emphasis on proportion in these passages was not lost on Hopkins. In fact, in one place in the *Journals* Hopkins records that Jowett "held forth about proportion" (p. 136).

[25] As Hermann Lotze said, through words like "color" and "tone" "we instruct our consciousness to represent and compare the particular, perceptible tones and colors, and in this comparison to apprehend the common factor which, as our sensation tells us, is contained in them. . . ." *Logik*, 2d ed. (Leipzig: Hirzel, 1880), pp. 29ff.

the Signs of Health and Decay in the Arts," Hopkins states that the cause of our sense of beauty is "comparison, the apprehension of the presence of more than one thing, and that it is inseparable in a higher or lower degree from thought" (*Journals*, p. 74).[26] Even in this early work, Hopkins is announcing a program of an aesthetics working in conjunction with metaphysics that he will follow consistently in his later critical remarks and especially in his poetry. Art is never mere *aesthesis* or sensation; its beauty is symptom or signal of truth. Again, being and knowing are one.

In this essay, Hopkins outlines four degrees of comparison, each of which is subsumed in the one above it:

(i)   of existence with non-existence;

(ii) of a thing with itself so as to see in it the continuance of law . . . ; instances of this kind are a straight line or a circle;

(iii) of two or more things together, so as to include the principles of Dualism, Plurality, Repetition, Parallelism, and Variety, Contrast, Antithesis;

(iv) of finite with infinite things, which can only be done by suggestion; this is the ἀρχή of the Suggestive, the Picturesque and the Sublime. (*Journals*, p. 74)

We might infer that a philosopher like Parmenides was engaged in the first of these degrees of comparison and that a scientist might employ the second degree. For Hopkins states that art is concerned only with the third and fourth degree and, further, that "the pleasure given by the presence of Truth in Art" occurs only in the third degree, the comparison of two or more things together. Significantly, the fourth degree, comparison with the infinite, does not give this kind of plea-

---

[26] Plato, in his *Timaeus*, 37a, *Complete Dialogues*, p. 1166, had said much the same thing (in perhaps more rapturous language): "the soul, when touching anything which has being, whether dispersed in parts or undivided, is stirred through all her powers to declare the sameness or difference of that thing and some other, and to what individuals are related. . . ."

sure. Hopkins' aesthetic is to be thoroughly this-worldly and incarnated. It is also interesting to notice that in the expression, "the *pleasure* given by the presence of *Truth* in Art," Hopkins has managed to combine what were dichotomized in Kantian-Coleridgean aesthetics. From that aesthetics, where art's purpose is pure pleasure, an art for art's sake can be born, but Hopkins' aesthetics prevents that. The kind of pleasure it proposes is actually holistic, beginning with the senses but eventually involving the whole being, even the soul, as pleasure becomes the awe or astonishment of instress.

For Hopkins, however, even an art of comparison can fail by falling into a "monotony or extravagance," the result of which is pain. While both strict regularity and total randomness fall outside the range of the beautiful or pleasurable, the middle range where neither monotony nor extravagance prevails is proportion. In the art of proportion the smaller is to the larger as the larger is to the whole, expressing the Greek ideal of the golden mean or golden section.[27] Hopkins sees the golden mean proportion as a state in which "comparison, contrast, the enforcement of likeness, is just and pleasurable" (*Journals*, p. 75). Later, he would see the sonnet form in terms of the golden mean; this intuitive-scientific notion stands behind many of his theories in drawing, poetry, and music.

In his insistence that "Science need not interfere with genius," and in his privileging of the third degree of comparison over the fourth degree of suggestiveness and sublimity, Hopkins is consciously adopting an anti-Romantic criticism of art, whose implications will become clearer in this and succeeding chapters. To understand Hopkins' rejection of the sublime in the fourth degree of comparison, we can consider Hegel's definition of the sublime as that in which "the relation of the Idea to objective reality becomes a *negative* one."[28] As realist, Hop-

---

[27] I owe this explanation to conversations with Kevin Hylton, a Scholar of the House at Yale Univ. in 1982.

[28] Hegel, *Lectures on Aesthetics*, in *On Art, Religion, Philosophy*, ed. J. Glenn

kins could not countenance the negation of reality for the ex-
altation of the Idea. The problem with the early Greek philos-
ophers, he said in notes for Pater, is that "they argued on the
Idea alone, on the thought in its first blush, unrealised"
("Notes on the History of Greek Philosophy," Unpublished
Oxford Notes, D12). Since Hopkins could find the Idea only
in and through the real, only an embodied, fully material art
would do. His more sacramental view of art resulted in his
concern both for the palpability of words and for the material
structure of poetry.

Hopkins' 1864 essay, "On the Signs of Health and Decay in
the Arts," sheds further light on the views he held of parallel-
ism and proportion in art, particularly in lyrical poetry. It de-
scribes two kinds of proportion, one by interval, where the
division is abrupt, parallelistic, "intervallary" (at intervals),
and quantitative; and one by continuance, where it is gradual,
continuous, chromatic, and qualitative. "The beauty of an in-
finite curve is chromatic, of a system of curves parallelistic,"
he says. Perhaps because our experience is of systems of curves
rather than of an infinite curve, Hopkins shows clear prefer-
ence for the parallelistic over the chromatic kind of propor-
tion. This preference probably owes something to his oppo-
sition to a philosophy of flux, without absolutes or forms, in
his philosophical essays. A chromatic beauty reflects a philos-
ophy like Hegel's, a philosophy of flux that Hopkins says can
only call forth a philosophy of Platonism in response (*Jour-
nals*, p. 120). In light of Hopkins' classification of drama's dic-
tion as chromatic and lyrical poetry's as parallelistic, we begin
to understand why Bridges' application of a "continuous lit-
erary decorum" in his introduction to the 1918 edition of
Hopkins' poetry was so inappropriate to what Hopkins him-
self intended. Rather than "chromatism" or continuity, Hop-
kins wanted an emphatic, concentrated diction—abrupt and

Gray, trans. Bernard Bosanquet (New York: Harper Torchbooks, 1970), p.
111.

parallelistic—unlike that of the Romantics and Victorians. This desire for an exceptional diction for poetry becomes increasingly evident in the undergraduate essays that follow.

Hopkins' 1865 essay, "On the Origin of Beauty: A Platonic Dialogue," probably written for presentation at the newly formed Hexameron Club (formed to promote Catholic doctrine),[29] presents a thoroughgoing aesthetics, organized largely under the rubric of parallelism. This essay is a lively, entertaining dialogue between a professor of aesthetics "whose lectures had been unattended during the term" (Pater?) and a young scholar of the college, no doubt a surrogate for Hopkins himself. Hopkins' young scholar, Hanbury, wants to overturn a subjectivist aesthetic of taste by means of a more "judicial," scientific system. Starting with the fan of the chestnut, Hanbury and the Professor conclude that "the beauty of the oak and the chestnut-fan and the sky is a mixture of likeness and difference or agreement and disagreement or consistency and variety or symmetry and change" (*Journals*, p. 90). Taking his point of departure from nature, as was his wont, Hopkins finds a union of opposites like that of Being and Non-Being in his "Parmenides," a union that here as throughout his work belongs to his concepts of parallelism and of inscape. Avoiding both strict regularity and lawless irregularity, Hopkins gives us a notion of beauty much like Schiller's "triumphant form [which] rests equidistant from uniformity and confusion."[30]

Though Hanbury has asked for a "judicial" aesthetics, one grounded in scientific principles, it is he who proves himself a Romantic in this essay. The Professor must counter Han-

[29] The object of this club, organized by H. P. Liddon and composed of "the abler undergraduates" whom he knew, was to "promote discussions upon subjects of interest so far as may be consistent with adherence to the doctrines of the Catholic Faith." Liddon Papers, quoted in Notes to Early Diaries, *Journals*, p. 328.

[30] Friedrich Schiller, *On the Aesthetic Education of Man*, trans. Reginald Snell (New York: Frederick Ungar, 1965), p. 34.

bury's notion of beauty as "something mystical," a unity of spirit, by recourse to a structural unity in art. (If Hanbury does represent Hopkins himself, we can only speculate, judging from the somewhat mystical poems like "Heaven-Haven" that Hopkins was writing at about this time, that this was a tendency he was tempering in himself.) Calling attention to parallelism as the distinguishing feature of Hebrew poetry, Hopkins' Professor makes it the common principle of metaphor and simile, comparisons for likeness' sake, as well as antithesis and contrast, comparisons for unlikeness' sake. Parallelism, because it causes metaphor, simile, and antitheses in poetry, is, as in Hebrew poetry, a primitive poetic form. Rhythm, the regular repetition of a sequence of syllables; meter, the repetition of regular sequence of rhythm; rhyme, an agreement of sound coupled with disagreement of sense; alliteration and assonance—all the structural properties of verse that may be seen to mingle likeness and unlikeness—are species of parallelisms. With the use of parallelism as the generic term, thanks to Bishop Robert Lowth's division of it into synonymous and antithetical parallelisms, Hopkins can encompass the negative in the ontology of the poem. Both metaphor, simile, and antithesis—the thought comparisons—as well as rhythm, rhyme, and alliteration—the sound comparisons—offer the coincidence of difference with likeness.[31]

Hopkins' preference for parallelistic over chromatic beauty may stem in part from his unwillingness to see the world strictly in terms of an undifferentiated, mystical agreement. Of course, the very notion that antitheses are also somehow "parallelisms" presupposes what we would call a paradox, the view that sheer opposition is bound into a higher unity. Even though Hopkins once commented that Patmore's delight in

---

[31] In a recent issue of *Hopkins Quarterly*, Leonard Cochran points out that Hopkins' preference for dappled imagery stems from his principle of unity of difference, which in his poetics is the principle of parallelism. "A World of Difference(s): Images of Instress in Hopkins' Poetry," *Hopkins Quarterly* 12 (October 1985–January 1986): 94–96.

paradox did not rest the mind,[32] and even though Hopkins did not cultivate paradox, he nonetheless did make *antithesis* a principle of his theology as well as of his aesthetic. Heraclitus, whose emphasis was on the opposition that brings concord, had preceded him in this; in Fragment 117, Heraclitus had said, "People do not understand how that which is at variance with itself agrees with itself. There is a harmony in the bending back, as in the case of the bow and the lyre."[33] Hopkins, straining to the point of antithesis in life as in art, did understand the harmony hidden in discord, although he could not always achieve it. In Chapter 3 of this study I look at the role of antithesis in Hopkins' thinking and poetry. To those who might assert that Hopkins' emphasis on proportion was no more than a renewed classicism, it should be pointed out that in Heraclitean fashion he prescribed that "Recovery [in art] must be by a breaking up, a violence" (*Journals*, p. 79).

Like Coleridge and other literary critics of his day, Hopkins is concerned to distinguish verse from prose, and he does so by means of parallelism. Parallelism, the intermittent, diatonic comparison, is verse's distinguishing mark: verse is "a continuous structural parallelism, ranging from the technically so-called parallelism of the Psalms to the intricate structure of Greek or Italian or English verse" (*Journals*, p. 108).[34] Parallelism, says Hopkins' Professor, is so universal a phenomenon that its existence can be illustrated even in English poetry. In fact, lyrical poetry lives in parallelisms, which "increase in number and distinctness with the rise of passion" (*Journals*, p. 109). This reference to passion at the origin of parallelistic utterance, so foreign to Hopkins' "judicial" aesthetics, is once again Bishop Lowth's legacy. Ultimately derived

---

[32] *The Correspondence of Gerard Manley Hopkins and Richard Watson Dixon*, ed. Claude Colleer Abbott (London: Oxford Univ. Press, 1935), p. 63.

[33] Heraclitus, Fragment 117, *The Presocratics*. Cf. also Fragments 116 and 98.

[34] On parallelism's presence in English poetry, Hopkins remarked in this essay, "I think it will surprise anyone when first pointed out."

from Longinus, this sort of passion is assimilated in Lowth to an *elevatio mentis*, a self-alienation and *ecs-stasis* that could have provided Hopkins with an almost anti-Romantic emotion at the origin of poetry, one closer to what his tutor, Pater, calls "biblical awe."[35] Indeed, in his letters, Hopkins uses the terms "passion" and "astonishment" interchangeably, and therefore we may be justified in seeing the birth of the poem in an elevated passion or "astonishment." He refers to this originating emotion as the poet's "flush" or "prepossession," and we will see by the end of this chapter that the poet re-creates and transfers that astonishment to the reader in the poem's surprises.

To illustrate the presence of parallelism in English poetry, Hopkins' Professor chooses the lines from Shelley: "—thy thoughts, when thou art gone, / Love itself shall slumber on." In these lines, the Professor finds the idea of the place of memory in love shaped as an antithesis, "thy thoughts" contrasted with the absence of the lover in "when thou art gone." He believes the idea probably rose in just this form of expression, "thought and expression indistinguishable." Again, we can see how important the embodiment of the idea in material form is for Hopkins; material form is not secondary but is given with the thought. Shelley's poem, he continues, consists of a system of parallelisms, whose antitheses are not merely necessary to their intelligibility but are "part of the substance of their beauty besides." Hopkins is concerned here to give a less rationalistic account of the effects of poetry. Its beauty lies for him not simply in the ideas but in the very form of expression, its parallelism. Without form, with a prepossession disengaged from the organic, there follow not only Romanticism, the suggestive way, but also, and almost inevitably, rationalism, the way of dialectic (*Journals*, p. 126). Where thought and

[35] Pater, "The Child in the House," first published in 1878; reprinted in *The Victorian Age*, ed. John W. Bowyer and John Lee Brooks, 2d ed. (New York: Appleton-Century-Crofts, 1954), p. 736. The influence of Keble and the Tractarians on this spiritual autobiography should be noted.

expression are truly indistinguishable, the poem has "transparent, almost spontaneous, artifice," an "exquisite artifice" that belongs to simple expression.

Hopkins' is the incarnational ideal of all great poetry, a return to an unfallen language that is "the utterance and assertion of [Being]." Not only meaning, then, but beauty itself—the beauty of proportion, that is—requires parallelism. When any clauses are joined by *and* (which we explore in Chapter 2 as parataxis), neither the nature of the subject nor utilitarian reasons require it. This kind of parallelism, which comes closest to the technical *parallelismus membrorum*, the parallelism of clauses of Hebrew poetry, occurs because of "the instinctive feeling of the requirements of the precise pitch of idealism." The poem's idealism is its beauty, its unity amid diversity; the "pitch" of that idealism is its tendency to elevate or "pitch" the naturalistic elements of the poem beyond beauty to truth. We have no trouble seeing in Hopkins' poetry that his realism is "pitched"; his realism is not naturalism. The beauty of parallelism, discovered where one had expected chaos, in nature or in the poem, is the truth shining through matter.

Recalling what Hopkins has said in his earlier essay, "On the Signs of Health and Decay in the Arts," that comparison can fail by falling into monotony, we see him illustrating it here by reference to the parallelisms of the Anglican Book of Common Prayer.[36] "It uses parallelism," he says, "to attain dignity but attains, shall we say? only pomposity, because the members of the parallelism do not bear the just proportion to each other" (*Journals*, p. 113). Expressions like "acknowledge and confess," "assemble and meet together," "pray and beseech," a false imitation of Hebrew parallelism, are not only parallel but equal—"they are just the same thing in other words." It should be clear by now that, because of his emphasis on asymmetry and difference, Hopkins does not interpret

---

[36] He is still an Anglican for another year and a half when he writes this essay.

the parallelism of Hebrew poetry as "just the same thing in other words," even though that interpretation was current and accepted even by Matthew Arnold.[37] Hopkins says, rather, that it is "rhyme we like, not echo"; he chose parallelism as the root principle in poetry because it encompasses the Heraclitean inequality, asymmetry, and "dappledness" that are more true to reality. Consistently, in both his poetics and his ontology, he sees difference in the very order of things.

PARALLELISM AS INSTRESS

Interpreting Hopkins, we could say that asymmetry, inequality, difference, and antithesis, which are taken up and tensively held by parallelism, involve what we are tempted to call a wounding and a healing. In fact, for him as for Jacques Maritain, the immobile, perfect art of the Greeks was not the greatest; rather "nothing is more precious than a certain sacred weakness, and *that kind* of imperfection through which infinity wounds the finite."[38] So far, we have remained within formal-aesthetic bounds in describing parallelism, but here we must open up the discussion to consideration of the questions, What did Hopkins want from parallelism? What psychological effect did he hope to achieve with it?

The answer in his essays is quite clear. Hopkins wanted to achieve surprise. Parallelism's resemblances and antitheses "make of each resemblance a reason for surprise in the next difference and of each difference a reason for surprise in the next resemblance; *and yet* or such words run before each new

---

[37] Matthew Arnold, for example, subscribed to a strictly synonymous definition of parallelism in *Literature and Dogma* by saying: " 'The fear of the Eternal' and 'To depart from evil' here mean, and are put to mean, and by the very laws of Hebrew Composition which make the second phrase in a parallelism repeat the first in other words, they *must* mean, just the same thing" (New York: Macmillan, 1883), p. 43.

[38] Jacques Maritain, *Creative Intuition in Art and Poetry* (Cleveland: World Publishing Co., 1954), p. 128.

point of comparison, and resemblances and antitheses themselves are made to make up a wider antithesis" (*Journals*, p. 105). He restated the point in his letter to A. W. Mowbray Baillie of 1864, explaining the difference between inspired and uninspired ("Parnassian") language in poetry: "In a fine piece of inspiration every beauty takes you as it were by surprise. . . ."[39] We can understand surprise as a jolting out of preconceptions, a disarming the reader of pretensions, in effect a self-diminishing response to the poem. By creating surprise with parallelisms, Hopkins could hope to correct or purge the reader's preunderstanding and to elevate the reader's understanding, to put it in hermeneutical terms.[40] Surprise was Hopkins' means of instressing the reader, of creating an awe that comes only in contact with otherness.

In understanding surprise as a self-diminishing response, we can see the effect of Aristotle's *Rhetoric*, a work Hopkins counted first among the great books.[41] Aristotle says: "Most smart sayings are derived from metaphor, and also from misleading the hearer beforehand. For it becomes more evident to him that he has learnt something, when the conclusion turns out contrary to his expectation, and the mind seems to say, 'How true it is! but I missed it.' "[42] Before Aristotle, Her-

---

[39] *Further Letters*, p. 217.

[40] That Hopkins saw this purging and elevation as necessary can be inferred from remarks made in the letters. To Dixon, he said, "people cannot, or they will not, take in anything however plain that departs from what they have been taught and brought up to expect: I know from experience." *Correspondence*, p. 31. And to Bridges, after recommending that he give alms, Hopkins somewhat more optimistically says, "It changes the whole man, if anything can; not his mind only but the will and everything." *Letters to Bridges*, p. 61. (We might note the early influence of Newman in this emphasis on the "whole man.")

[41] See *Journals*, p. 49.

[42] Aristotle's *Rhetoric*, 3.11.6; Hopkins' emphasis on antithesis may also have derived from Aristotle. In this connection he says, "The more special qualities the expression possesses, the smarter it appears; for instance, if the words contain a metaphor, and a metaphor of a special kind, antithesis, and equality of clauses, and actuality" (3.11.10).

aclitus, in his far more oracular way, had warned: "Unless you expect the unexpected, you will never find [truth], for it is hard to discover and hard to attain."[43] Up to this point, we have been discussing the Heraclitean moment or element in the *inscape* or composition of the poem, but with the Heraclitean moment of surprise we open onto the subject of the poem as *instress*. As inscape, parallelism, we have said, is an integrative device, encompassing negativity or otherness on the ontological plane; as instress, parallelism is now seen to be a psychological or epistemological tool, enabling the poem to instress itself on the hearer-reader by its surprises. For the idealist-realist or Parmenidean-Heraclitean poetics we are constructing from Hopkins' thoughts, we can infer that as resemblance emerges from difference, we are surprised by the ideal; as difference emerges from resemblance, we are surprised by the real. Neither moment is lost or subjected to the other.

We should note, however, that in the statement quoted above, "resemblances and antitheses themselves are made to make up a wider antithesis," it is antithesis that has the final word, becoming the inclusive frame of the poem. If antithesis is the final word, then brokenness of form and lack of repose in the reader seem to prevail. Instress prevails over inscape, discord over harmony. Though Hopkins is no Romantic, he can no longer return to the achievement of perfect symmetry and rest found in classical architecture. For while opposition in architecture, if equal, creates symmetry, and opposition or counterpoint in music creates an answer or variation to a theme, antithesis in poetry is really a kind of asymmetry because of the lack of resolution it creates. A broken symmetry, an asymmetrical parallelism, resembles what James Kugel in *The Idea of Biblical Poetry* has called a "what's more," or in Hopkins' words, an "and yet." The second part of this antithetical "parallelism" goes beyond and corrects the first. As a

---

[43] Heraclitus, Fragment 19, *The Presocratics*. Cf. also Fragment 72: "Fire in its advance will catch all things by surprise and judge them."

poetic illustration of this "what's more" in Hopkins' own po-
etry, take "The Windhover" 's Lord in "AND the fire that
breaks from thee then." He is at one and the same time united
in comparison with the awesome bird but overriding it by his
greater danger, his more awful might, his transcendence. (We
will return to discussion of this poem in Chapter 3.) "The
Windhover" is in short a "wider antithesis." This instance
should demonstrate that comparison for Hopkins is not
equivalence or rhyme.[44]

That Hopkins wanted the poem to surprise its readers is
clear from other remarks made in his letters. Defending his
"obscurity" to Bridges, he says, "One of two kinds of clear-
ness one should have—either the meaning to be felt without
effort as fast as one reads or else, if dark at first reading, when
once made out *to explode.*"[45] The "darkness" of the first read-
ing entails the reader's grappling with otherness rather than
self-confirmation. Great men like Plato, and Wordsworth in
his Intimations Ode, he adds in the letter, are those who have
themselves got a shock and have communicated that shock so
that "the tremble from it is spreading."[46]

Schiller's notion of the "naive of surprise" may help to ex-

---

[44] For this reason I disagree with Roman Jakobson's assimilation of paral-
lelism to equivalence in his celebrated definition of poetry as projecting the
principle of equivalence from the axis of selection to the axis of combination.
"Grammatical Parallelism and Its Russian Facet," *Language* 42 (1966): 399–
429. I also disagree with J. Hillis Miller who, in his essay on Hopkins, "The
Univocal Chiming," in *The Disappearance of God*, calls rhyme the fundamental
method of Hopkins' poetry. Insofar as an emphasis on rhyme implies confir-
mation of response rather than surprise, and likeness rather than unlikeness
(which we have seen it did not imply for Hopkins), it loses precisely the neg-
ative element of antithesis preserved by an emphasis on parallelism as the ge-
neric term. *The Disappearance of God: Five Nineteenth-Century Writers* (Cam-
bridge, Mass.: Harvard Univ. Press, 1976), p. 277.

[45] *Letters to Bridges*, p. 90.

[46] *Correspondence*, p. 148. The passage continues, "You know what hap-
pened to crazy Blake, himself a most poetically electrical subject both active
and passive, at his first hearing: when the reader came to 'The pansy at my
feet' he fell into a hysterical excitement."

plain its continuing appeal for Hopkins. In his famous distinction between naive and sentimental poetry, Schiller describes the naive mode of thought as conveying the pure, free strength, the integrity and eternality, of the child.[47] The childlike simplicity of the naive is not incapacity but rather a higher strength. The naive for Schiller is simply "childlikeness where it is no longer expected"; thus it results in surprise and even shame. As "nature's victory," the naive of surprise runs counter to the knowledge and will of the individual perceiving it, causing shame or regret over his own artificiality in contrast to the sincerity of nature.[48] For one like Hopkins who judges a work of art by the presence or want of earnest, for whom "transparent, spontaneous artifice" is the goal, surprise is best achieved by the naive. Hopkins grounds his poetry in a knowing and willing *naiveté*, an ignorance of ultimate explanations about the simple fact of being. Things are dappled "who knows how?" The naive presents itself in his work, I believe, by "simple *yes* and *is*," by affirmation rather than irony, and by an iconic presence of things rather than a reflective absence, as in Wordsworth's poetry.

HOPKINS AND WORDSWORTH

Nowhere does it seem truer that Hopkins' aim was "to admire and do otherwise"[49] than in the case where his anxiety of influence may have been greatest—in the case of Wordsworth. I believe Hopkins was at special pains to distance himself from

[47] Friedrich Schiller, *Naive and Sentimental Poetry and On the Sublime*, trans. Julius A. Elias (New York: Frederick Ungar, 1966), p. 87.

[48] Ibid., pp. 89–92; Schiller appends an instructive footnote from Kant's *Critique of Judgment* on the naive: "Something compounded of both [the animal feeling of pleasure and the spiritual feeling of respect] is found in naivety, which is the bursting forth of that sincerity originally natural to mankind in opposition to the art of dissimulation . . . the scoundrel in us, as it were, is revealed—sets the mind in motion in two opposed directions one after the other, giving the body a salutary shock" (p. 88).

[49] *Letters to Bridges*, p. 291.

Wordsworth throughout his work, and this effort first appears in the youthful essay he titled "Poetic Diction." The essay begins, "Wordsworth's view was that poetic diction scarcely differed or ought to differ from that of prose: he said 'The most interesting parts of the best poems will be found to be strictly the language of prose when prose is well written.' "[50] Although Hopkins sees Wordsworth's lowering of poetic diction as a corrective, useful for its time, he feels that it cannot be decisively accepted without modification. For Hopkins cannot see meter, rhythm, and rhyme as extraneous elements of poetic form superadded to prosaic content. As he says elsewhere, thought and expression should be indistinguishable. Therefore, "all the structure which is called verse both necessitate and engender a difference in diction and thought" (*Journals*, p. 84). Poetic structure calls for poetic diction and poetic thought. In his essay, "On the Origin of Beauty," Hopkins illustrates his thesis by actually removing the structure from Wordsworth's poem, "To the Cuckoo," and demoting it to prose: "Blithe New-comer, I have heard thee, even now/ I hear thee and my heart rejoices. O Cuckoo!/ is it Bird I must call thee or a wandering Voice?" The Professor comments, "The changes necessary to make it unrhythmical have inevitably destroyed some of the grace of expression" (*Journals*, p. 102). Hopkins' point is that a threefold dynamics involving structure, expression, and thought should occur in poetry, making it *sui generis*. "The effect of verse," he says, "is one on expression and on thought, viz. concentration and all which is implied by this" (*Journals*, p. 84). By "concentration" he

---

[50] Hopkins is quoting from the preface to the second edition of *Lyrical Ballads* (1800): "not only the language of a large portion of every good poem, even of the most elevated character, must necessarily, except with reference to the meter, in no respect differ from that of good prose, but likewise that some of the most interesting parts of the best poems will be found to be strictly the language of prose when prose is well written." In *Wordsworth's Literary Criticism*, ed. Nowell C. Smith (London: Humphrey Milford, 1925), p. 19.

means not merely terseness, selectivity, or definiteness, but "vividness of idea." In contrast to Wordsworth, for Hopkins, the energy of the poem concentrates or intensifies in its parallelisms.

If Wordsworth, on the one hand, wanted to create what Hartman has called a "Vulgate"[51] by making poetry "a selection of the real language of men in a state of vivid sensation,"[52] Hopkins, on the other, wanted to "re-sacralize" poetry, to make its utterance special and discontinuous with ordinary prose. For Wordsworth there can be no essential difference between prose and poetry; the only distinction is between poetry and science.[53] In making this Kantian move, Wordsworth is also liable to the charge of setting truth or matter of fact on the side of science and leaving emotion for poetry. Coleridge too in his definition of the poem makes this point quite explicit: poetry is "that species of composition, which is opposed to works of science, by proposing for its immediate object pleasure, not truth."[54] Alba Warren, surveying the poetic theory of the Romantics, shows that both Wordsworth and Coleridge accept a dichotomy between objective and subjective truth.[55] Hopkins' ultimate purpose in insisting on a special mode of utterance for poetry is, I believe, to safeguard the possibility of truth in poetry.

With regard to the Romantic idea of the genius who works *je ne sais quoi*, Hopkins feels the structural constraints necessitated by poetry actually activate the genius of the poet, for "genius works more powerfully . . . when conditioned than when unconditioned" (*Journals*, p. 108). This subordination

[51] See Hartman's chapter on Wordsworth in *The Unmediated Vision*.

[52] Wordsworth, Preface to the *Lyrical Ballads* (1800 ed.), in *Wordsworth's Literary Criticism*, p. 11.

[53] Ibid., p. 21n.

[54] Samuel Taylor Coleridge, *Biographia Literaria*, 3 vols., 2d ed. (London: William Pickering, 1847), 2:10.

[55] Alba H. Warren, Jr., *English Poetic Theory, 1825–1865* (Princeton: Princeton Univ. Press, 1950), p. 11.

of genius to the constraints of structure, this finding of free-
dom *in* necessity, is a typically anti-Romantic move on the
part of Hopkins. Throughout the Romantic and post-Roman-
tic periods, the role of genius in the making of a poetry seen
as creation or *poiesis* rather than mimesis, and of creation as a
somnolent, unconscious *je ne sais quoi*, held nearly absolute
sway in critical theory.[56] One of Hopkins' purposes is to undo
this dominance and to return the poet to a submission to his
materials.

In making his case for a unique poetic language, Hopkins
underlines the fundamental structural principle of poetry—
parallelism: "The artificial part of poetry, perhaps we shall be
right to say all artifice, reduces itself to the principle of paral-
lelism. The structure of poetry is that of continuous parallel-
ism, ranging from the technical so-called Parallelisms of He-
brew poetry and the antiphons of Church music up to the
intricacy of Greek or Italian or English verse" (*Journals*, p.
84). Parallelism, the structure of poetry, including rhythm,
meter, alliteration, assonance, and rhyme, accounts for its dis-
tinctness. Poetry is not a concentrated prose nor is prose a
more diffuse poetry. Poetry is of a different kind from prose
because "the force of this recurrence [in the structure] is to
beget a recurrence or parallelism answering to it in the words
or thought and . . . the more marked parallelism in structure
whether of elaboration or of emphasis begets more marked
parallelism in the words and sense" (*Journals*, pp. 84–85).

Parallelism, then, operates on three levels in the poem: in
the structure (meter, rhythm, rhyme, etc.), in the diction
(metaphor, simile, parable), and, finally, in the thought,
which takes us outside the poem. The parallelism begun in the
structure, as sounds repeat themselves, causes parallelism or
comparison to occur in the choice of diction so that meta-

---

[56] See M. H. Abrams' *The Mirror and the Lamp: Romantic Theory and the
Critical Tradition* (New York: Oxford Univ. Press, 1958) and Alba H. War-
ren's *English Poetic Theory*.

phorical resemblances and antithetical contrasts are made. "And moreover," as Hopkins says, "parallelism in expression tends to beget or passes into parallelism in thought" (*Journals*, p. 85). Hopkins' theory of poetry asserts that the parallelism of expression in metaphor, parable, and antithesis, all forms of comparison, strengthens or elevates even human thought. Elevated expression and thought can be won only by a diction peculiar to poetry. In a final statement, Hopkins summarizes the modification he would make of Wordsworth: "Accordingly we may modify what Wordsworth says. An emphasis of structure stronger than the common construction of sentences gives asks for an emphasis of expression stronger than that of common speech or writing, and that for an emphasis of thought stronger than that of common thought" (*Journals*, p. 85). Common speech, as both Parmenides and Hopkins saw, can all too easily betray and engender common thought, an ordinary perception of things. Hopkins clearly wants an expression that can give rise to the extraordinary. Parallelism must be transferred from seeing to saying so that it can recur in seeing—the reader's contemplative seeing of the poem.

Hopkins was not the first to oppose Wordsworth's elision of poetic diction and the "real language of men." In the second volume of his *Biographia Literaria*, Coleridge, applying the Romantics' theory of organic poetry, insisted that "if metre be superadded all other parts [of the poem] must be made consonant with it."[57] The parts must harmonize with and support the poem's metrical arrangement, and, further, they must justify the attention "which recurrences of accent and sound are calculated to excite."[58] In Coleridge's phenomenology of metrical effects, meter, as the balance in the mind that holds passion in check, represents a partnership and interpenetration of passion and will. Meter produces a kind of "tacit compact" between the poet and the reader. Like the biblical interpreters

[57] Coleridge, *Biographia Literaria*, 2:10.
[58] Ibid., 2:70–71.

of parallelism, Coleridge sees the poetic compact inaugurated by meter as an agreement on the part of the reader to both spontaneity and order. It increases in the reader the vivacity and susceptibility of the attention "by the continued excitement of surprise, and by the quick reciprocations of curiosity still gratified and still re-excited."[59] As a final blow to a Wordsworthian theory of meretricious meter, Coleridge compares the effect of reading a poem where language and thought do not fit the presence of meter to leaping in the dark from a last step when the muscles are prepared for three or four more.[60] Coleridge's masterly discussions of metrical effects have quite possibly formed a source for Hopkins' own thoughts on parallelism; Hopkins, however, with Hebrew poetry as a paradigm, sees parallelism as a more original and fundamental constitutive principle of poetry than is meter.

But Coleridge, who studied with German biblical critics like Eichhorn, most probably influenced Hopkins in other ways. He possessed a keen appreciation for biblical modes of utterance, seeing the first chapter of Isaiah as poetry in the most emphatic sense, though it existed, he said, without meter.[61] Coleridge remarks that Wordsworth's men speak an elevated language only because they have been schooled on the poetic dictions and rhythms of the Bible. The "real language of men" as Wordsworth found them was in fact biblical language! Coleridge pointed to the repetitions of the Song of Deborah as a "beauty of the highest kind" where the passion is greater and of longer duration than to be exhausted in a single representation.[62] Above all, his description of the nuanced effect of prophetic style would certainly have provided Hopkins, another student of form and style, much food for thought. Coleridge says of the style of the prophetic books that it consists in the "excitement of surprise by juxtapositions

[59] Ibid., 2:72.
[60] Ibid.
[61] Ibid., 2:13.
[62] Ibid., 2:62.

and *apparent* reconciliation of widely different or incompatible things."[63] Coleridge's remarks on surprise by juxtaposition and on *apparent* (the emphasis is his) reconciliation of opposites probably accounted in part for Hopkins' own emphasis on likeness and unlikeness, metaphor and antithesis, in parallelism. Coleridge's "surprise by juxtaposition," an effect Erich Auerbach refers to as the paratactic style of biblical speech,[64] the peculiar form of its simple connections and transitions, occupied literary critics of the nineteenth century as well. But where Coleridge sees "surprise by juxtaposition" as indigenous to the Bible, Hopkins makes it the fundamental principle of all poetry.

In his opposition to Wordsworth's reductionist view of poetry, Hopkins had another, more contemporary, ally—his friend and correspondent, Coventry Patmore. Since Patmore first published his "Essay on English Metrical Law" in 1856, it is possible that Hopkins was familiar with Patmore's theory of metrics when he wrote his undergraduate essays. He says in his early diaries that he has discovered the poetry of Patmore, and he refers to the essay later in his letters. Their views are amazingly consonant. Patmore too indicts Wordsworth: "Wordsworth's erroneous critical views of the necessity of approximating the language of poetry, as much as possible, to that of prose, especially by the avoidance of grammatical inversions, arose from his having overlooked the necessity of manifesting, as well as moving in, the bonds of verse."[65] In an

---

[63] Ibid., 2:92–93. This emphasis on the reconciliation of opposites occurs throughout the *Biographia Literaria*. Coleridge says in the first volume that the law of association accounts for ability to make connections in time, in space, by interdependence, by cause and effect, and lastly, by likeness and contrast (1:105–107). In the second volume, he defines imitation, in opposition to mere copying, as "the interfusion of the same throughout the radically different, or of the different throughout a base radically the same" (2:78).

[64] Erich Auerbach, *Mimesis: The Representation of Reality in Western Literature*, trans. W. R. Trask (Princeton: Princeton Univ. Press, 1953), pp. 70–71.

[65] Coventry Patmore, "Essay on English Metrical Law," *Poems*, vol. 2 (London: George Bell and Son, 1886), p. 222.

age of great spiritualization of the language of poetry, an age of Romanticism as defined by Hegel, the *material* element of poetry must make itself recognized, according to Patmore. He actually views the "over-smooth and accurate" meter of the eighteenth century as defective, and grammatical inversions, "the very deformities produced . . . in the phraseology of a great poet by the confinement of metre, [as] beautiful."[66] "A cultivated ear," says Patmore, "delights in remission, inversion, or omission of the recurrent ictus when there is an emotional motive."[67]

This antinomian strain in Patmore's metrical theory could have provided Hopkins ample support for his own departures from metrical and grammatical regularity. Hopkins' "deformities" and grammatical inversions, however, were produced not only by the "confinement of metre" but by his sense that poetic language should be different in kind from that of prose. In his emphasis on rhyme and alliteration as the accompaniment of meter, Patmore supplies Hopkins with an additional incentive for multiplying these elements in his own poetic practice. But what is even more characteristic of Patmore's system of prosody, and what certainly came to be an influence on Hopkins' use of parallelism, was his emphasis on caesura or pause in the poetic line. The caesura, whose alteration Patmore sees as "a mode of expressing real emotion,"[68] constitutes the "punctuation mark" of a strict parallelism.

Although Hopkins rejected Wordsworth's common language for poetry, it is ironic that both Hopkins and Wordsworth, in presenting their conflicting theories of poetic diction, use Hebrew poetry as their point of departure. In his 1802 Appendix to the *Lyrical Ballads*, Wordsworth says no better example could be given of the phrase "poetic diction" than a comparison of poets' metrical paraphrases of passages

[66] Ibid.
[67] Ibid., p. 238.
[68] Ibid., p. 266.

from the Old and New Testaments with those passages in the common translation (meaning the King James Version).[69] Using metrical paraphrases from Pope's *Messiah* and Prior's 1 Cor. 13, Wordsworth invites us to pass "from this hubbub of words" to the "original"; then he quotes the famous passage on the ant from Prov. 6:6 in the King James Version.[70] This passage proves to Wordsworth that "meter is but adventitious to composition."[71]

It may be that Wordsworth's remarks prompted both Coleridge and Hopkins to jump to the defense of the Bible as poetry. Although all see meter as lost both in the Hebrew original and in the "original" King James, some poetic principle is at work here that Wordsworth fails to note.[72] This passage can hardly be a selection of real human language. Let us look at the passage as translated in the King James Version:

> Go to the ant, thou sluggard;
> consider her ways and be wise:
> How long wilt thou sleep, O sluggard?
> When wilt thou arise out of thy sleep?
> Yet a little sleep, a little slumber,
> a little folding of the hands to sleep:

What Wordsworth perceives here is proximity to ordinary language and the absence not only of meter but of any other poetic artifice. This prosaic impression may be reinforced by a reading in the King James Version, his "original text." For this version, with its prepositional phrases and connectors, is

[69] See *Wordsworth's Literary Criticism*, p. 44.

[70] Ibid.

[71] Ibid., p. 46.

[72] In his preface to the 1815 ed. of the *Poems*, thirteen years later, Wordsworth does, however, remark that "The grand storehouses of enthusiastic and meditative Imagination, of poetical, as contra-distinguished from human and dramatic Imagination, are the prophetic and lyrical parts of the Holy Scriptures, and the works of Milton" (*Wordsworth's Literary Criticism*, p. 162). We could conclude that the Bible's prophetic and lyrical passages are poetry because of their content, not because of their form.

far looser and more polysyndetic than the Hebrew original. The compactness of the Hebrew is lost in the King James translation. Yet, the repetition and parallelism of the Hebrew original are reproducible in translation.[73] The repetition of the word *sleep*, repetition of the liquid "l" sound, the parallelistic structure, and the bold comparison are all unmistakably poetic devices. Deliberately departing from Wordsworth's vernacular verse, Hopkins notes that a concentrated, parallelistic style is vivid, surprising, and elevated. As he became increasingly more familiar with the Hebrew original in his Jesuit studies, Hopkins recognized its concentrated style as clearly poetic.

Biblical Interpreters of Parallelism

In his references to Hebrew poetry, Hopkins is drawing on a tradition of biblical criticism that had had its origin at Oxford one century before. Hopkins' familiarity with this tradition is not surprising, since Bishop Robert Lowth, the first Englishman to make a significant contribution to the literary study of the Bible, had held the very influential chair of Professor of Poetry at Oxford. Lowth's lectures, published in 1753 as *De Sacrā Poesi Hebraeorum*, passed over classical models, choosing instead to examine the peculiar beauty of Hebrew composition. Lowth's choice had an enormous effect, not only on future occupants of the Chair of Poetry like Keble and Arnold, but on the actual writing of English poetry in the following century, especially among the Romantics.[74]

---

[73] See Ruth Ap-Roberts, "Old Testament Poetry: The Translatable Structure," *PMLA* 92 (1977): 987–1004, for a discussion of parallelism and translation.

[74] Murray Roston, in his *Prophet and Poet: The Bible and the Growth of Romanticism* (Evanston: Northwestern Univ. Press, 1965), discusses biblical parallelism and biblical imagery in Christopher Smart, William Blake, Wordsworth, and Coleridge. Although Roston is sensitive to the influence of biblical poetry on these Romantics, he makes too sharp a distinction between the "ar-

One reason for tracing parallelism from Hopkins' essays back to its biblical roots is that it allows us to treat Hopkins' recurrent alliteration, assonance, and rhyme, the sound repetitions that he called "parallelism of structure," not as isolated, and merely idiosyncratic, phenomena but as aspects of an overall, coherent schema. His schema encompasses not only these phonetic recurrences but grammatical and even semantic recurrences as well. As we recall, parallelism is a threefold occurrence in Hopkins' idea of poetry: parallelisms of structure engender parallelisms of expression that in turn engender parallelisms of thought. "Parallelism" is meant to occur on more than the auditory level; yet many interpreters ignore the fuller phenomenon that Hopkins intended parallelism to be in their discussion of the auditory effects of Hopkins' poems.

Parallelism in Hebrew poetry, as Hopkins rightly interpreted it, is primarily "figure of grammar" (*Journals*, p. 267). Yet what does it *mean* when we encounter a biblical text such as the following from Ps. 19:1:

> The heavens are telling the glory of God;
> and the firmament proclaims his handiwork.

or this from Isa. 40:18:

> To whom then will you liken God,
> or what likeness compare with him?

Confronted with texts such as these, we have two interpretive options. The exegete or pious reader can either assume that the second line, or really half-line,[75] merely repeats the same sentiment as the first in other words. That assumption seems

---

tificial" devices of classical poetry and the "directness" of the Hebrew. Versifiers like Coleridge were not so indifferent to the formal idiom of Hebrew poetry.

[75] Half-lines are variously called hemistichs or bicola. We will simply refer to them as half-lines, meaning the two parts of the parallel line before and after the medial pause (represented by /) and before the final pause (represented by //) in the configuration: /   /   //.

particularly appropriate for the line from Isaiah. Or the inter-
preter can assume a nuanced difference in meaning between
the first and second half-lines. That assumption seems to fit
the line from Ps. 19, for "telling" can be easily distinguished
from "proclaiming," just as can "glory" and "handiwork."
The options reduce, then, to synonymity, with its "elegant
variation," different words for the same thing,[76] or to real dif-
ference of some kind. We may designate these options the aes-
thetic, where the effect is chiefly sensuous and musical, and
the cognitive or semantic, where the effect is a heightening or
sharpening of the thought. The aesthetic option involves a
frank recognition of the phenomenon but transvalues it. It is
no longer verbal repetition but rather symmetry, an analogy
to architecture, or thought-rhythm, an analogy to music. The
semantic or cognitive option attempts to go beyond the aes-
thetic, to connect form with content and with meaning.

Bishop Robert Lowth is largely responsible for the tenacity
of the notion that biblical verses are synonymous and thus that
their variations are aesthetic. Lowth, parallelism's "discov-
erer," made his first extended definition of what he called *par-
allelismus membrorum*, the parallelism of clauses, in Lecture 19
of his *De Sacrā Poesi Hebraeorum*. In this work, the fruit of ten
years of lectures at Oxford, he first defined parallelism: "The
correspondence of one verse, or line, with another, I call *par-
allelism*. When a proposition is delivered, and a second is sub-
joined to it, or drawn under it, equivalent, or contrasted with
it, in sense; or similar to it in the form of grammatical con-
struction; these I call parallel lines, and the words or phrases,
answering one to another in the corresponding lines, parallel
terms."[77] Contained in the definition of parallelism is its clas-
sification into three "species" essential to Lowth's treatment.
In the first and most common species, synonymous parallel-

[76] W. K. Wimsatt in *The Verbal Icon* (Lexington: Univ. of Kentucky Press,
1954) describes "elegant variation" as a failure in rhetoric.

[77] Bishop Robert Lowth, *Lectures on the Sacred Poetry of the Hebrews*, trans.
G. Gregory, 2 vols. (London: J. Johnson, 1787), 2:32.

ism, "the same sentiment is repeated in different, but equivalent terms." Lowth, to a great extent a representative of the neoclassical age, rejoiced in the "accuracy and neatness" of synonymous parallelisms, selecting a nearly perfect example from Ps. 114, which begins:

> When Israel went out from Egypt;
> The house of Jacob from a strange people:[78]

and an equally "symmetrical" example from Isa. 60:1–3, beginning:

> Arise, be thou enlightened; for thy light is come;
> And the glory of Jehovah is risen upon thee.

Lowth also cites examples of synonymous parallelism that rely on sheer iteration or word repetition as in Ps. 129:1–2 and Ps. 94:1 and 3. Under this category, however, he must include instances where the parallelism as such breaks down, where, as he puts it, there is "something wanting in the latter member,"[79] as, for example, in Isa. 49:7:

> Kings shall see him and shall rise up;
> Princes, and they shall worship him:

and "synonymous parallelisms" where the whole second half-line answers only to some part of the first, including here the same verses from Isa. 60:1 that he had quoted above to illustrate the perfect conformity and symmetry of synonymous parallelism. Lowth's "system" may not be so formidable after all. He had himself caught the Latin Father, Jerome, in just such a slip. At one time Jerome had referred to the Song of Moses in Deuteronomy as composed in hexameters and pentameters and at another time in tetrameters, a blunder Lowth, who views the Bible's meter as unrecoverable, takes pride in exposing.[80]

---

[78] I follow here the translation made by Gregory from Lowth's Latin.
[79] Lowth, *Lectures*, p. 41.
[80] Ibid.

The second species of parallelism Lowth classifies as "antithetic," which occurs "when a thing is illustrated by its contrary being opposed to it."[81] Antithetic parallelism turns out to be the exact opposite of the synonymous, since opposition instead of agreement is intended. For example, the practical wisdom and prudence that oppose a life of aimlessness and wickedness in the Book of Proverbs lend themselves to antithetic formulae such as the following:

> A wise son hears his father's instruction,
>   but a scoffer does not listen to rebuke. (Prov. 13:1)

or:

> A soft answer turns away wrath,
>   but a harsh word stirs up anger. (Prov. 15:1)

Examples of antithetic parallelism abound in Prov. 10–22 and Prov. 25–29, from which Lowth quotes several. He observes that this form of composition agrees well with adages, whereas "sublimer poetry seldom adopts this style."[82]

The third species of parallelism Lowth calls the "synthetic" or "constructive," where sentences answer to each other "merely by the form of construction."[83] Actually, this is a thinly veiled catch-all category that was soon to come under attack from Lowth's successors. Most of them agreed that "synthetic" parallelism meant the absence of parallelism.[84]

This neat system of kinds of parallelism Hopkins inherited but transformed. The congruence between form and content found in parallelism explains why Hopkins too passed over

---

[81] Ibid., p. 45.

[82] Ibid., pp. 46–48.

[83] Ibid., p. 49.

[84] George Buchanan Gray, *Isaiah*, vol. 1, in *International Critical Commentary*, vol. 21 (New York: Charles Scribner's Sons, 1912), p. lxi. Gray asserts that parallelism "is not a constant phenomenon of Hebrew poetry. What Lowth called 'synthetic' parallelism is in reality absence of parallelism in lines such as 'Yet I have set my kind/ Upon Zion, my holy hill.' "

the Greek classical forms so familiar to him from his classical education at Oxford to choose Hebrew parallelism as his point of departure for a discussion of the structure of poetry. When, as a Jesuit, he had studied the original Hebrew of the Bible,[85] he once again turned to Hebrew poetry in his lecture notes compiled on rhetoric and verse for his teaching at the Jesuit novitiate at Roehampton. Defining verse as "figure of spoken sound," Hopkins notes that the figure of Hebrew poetry is not in the sounds but in the grammar. We might say it therefore seems to be an exception, occupying the only place in the category, "poetry which is not verse," that is, not metrical. Using the terminology of Hopkins' earlier essays, we could say Hebrew poetry lacks that very parallelism of structure, including meter, rhythm, and other sound recurrences, that made Hopkins choose it as paradigmatic in the first place! How is this discrepancy to be accounted for? Hopkins' answer takes the form of a knowledgeable analysis of the form of Hebrew poetry:

> there is a marked figure and order not in the sounds but in the grammar and this might be shifted to other words with a change of specific meaning but keeping some general agreement, as of noun over against noun, verb against verb, assertion against assertion, etc., e.g., Foxes (A) have (B) holes (C) and birds of the air (A') have (B— not B' here) nests (C'), or more widely even than this/ with a change of words but keeping the grammatical and logical meaning—as/Foxes have holes and birds of the air have nests (that is/Beasts have homes to live in) but the Son of Man has not where to lay His head (that is/Man has not a home to live in): the subjects of the clauses being changed the one does no more than say yes, the other no. (*Journals*, p. 267)

These notes, written some eight or nine years after Hopkins'

[85] *Further Letters*, p. 241.

first speculations on parallelism, show him still interested in the *Gestalt* of Hebrew poetry. Although it does not exhibit the metrical regularity of verse,[86] Hebrew poetry possesses grammatical recurrences and correspondences that in turn effect logical correspondences with semantic differences ("with a change of specific meaning but keeping some general agreement"). Hopkins is again demonstrating the containment of difference within sameness; the logical and grammatical meanings form the sameness that includes specific semantic differences. At the same time he shows, as in the earlier essays, the inclusion of sameness within difference, for his biblical quotation is a perfect example of how "resemblances and antitheses are themselves made to make up a wider antithesis" (*Journals*, p. 105). It is of course remarkable that Hopkins is drawing from the *Greek* New Testament to illustrate a point about Hebrew poetry. This passage from Matt. 8:20 is neither poetry nor written in Hebrew.[87] Yet, in the nineteenth century, other interpreters like Bishops Jebb and Forbes found parallelism throughout the New Testament.

It has been said that parallelism was seen in the nineteenth century as just the same thing in other words, mere tautology in effect. One interpreter, Bishop Forbes, attempted to rescue parallelism from "disrepute" and from this imputation of tautology. He defended parallelism with a semantic interpretation where the second or responsive clause "always diversifies the preceding clause, generally so as to rise above it forming a sort of climax in the sense."[88] Hopkins, of course, in his em-

---

[86] This assumption has been anything but proved. The search for the metrical law of Hebrew poetry still continues.

[87] Rudolf Bultmann, however, also recognizes in this passage a clear development from the Jewish *mashal*: "It is but a slight development of the two-stranded *mashal* when one part is divided into two synonymous halves." Rudolf Bultmann, *History of the Synoptic Tradition*, trans. John Marsh (New York: Harper and Row, 1963), p. 81.

[88] Rev. John Forbes, *The Symmetrical Structure of Scripture or the Principles of Scripture Parallelism Exemplified* (Edinburgh: T. and T. Clark, 1854), p. 6.

phasis on parallelism's effect of surprise, would subscribe to this view. Despite more sensitive renderings of parallelism, the attitude that it is merely monotonous tautology is not entirely absent today, as evidenced in the view of so respectable a translator as John Knox: "to our notions of poetic composition, these remorseless repetitions are wholly foreign; when you have read a page or two on end, they begin to cloy."[89]

But there is another attitude toward the parallelism of the Hebrew Bible that turns on one's acceptance or rejection of the central notion of repetition. Those who, like Lévi-Strauss, can dispel the myth of primitive impoverishment, can see parallelism's capacity for creating recurrences at all levels as positive. Roman Jakobson is such a thinker. For him, "pervasive parallelism inevitably activates all the levels of language."[90] Jakobson recognizes Hopkins as a practitioner of "pervasive parallelism" and pays him homage because "he recognized the principle of parallelism as the fundamental problem of poetry," demonstrating his "prodigious insight into the structure of poetry." In Jakobson's linguistic, formalistic terms, "Phonemic features and sequences . . . when occurring in metrically or strophically corresponding positions, are necessarily subject to the conscious or subconscious questions whether, how far, and in what respect the positionally correspondent entities are mutually similar."[91] According to Jakobson, this positional correspondence is parallelism, the bond between form and meaning, language and thought, that Hopkins saw it to be. Or, as he put it in his famous, and enigmatic, definition of poetry in the Closing Statement of a 1960 conference on linguistics, "Poetry projects the principle of equivalence from the axis of selection to the axis of combination."[92] Poetry

[89] John Knox, *On Englishing the Bible*; quoted in F. F. Bruce, *The English Bible: A History of Translations* (London: Oxford Univ. Press, 1961), p. 97.

[90] Jakobson, "Grammatical Parallelism," p. 423.

[91] Ibid., p. 399.

[92] Jakobson, "Linguistics and Poetics: A Closing Statement," in *Style in Language*, ed. Thomas A. Sebeok (Cambridge, Mass.: MIT Press, 1960).

does not work simply in the linear direction of ordinary speech, but its recurrences, in sound, grammar, and syntax, create recurrences in thought. For Jakobson, poetry, unlike prose, actively works to overcome the "prejudice that the metonymic correspondences—such as partition and enumeration of particulars—which link 'constructively similar' lines are merely cumulative and not integrative."[93]

Jakobson's study is extremely helpful because it provides an alternate, and quite sophisticated, set of terms with which to compare Hopkins' poetics. With his emphasis on equivalence in parallelism, however, he may miss to some extent the Heraclitean need for variety and asymmetry that we have seen as a strong element in Hopkins' work. Parallelism is an integrative device for Hopkins, but one that achieves for the poem equality without equation or mere synonymity. Usually, in each "aftering" there is "othering." For Hopkins knew he had to preserve the eachness, or haecceitas, of all things while still effecting a retrospective return, a first step toward the poem's retiring unity.[94] The presence of parallelism within the body of the poem points toward that reticent unity at the same time that it begins in thought the gathering, elevating process toward it. As soon as the equal sign is done away with, and the illusion of synonymity dispelled, parallelism becomes a phenomenon that has as much to do with difference as it does with unity and therefore with the profound presence of difference within unity. The repetitions of parallelistic style hint at the inexhaustibility, but not the utter ineffability, of what lies behind and outside language. No one statement suffices to express the inexpressible. Parallelism, while abrogating the univocal, one-to-one fit that scientific discourse requires between thought and language,[95] still closes up the thought after

[93] Jakobson, "Grammatical Parallelism," p. 402.

[94] "All words mean either things or relations of things," he wrote on February 9, 1868, in *Journals*, p. 125.

[95] As Louis Newman puts it, "The human mind, richly stored, rarely contents itself with a single formulation of a theme close to its interests." *Paral-*

two or three half-lines, rather than running on line after line in an endless, futile attempt to capture it. Such a structure might suggest that language is equivocally related to thought, that it may, in fact, be a lie. With parallelism, language and reality, thought and being, are still related.

Returning to Hopkins' interpretation of parallelism in Hebrew poetry, even if Hebrew poetry does not display the "figure of spoken sound" that constitutes what he had called parallelism of structure, it still makes an approach to it. For, according to Hopkins, Hebrew poetry's origin in music "will supply the element of structure instead of verse and when it is no longer sung will be so far supplied by the reader in thought as to justify at least the poetic wording, stress, dwelling, impressiveness, formal antithesis, etc." (*Journals*, p. 267). This reference to a musical origin of Hebrew poetry that supplies the "element of structure" and justifies poetic expression may owe something, directly or indirectly, to the thinking of J. G. Herder.

It may be no exaggeration to say that Herder is as much Lowth's antithesis as Romanticism is neoclassicism's. Indeed, Herder is in large part the inspiration of the German Romantic movement. Curate of Weimar, confidant of Goethe, pupil of Hamann and Kant, Herder stood at the center of Romanticism, looking in one direction to the mysticism of his mentor, Hamann, and in the other to the naturalism of his friend, Goethe. Where Lowth was the great systematizer, Herder was the great synthesizer. In fact, he was more monist than synthesizer. And when a monist looks at a phenomenon as poten-

---

lelism in Amos. Part I of *Studies in Biblical Parallelism* (Berkeley: Univ. of California Press, 1918), p. 57. James Kugel has it that repetitions are prized in the poems of all peoples "for the sense of return and completion on which every poetry thrives." *The Idea of Biblical Poetry: Parallelism and Its History* (New Haven: Yale Univ. Press, 1981), p. 39. See, on the distinction between technical and literary language in regard to the Bible, Luis Alonso Schokel, S.J., *The Inspired Word*, trans. Francis Martin, O.C.S.O. (New York: Herder and Herder, 1965), pp. 135–172.

tially diverse and classifiable as Hebrew poetry, he sees *spirit*, spirit evidenced in and through the individual poets and the *Volk* they represent. And so, Herder's study of Hebrew poetry became, in deliberate contrast to Lowth's, *Die Geist der Hebräischen Poesie* (*The Spirit of Hebrew Poetry*)[96] first published in 1783, just thirty years after Lowth's *Lectures*.

Herder wrote his *Spirit of Hebrew Poetry* in large part, I believe, to polemicize against Lowth.[97] A casual reading of Herder's book might note only his indebtedness to Lowth and the vague assertion that it treats a sphere "distinct" from that of Lowth's. In his series of letters, *Über das Studium der Theologie*, on the reading of the Old Testament, however, Herder makes his objections to Lowth's treatment of Hebrew poetry quite clear.[98] Herder accuses Lowth of being unable to free himself of the Greek and Roman models he offers at times as contrasts. Of course, in Lowth's defense, we might say his task differed essentially from Herder's. Lowth had to convince a neoclassical Enlightenment audience that the writings of Moses, David, and Isaiah had equal claim to attention and praise with those of Homer, Pindar, and Horace.[99] In a sense, his apologies for Hebrew poetry resemble those of Jerome speaking to an audience bred on the great pagan rhetoricians. On the other hand, Herder's dismissal of classical models resembles that of Bede, for whom the models of antiquity were no longer authoritative. Once the hold of absolutized classi-

[96] See J. G. Herder, *The Spirit of Hebrew Poetry*, trans. James Marsh, 2 vols. (Burlington, Vt.: Edward Smith, 1833).

[97] See Hans W. Frei, *The Eclipse of Biblical Narrative* (New Haven: Yale Univ. Press, 1974), chap. 10, "Herder on the Bible: The Realistic Spirit in History," where this point is also made.

[98] J. G. Herder, *Über das Studium der Theologie*, Letters 1–24 (Leipzig: Dechent, 1905). His words are: "Samt und sonders gehoren sie unter keine dieser Klassen und Arten: nicht bloss weil (Regeln nach) keine dieser Klassen und Arten noch erfunden war, sondern weil uberhaupt kein biblischer Skribent (im Sinn der Griechen und Romer, geschweige der neueren) Dichter sein wollte. Seine Poesie war nicht Kunst sondern Natur" (p. 6).

[99] Lowth, *Lectures*, 1:26.

cism had been broken, Herder was free to interpret biblical poetry as *sui generis*. Yet, Herder was clearly incensed that Lowth, despite his disclaimers, tended to classify this "*most ancient* poetry" using art forms (epic, drama, ode) that did not even exist when the biblical scribes were writing. Lowth's analysis is simply "zu kunstliche"[100] for this "*most simple* poetry." Nothing would do but "a new Lowth who did not know the poetry of later times." Herder resented not only Lowth's classification but also his restriction of poetry to *written* forms; for him, poetry was indistinguishable from life.

Hopkins, as we have seen, did not share Herder's antiformalist and largely antinomian conception of poetry. Nevertheless, although Hopkins' tendencies were as formalistic as Lowth's, he, like Herder, wanted to achieve the full spiritual potential of form. Whether he ever read or knew of Herder's work is uncertain, but at least one Hopkins interpreter sees a possible influence there. Winifred Nowottny, in the Hopkins Society Fourth Annual Hopkins Lecture, assuming that Hopkins would have consulted the 1833 English translation of Herder's work, sees an affinity between several passages in Herder and the poetics implicit in Hopkins' poems.[101] The most relevant of these passages for our purposes is found in Herder's definition of the lyric or ode:

> So soon as a lyrical effusion, either from the comprehensiveness of its subject, or the fuller expression of emotion, becomes extended, it requires variety, contrasts, a manifoldness of parts. . . . Here, according to the Oriental style, a great effect is produced by change of person, questions and answers, sudden appeals to inanimate or absent objects. . . . This is what the critics call the beau-

[100] Herder, *Studium*, p. 7.
[101] Winifred Nowottny, "Hopkins' Language of Prayer and Praise," *Hopkins Society Fourth Annual Lecture*, Univ. of London (March 5, 1973), pp. 4 and 14.

tiful irregularity, the ambitus, of the Ode, *the flight*, in which it strays, but is never *lost.*[102]

We have seen Hopkins using just such terminology, of "variety," "contrasts," and the beauty of irregularity, in his early essays. And, like Herder, he insists on the irreplaceability of each element of the poem. And certainly, his poetry evidences "the Oriental style" as defined here by Herder; his first mature poem, *The Wreck of the Deutschland*, exhibits continual changes of images, dramatic situations, questions, and abrupt reversals. We must remember that he defined it to Bridges as "an ode and not primarily a narrative."[103] It does seem that throughout his work he aimed for the "variety" and "manifoldness of parts" of Oriental style rather than the simplicity and austerity of the Greek.[104]

Yet, it was in his definitions of parallelism that Herder could have had the greatest effect on Hopkins' thought, opening his eyes to parallelism as a principle of the universe and thus providing Hopkins with an analogue to his future notion of inscape. For, in polemicizing against Lowth, Herder greatly extended the notion of parallelism until it became not merely a formal, artistic device but a psychological and ontological principle as well. Herder responded to the Enlightenment's stereotypical notion of parallelism as "monotonous, an everlasting tautology,"[105] which merely says things twice, by making a comparison to the dance and the choral ode and by asking, "Does not all rhythm, and the metrical harmony both of motion and of sound, I might say all, that delights the senses in forms and sounds, depend on symmetry? And that too a symmetry easily apprehended, upon simplicity and equality in the proportion of its parts?"(1:39). The hexameter verse of

[102] Herder, *The Spirit of Hebrew Poetry*, 2:233.

[103] *Letters to Bridges*, p. 49.

[104] Indeed, as far as classical models were concerned, he always chose Pindar, the most antinomian of classical poets, whose verse was often compared, by Lowth and others, with biblical style.

[105] Herder, *The Spirit of Hebrew Poetry*, 1:27. Page and volume references to this work appear in the text hereafter.

the Greeks, even all rhyme, is for Herder a continued parallel-ism (ibid.). But, whereas the Sapphic odes are "finely woven," in the poetry of the Hebrews "the two strings of pearls are not twisted into a garland, but simply hang one over against the other"(1:40). The symmetry and proportion of Hebrew verse, perceptible to the dullest ear, gratify the senses.

Yet Herder, always the holistic psychologist, sees parallel-ism as involving not only the sensuous, phonetic element of symmetry, but also the "breathing of emotion": "As soon as the heart gives way to its emotions, wave follows upon wave, and that is parallelism. . . . So soon as the first wave has passed away, or broken itself upon the rocks, the second swells again and returns as before. This pulsation of nature, this breathing of emotion, appears in all the language of passion" (1:41). But Herder did not stop at describing the sensuous and emotional aspects of parallelism, its ability to "gratify the ear" and to represent "the breathing of emotion"; he went on to describe parallelism as an ontological principle. Parallelism actually ex-ists in the universe, in the contrast between "the boundlessness of the heavens [and] the nothingness of the earth, their eleva-tion [and] our abasement" (1:58). Herder, not satisfied with making parallelism merely rhetorical or even merely psycho-logical, must make it also cosmological. We have seen how much Hopkins makes of symmetry and proportion in his own poetics, and how strong is his emphasis on the "body" or pho-netic element of poetry. As the journal entries indicate, Hop-kins too found parallelism as an ontological principle in na-ture, and he spoke of "the principle of parallelism" as a comparison made between art and life (*Journals*, p. 75).

When we turn back to Hopkins' reading of parallelism, however, we can see that although he shares with Herder a tendency to make of parallelism a universal principle, he more carefully grounds this principle in the form. Although he adopts Lowth's distinction between synonymous and anti-thetical parallelism, he makes them convey not equivalence and agreement but surprise, the *and yet* that corrects as much as confirms what went before. In short, he sees both the aesthetic and semantic potential of parallelism. Hopkins went beyond both the rationalist alternative offered by Lowth and the Romantic one offered by Herder to see in parallelism a holism of feeling, the poet's prepossession, wedded to thought and expression.

Parallelism became in Hopkins' thought and in his hands the way of heightening the current language, of taking the "natural and national" speech and marking or inscaping it. Poetic language in Hopkins' theory of poetry had to be special, not only in its diction, images, and lofty sentiments, but especially in its repeated figures, its parallelisms. In his lecture notes titled "Poetry and Verse," written in 1873–1874 while teaching at Manresa House, Roehampton, Hopkins again stresses the repetitions of verse and identifies them as poetry's inscape:

> (Poetry is in fact speech only employed to carry the inscape of speech for the inscape's sake—and therefore the inscape must be dwelt on. Now if this can be done without repeating it *once* of the inscape will be enough. . . . If not/repetition, *oftening, over-and-overing, aftering* of the inscape must take place in order to detach it to the mind and in this light poetry is speech which afters and oftens its inscape, speech couched in a repeating figure and verse is spoken sound having a repeating figure.) (*Journals*, p. 289)

Hopkins' "speech which afters and oftens its inscape" becomes in this essay "speech framed for contemplation of the mind." The subject of contemplation is briefly addressed here, although it will be taken up extensively in the last two chapters of this study.

BIDDING TO CONTEMPLATION

It is to the element of reader response that we now turn in our reconstruction of a Hopkins poetics. Of course, we have been there already, for in the surprise created by the *and yet* of each parallelism and in the parallelism of thought created by any parallelism of expression, Hopkins is pointing to the reader or spectator. And, as with any idea that meant a great deal to him, he has invented his own term for it. Hopkins called it "bidding," which he defined as "the art or virtue of saying everything right *to* or *at* the hearer, interesting him, holding him in the attitude of correspondent or addressed or at least concerned, making it everywhere an act of intercourse—and of discarding everything that does not bid, does not tell."[106] Geoffrey Hartman has called attention to this vocative element in Hopkins' poetry as has Marylou Mott in her recent study.[107] Hopkins' addresses to the reader, his imperatives to "Look" or "Buy" or "Bid," are one aspect of the bidding of his own poems. But in his early poetics, this element of bidding the reader also takes the form of surprise, of parallelism of thought and especially of asking the reader to encounter the poem in contemplation.

The repetitions of parallel form convey the "biblical awe" of contemplation that comes from standing before the holy. Hopkins disallowed absolute contemplation except in a trance (*Journals*, p. 126), because with absolute contemplation there would be only speechless awe and not the conscious, poetic rendering of the awesome. Parallelism was therefore appealing to him because it combines literary ingenuity with an extreme of contemplative awe that approaches trance. The type of this combination is Balaam, who "falls in trance but has open eyes" (Num. 24:4), the visionary who speaks in well-ordered sentences.[108]

---

[106] *Letters to Bridges*, p. 160.

[107] Hartman, "Introduction: Poetry and Justification," in his *Hopkins: A Collection of Critical Essays* (Englewood Cliffs: Prentice-Hall, 1966), pp. 7–8; Marylou Mott, *"Mined with a Motion": The Poetry of Gerard Manley Hopkins* (New Brunswick: Rutgers Univ. Press, 1984).

[108] See James Muilenburg, "A Study in Hebrew Rhetoric: Repetition and Style," *Supplements to Vetus Testamentum*, vol. 1 (Leiden: E. J. Brill, 1953), p.

We can observe a tendency toward increasingly parallelistic form as utterance becomes gradually more passionate and God-inflamed in the eleventh chapter of the book of the prophet Hosea, a book considered to exhibit little parallelism. In the opening lines (Hos. 11:1), the prophet has God speaking about His love by means of parallelism:

> When Israel was a child I loved him,
> and I called my son out of Egypt. [109]

As the catalog of Israel's falling away from God's love begins, however, the text drops completely out of parallelism, as seen in lines such as these:

> My people are diseased through their disloyalty,
> they call on Baal,
> but he does not cure them. (Hos. 11:7)

Yet, all references to the tender, intensely parental love of God are couched in nearly complete parallelism:

> I myself taught Ephraim to walk,
> I took them in my arms; (Hos. 11:3)

> Ephraim, how could I part with you?
> Israel, how could I give you up? (Hos. 11:8a)

> My heart recoils from it,
> my whole being trembles at the thought. (Hos. 11:8c)

As in these verses from Hosea, parallelism was associated in biblical speech with the uncommon and uncanny—with the holy. Hopkins did not want "what oft' was thought but ne'er so well expressed" but rather uncommon thought, the surprise or instress of the extraordinary. Wanting to erect differ-

---

106. Muilenberg's article is one of the best in English on the phenomenon of repetition. Louis Newman too notes that "Inspiration equal to biblical grandeur and complexity of poetic forms are compatible," in *Parallelism in Amos.* Part 1 of *Studies in Biblical Parallelism*, p. 135.

109 The translations that follow are from the *Jerusalem Bible.*

ence, even reversal, on the foundation of parallelism's agreement, he multiplied parallelisms to convey the sense of the holy in his verse. In the series of paradoxes from stanza 9 of *The Wreck of the Deutschland*, for example, there is apparent symmetry in the joining by the coordinate *and*, and the breakup of such symmetry in the stressful, surprising part:

> Thou art lightning and love, I found it, a winter and
>   warm;
> Father and fondler of heart thou hast wrung:
> Hast thy dark descending and most art merciful then.

Even in its content, Part I of *The Wreck*, with its uneasy alliance between God's mastery and mercy, resembles the debate in God's heart between his anger and his love in Hosea:

> My heart recoils within me,
>   my compassion grows warm and tender.
> I will not execute my fierce anger,
>   I will not again destroy Ephraim.
>   (Hos. 11:8c–9a; Revised Standard Version)

Hopkins, too, used parallelism, as we shall see in the next chapter, to express the height of religious emotion in the face of the sacred in *The Wreck of the Deutschland*. In doing so, he was bidding the reader to contemplation of the mystery of holiness.

Hopkins uses the word *contemplation* to describe both an energy of the mind and the nature of art in notes dated February 9, 1868, which begin "All words mean either things or relations of things" (*Journals*, pp. 125–126). After discussing the three ὅροι or moments of the word alluded to above—its prepossession, definition, and application—he concentrates on the middle term, the definition or expression, which he reads back into the mind as an energy, an "inchoate word." He perceives two kinds of energy in the mind, "a transitional kind, when one thought or sensation follows another," and "an abiding kind . . . in which the mind is absorbed (as far as that may be), taken up by, dwells upon, enjoys, a single thought: we may call it contemplation" (*Journals*, pp. 125–126). Twentieth-century epistemologists and psychologists have invested a great deal of thought in identifying these two ways of knowing, which have been called on the one hand the discursive, linear, analytic, and rational, and on the other the intuitive, spatial, synthetic, and nonrational.

For the contemplative tradition inaugurated by Plato and Plotinus, contemplation means simply beholding, seeing, but in more than a sensory way. It means letting the world speak first, rather than remaining in the chaos of feeling, or ordering that chaos in the self and world through intellection. As Evelyn Underhill explains it, in the contemplative mode of experiencing, there is "a self-forgetting attentiveness, a profound concentration, a self-merging, which operates a real communion between the seer and the seen."[110]

If by contemplation one understands a "mental attitude in which all things give up to us the secret of their life,"[111] then Hopkins' instress and inscape are a contemplative way of experiencing the world. The instress is the awe and astonishment that accompany the act of vision; the inscape is the secret of the world's inner beauty opened up by that seeing. Insofar as possible, Hopkins has transposed both the "what" of his contemplative seeing, the inscape, and the "how," the instress, into the poem, and therefore into the contemplative act of encountering the poem. Parallelisms in sound and expression engender parallelism of thought: form itself becomes eloquent. It is an eloquence heard only in contemplation.

[110] Evelyn Underhill, *Mysticism* (New York: E. P. Dutton, 1961), p. 300.
[111] Ibid., p. 301.

2

"Meaning Motion": Parallelism in
The Wreck of the Deutschland,
Part the First

WHEN ONE TURNS from Hopkins' critical theory to his actual poetry, especially to *The Wreck of the Deutschland*, the first poem to break his seven-year self-imposed silence as a poet, one may well ask, How much, if at all, does his literary theory influence his own writing of poetry? How much, therefore, do his thoughts about parallelism inform his own poetry? Almost anyone who reads his essays, his letters, and his spiritual writings would concur with the early reaction to the publication of his prose writings—his work is all of a piece. Indeed, his own thought, whether expressed in essay, letter, sermon, or poem, has been "an effort at unity." Yet, the nature of that unity is not immediately apparent.

A translation from Plato's *Philebus* that Hopkins made as a young undergraduate could well be taken as a commission to those seeking the underlying unity of that thought: "we have always one idea to presuppose in everything and in each case to look for that; for it is there and we shall find it."[1] The one

---

[1] From Unpublished Oxford Essays, D6, no. 5; some unpublished material

idea that we presuppose in all Hopkins' work is inscape, the outer form of inward beauty that defines a thing. Hopkins' theoretical interests, therefore, remained constant over his whole life; though the terms might change from parallelism, proportion, symmetry, and surprise, to inscape and instress, the forms explored in his university essays showed themselves part of his intuitive life, carrying over into the shape of his poetry. Once it is seen in its broader dimensions and not simply as a theory of sprung rhythm that forms only one aspect of it, Hopkins' theory of poetry does not overwhelm but actually illuminates the poetry. Because in him "thought and expression" are truly "indistinguishable," his thinking about parallelism, rather than being a passing interest, informs and energizes his peculiarly inscaped art. Parallelism is the inscape or individuating principle of Hopkins' poetry.

Hopkins himself tells us that he aims at inscape in poetry: "but as air, melody, is what strikes me most of all in music and design in painting, so design, pattern or what I am in the habit of calling 'inscape' is what I above all aim at in poetry."[2] Yet, even with all the definitions accrued by scholars for the notion of inscape, and even with the considerable number of exegeses offered for *The Wreck of the Deutschland*,[3] in terms of

---

is appendixed in James Finn Cotter, *Inscape: The Christology and Poetry of Gerard Manley Hopkins* (Pittsburgh: Univ. of Pittsburgh Press, 1972), Appendix I.

[2] *Letters to Bridges*, p. 66.

[3] Among interpretations of this poem are W. H. Gardner's in *Gerard Manley Hopkins: A Study of Poetic Idiosyncrasy in Relation to Poetic Tradition*, 2 vols. (New Haven: Yale Univ. Press, 1948), 1:38–70; Robert R. Boyle, S.J.'s "The Thought Structure of *The Wreck of The Deutschland*," in *Immortal Diamond: Studies in Gerard Manley Hopkins*, ed. Norman Weyand, S.J. (New York: Sheed and Ward, 1949), pp. 333–350; Todd K. Bender's in *Gerard Manley Hopkins: The Classical Background and Critical Reception of His Work* (Baltimore: Johns Hopkins Univ. Press, 1966), pp. 71–96; John Pick's in *Gerard Manley Hopkins, Priest and Poet*, 2d ed. (New York: Oxford Univ. Press, 1966), pp. 40–51; and the essays in *Readings of The Wreck: Essays in Commemoration of the Centenary of G. M. Hopkins' The Wreck of the Deutschland*, ed. Peter Milward, S.J. and Raymond Schoder, S.J. (Chicago: Loyola Univ. Press, 1976).

its inscape this poem still remains what his friend and fellow
poet, Robert Bridges, called it, "the dragon in the gate." In
this chapter I propose looking at Part I of this poem in terms
of the structural device Hopkins elaborated not only as an un-
dergraduate at Oxford but again as a teacher of rhetoric only
one or two years before he began his great ode. The proximity
of his speculations on parallelism to the actual writing of *The
Wreck*, as well as references to this rhetorical mode in letters
that date from 1875 to 1876, the time of its composition, war-
rant an examination of the poem to see how important a role
parallelism actually played.

From comments in his letters we can discern that Hopkins
continued thinking about parallelism long after his remarks in
the essays. For example, to Richard Watson Dixon he illus-
trates the principle of equal stress with "an antithesis or par-
allelism, for there the contrast gives the counterparts equal
stress; e.g. 'sanguinary consequences, terrible butchery,
frightful slaughter, fell swoop': if these are taken as alternative
expressions, then the total strength of *sanguinary* is no more
than that of *terrible* or of *frightful* or of *fell* and so on of the
substantives too."[4] In a letter defending his poem against
Bridges' charges of obscurity, Hopkins offers a contemplative
method for reading it based on its parallelisms: "Granted that
it needs study and is obscure, for indeed I was not over desir-
ous that the meaning of all should be quite clear, at least un-
mistakable, you might, without the effort that to make it all
out would seem to have required, have nevertheless read it so
that lines and stanzas should be left in the memory and super-
ficial impressions deepened."[5] In the words of his early essays,
Hopkins is telling Bridges that parallelisms of expression in
the lines and stanzas lead on to parallelism of thought. What
Hopkins offers Bridges as a hermeneutic strategy is in effect a
contemplative mode of reading his poem. Because Hopkins

[4] *Correspondence*, p. 22.
[5] *Letters to Bridges* (May 13, 1878), p. 50.

intended his poem to be an ode rather than a narrative,[6] it involves not the linear, "transitional" energy appropriate to narrative poetry, but the "memory kept on the strain," the "abiding energy" of contemplation. "Lines and stanzas should be left in the memory," since the predominant artifice connecting line to line and stanza to stanza is parallelism. Parallelisms of expression serve to deepen "superficial impressions." Hopkins puts precisely the effect of parallelism in rendering a contemplative experience of the poem. If parallelism is the outer form of inscape, contemplation is its inner form or soul.

This chapter takes up the subject of parallelism of *resemblance*, the supreme instance in which form imitates meaning, or, as Hopkins put it, parallelisms of structure (sound) and expression (diction) generate parallelism of thought. Because parallelisms of sound—in alliteration, assonance, and rhyme—have been thoroughly examined in Hopkins' poems, we will concentrate here on grammatical and syntactic recurrences, that is, words, phrases, or whole lines that take up the thought of other words, phrases, and lines while imitating their formal sequence. Parallelism of resemblance is an almost ironic expression, for every "resemblance" in a Hopkins poem still manages to surprise us by its nuanced difference. In its "aftering" (*Journals*, p. 289), it is also instressing what has gone before. Hopkins' definition of poetry as "speech which afters and oftens its inscape, speech couched in a repeating figure," from the Roehampton lecture notes of about 1873, makes parallelism of resemblance an important, perhaps the most important, structural principle of the poem he was about to write two years later—*The Wreck of the Deutschland*.

From comments in his letters and lecture notes, then, we can infer that Hopkins intends the many appositives and conjunctive forms, the groups of two, three, or more words or phrases found as a constant characteristic of his poetic style, to be parallelisms, that is, "counterparts" but yet maintaining "contrast." In Jakobson's terms, the effect is integrative as well

[6] Ibid., p. 49.

as cumulative.[7] Metonymy becomes metaphor as the world begins to converge. Parallelism of resemblance constitutes the Parmenidean moment, the unity, of Hopkins' poem. Yet, the resemblances of *The Wreck* afford only a reticent unity, like that of a biblical psalm, where images and emotions abruptly follow one another in Heraclitean fashion, exacting of the reader an energy of contemplation to rediscover the poem's unity. To discover unity in *The Wreck of the Deutschland* is analogous to its discovery in an entropic world. Though parallelism integrates, it leaves still surging beneath the surface the tensions that continued to be the impetus of much of Hopkins' great poetic work. These tensions proved to be a grace in Hopkins' life, as this his major poem recognizes.

Although no critic has actually taken up the subject of parallelism in Hopkins' poems, W. H. Gardner, one of the most thorough critics to date, has noticed its prevalence. "Parallelism in thought and syntax," he says, "is one of the outstanding features of Hopkins' style."[8] Despite this admission, and the later one that an important structural characteristic is the "asyndetic series of parallel statements,"[9] parallelism as a subject is not treated further in Gardner's chapter on "Diction and Syntax" (chap. 4) and is not listed in the index.[10] Commenting on *The Wreck* Robert Boyle says, "The essential unity of the

[7] Jakobson, "Grammatical Parallelism," pp. 399–429.

[8] Gardner, *A Study*, 1:109. Exceptions to the general silence on parallelism are Sr. Marcella Holloway's articles on antithetical parallelism and particularly with regard to *The Wreck* her " 'The Rarest-Veinèd Unraveller' ": Hopkins as Best Guide to *The Wreck*" in *Readings of The Wreck*, where she states, "Take the poem on any level, theme, character, setting, time—and the parallelisms are obvious, built into antithetical shapes" (p. 93).

[9] Gardner, *A Study*, 1:149.

[10] Gardner seems to maintain a preference for "chromatic parallelism," which he says provides "the intensity and *chiaroscura* of great poetry." As we have seen in Chap. 1, Hopkins himself preferred abrupt or "diatonic parallelism." Observing that Hopkins' images "frequently move forward in groups of twos and threes," Gardner relates the parallelism to the Welsh *dyfalu*. But Hopkins was thinking about parallelism long before he encountered a possible counterpart in Welsh.

whole poem is achieved by a perfect structural parallelism in which part is proportioned to part . . . [in Part I] the power of God masters the poet, in [Part II] the same power masters the nun."[11] Since, however, Boyle's article concentrates on the thought structure of the poem, he does not tie the parallelism of thought to the parallelism of structure. This interconnection between thought and expression is, as we saw in Chapter 1, Hopkins' aim in his essays about poetry. To do justice to this aim, then, and to the inscape of Hopkins' poem, we cannot look at the poem only in terms of form, as the New Critics have tended to do,[12] without regard to its religious meaning, an undeniably serious part of Hopkins' intention. We will look at the form as essentially directed to the religious meaning of the poem. The other possible error in treating these intensely personal stanzas would be to ignore the form entirely and give an exclusively existential, romantic, or biographical reading. Hopkins' poem precludes this sort of reading by its very difficulty, a difficulty he defended again and again to Bridges. It forces us to look at the form, seeing more than technical virtuosity, and ask Why?

Hopkins explained the impetus for writing the poem to his friend, Canon Dixon: "when in the winter of '75 the Deutschland was wrecked in the mouth of the Thames and five Franciscan nuns, exiles from Germany by the Falck Laws, aboard of her were drowned I was affected by the account and happening to say so to my rector he said he wished someone would write a poem on the subject."[13] Hopkins wrote his first poem as a Jesuit priest to be an ode of praise for a God who would allow the senseless drowning of passengers from a ship sinking on the very shores of England. From its conception, it was intended to encompass the negative and the absurd. It

[11] Boyle, "The Thought Structure," p. 342.

[12] See Todd Bender's treatment of the reception of Hopkins' poetry, beginning with I. A. Richard's epoch-making 1926 article, in the first chapter of Bender's *The Classical Background*, pp. 12–13ff.

[13] *Correspondence*, p. 14.

is interesting to compare this shipwreck with that of Paul as recounted by the author of Acts (27:9–44): after his wreck, Paul gets to Rome but only on scattered pieces of the ship. But Paul's shipwreck gives him one more opportunity to credit the mercy of God rather than the false security of human conveyances. In Hopkins' poem, too, the poet and the nun are thrown upon the grace of God rather than upon their own self-efforts. Their own "foundering" ("That Nature is a Heraclitean Fire") makes room for grace. Part I, the poet's account of his daunting religious experience, and Part II, the experience of the nun who cries to Christ in her extremity, mutually illuminate and strengthen one another. Struggling with despair, the poet needs to draw strength as much from the nun's faith as from his own resources. If she could "Read the unshapeable shock night/ and [know] the who and the why," so too could he. Equally, if he has experienced near disintegration and yet great mercy in God's "dark descending," so too will the nuns. The I-Thou language of prayer that frames Hopkins' autobiographical account in Part I overarches the terrible events of Part II.

The first ten stanzas of *The Wreck of the Deutschland*, because they form a self-contained whole within which to observe closely the movement of form, provide an obvious choice for a study of the parallelistic underthought of Hopkins' poetry. These stanzas, Part I of the two-part poem, also constitute the poet's confession of the turning points in his religious life. In these opening stanzas of *The Wreck*, parallelism, as Hopkins himself pointed out, seems to increase with the growing intensity of religious emotion. Thus, this section of the poem offers a good case for testing the assumption that parallelism is the formal inscape in Hopkins' work.

Stanza 1 contains in miniature the movement of the whole poem, from Creation ("Thou hast bound bones and veins in me,") to Fall ("And after it almost unmade") to Redemption ("And dost thou touch me afresh?"). This stanza hints too at

the dialectic in the spiritual life between death to self and re-
birth to a new life.

> Thou mastering me
> God! giver of breath and bread;
> World's strand, sway of the sea;
> Lord of living and dead;
> Thou hast bound bones and veins in me, fastened me flesh,
> And after it almost unmade, what with dread,
> Thy doing: and dost thou touch me afresh?
> Over again I feel thy finger and find thee.

The first stanza begins on the downbeat as it were, with a
heavy emphasis given its first word, "Thou." In the first four
lines, all end-stopped but the first, which rushes to a halt on
the word "God!," there are no verbs but the participial "mas-
tering." All is stasis, bound in a rigid syntactic series of parallel
appositives. The very parallelism of these phrases seeks to
unite them, though there is powerful tension between them.
The series ends on the word, "dead," which, though it rhymes
with "bread," seems to give the lie to the assertion of that line.
A similar opposition exists in the third line, where this God is
both "strand," outside the world as a transcendent shore (es-
pecially that of a foreign country), and the very "sway of the
sea," the immanent motion that makes for the flux of the
world and the threat to creation in the floods of Genesis. But
God's *ruah* or breath, which hovered over the deep, was
breathed into human life, making it "living spirit." Once we
begin to see these lines as a tissue of contrasts, even the
rhymed words "me" and "sea" appear as antitheses, the sea
threatening to swallow up and almost unmake the individual
"me." Only at the end of the stanza does this "me" find an-
other rhyme in "thee," ending the threat of extinction of "me"
and bridging the gulf between "me" and this God outside of
time. The "Thou" and "thee" addressed to God at beginning
and end bind into fragile unity a stanza and in fact a poem
about the kind of God who makes and unmakes, who touches

both with mighty sway of the sea and with delicate finger. This intimate address to God encompasses not only the stanza but all of Part I, signalling that the poem's ultimate unifying reference is the all-encompassing grace of God.

In one sense, this is a poem about grace, the awakening ("momentary"), sustaining ("continuous"), and elevating graces that have drawn the poet toward God even as he experienced despair. Part I of the poem employs a trinitarian sequence or procession of graces: God the Father's lightning rod awakening, the Son's sustaining and correcting through Eucharist and gospel, and the Holy Spirit's transforming through elevating grace. "Grace," says Hopkins in his spiritual notes, "is any action, activity, on God's part by which, in creating or after creating, he carries the creature to or towards the end of its being, which is its self-sacrifice to God and its salvation."[14] He elsewhere calls the Father's grace "creative," the Son's " 'medicinal,' corrective, redeeming," and the Holy Spirit's "elevating."[15] Commentaries on this poem have not usually noticed the correlation between the dramatic events of the poet's interior life in Part I and Hopkins' writings on grace. Before writing this poem, Hopkins had struggled with, and been subdued, consumed, touched, and transformed by God. The poet's despair actually enabled him to experience God's threefold grace. Even St. Ignatius, the founder of The Society of Jesus, knew the graceful quality of doubt when he uttered the prayer, "Lord, I believe; help thou my unbelief."

The central question raised by both Parts I and II, "Is the shipwreck then a harvest?" (st. 31) remains a real, not a rhetorical, question throughout the poem. The question is answered as much on the formal, material level of the poem as on the semantic one. The coherence achieved by the poem's structural repetitions is part of its purpose as theodicy. Paral-

[14] See *The Sermons and Devotional Writings of Gerard Manley Hopkins*, ed. Christopher Devlin, S.J. (London: Oxford Univ. Press, 1959), p. 154.
[15] Ibid., p. 158.

lelisms glimmer amid the poem's dark events like the stars in stanza 5 that waft God out of themselves, yielding their inscape, that is, to the poet or reader who looks or acknowledges them in a contemplative act. In lecture notes on poetry and verse from this period, Hopkins actually speaks of intermittent repetition in verse as "brilliancy, starriness" (*Journals*, p. 290). Like the stars in the night sky, the structural repetitions of alliteration, internal rhyme, and syntax hint at the order and meaning hidden behind the world's opacity. In a letter to Baillie, Hopkins spoke of two strains of thought, the overthought and the underthought, running together and counterpointed in a lyric poem.[16] The underthought, only half-realized by the poet himself, he compares to "canons and repetitions in music."[17] Such repetitions can even counterpoint or give the lie to the overthought or manifest meaning of the poem. In fact, in several places Hopkins implies that the structure of repetitions, the underthought, may be the real meaning of the poem or work of art.[18]

This is not to deny that the poem has reference, but to ask that we look more closely at its "deep structure," or in Hopkins' words, that we deepen its superficial impressions. What

---

[16] *Further Letters* (January 14, 1883), p. 105.

[17] Ibid. He states further that he finds such a principle of composition in St. James', St. Peter's, and St. Jude's Epistles "an undercurrent of thought governing the choice of images used." Even though it is odd that he exempts St. Paul's Epistles from this list, it is clear from this statement and from the use he does make of Paul in his devotional work that the New Testament writers had a stylistic influence on Hopkins.

[18] In a letter to Bridges, Hopkins, speaking of Chopin's music, says its being and meaning lies outside itself in the harmonies. *Letters to Bridges*, p. 213. Similarly, he says of Purcell, "while he is aiming only at impressing me his hearer with the meaning in hand I am looking out meanwhile for his specific, his individual markings and mottlings, 'the sakes of him.' " *Letters to Bridges*, p. 170. He makes a more subtle and profound statement of the meaning of form in an unpublished essay, "The change or passing from [matter to form] is motion and its meaning is form, the realization of form in matter." "Connection of Aristotle's metaphysics with his ethics," Unpublished Oxford Essays D11, no. 4; published in Cotter, *Inscape*, pp. 310–312.

it references is order and design in an apparently chaotic, Heraclitean universe.[19] Hopkins' loosening or springing of rhythm from its centuries-old shackles in convention testifies to the very real entropy, the shipwrecks, we face in the universe, while his increasing the repetitions or harmonies of the verse gives his "half-realised" conviction that entropy is overcome. Thus, the central tensions of the poem, his despair and God's grace in both his own and the nun's life, play themselves out on the precognitive, sensuous level of the poem. The tension between the disunifying sprung rhythm and the unifying parallelisms reinforces the poem's expression of a dialectic in the spiritual life between despair and grace, Fall and Redemption. Hopkins has realized that even apparent entropy can be hidden redemption, that "chance left free to act falls into an order as well as purpose" (*Journals*, p. 230), that within each fall/Fall is the opportunity for God's grace. Both Parts I and II express this hidden paradox. The underthought of the poem, then, expressed in its parallelisms, works toward Parmenidean unity despite Heraclitean chaos.

Thus, each of stanza 1's tensive oppositions is held in unity by the parallel appositives, coordinates, and rhymes. For, despite the oppositions set up in the first four lines—death and life, creation and annihilation, transcendence and immanence—the form itself, the parallel syntactic structure reinforced by parallelism of sound, tends toward Parmenidean unity. The poem works because of its parallelism: Creation is paralleled to the Fall and to spiritual rekindling. All the events of Part I parallel stanza 1's last line, "Over again I feel thy finger and find thee," and reveal themselves as the Thou's acts of grace. Parallelism, tiresomely called "just the same thing in

---

[19] Hopkins' sympathy with Heraclitus is evidenced in another early essay where he describes him as one "who felt beyond any of his predecessors the chaos, uncertainty, and illusion of all things," but who "spoke nevertheless of a rhythm, something imposed by mind as an air on the notes of a flute." "The connection of mythology with Philosophy," Unpublished Oxford Essays, D6, no. 5; published in Cotter, *Inscape*, pp. 307–309.

other words" for the greater part of two centuries, does function to create sameness amid obvious difference. Hopkins exploits this function here to unite antithetical phrases. Parallelism in these phrases effects a convergence in the nature and activity of this one, modeless God.[20] Even Heraclitean multiplicity gives way to Parmenidean convergence if we look with the abiding energy of the mind, rather than in discrete, atomistic frames. The Parmenidean side of Hopkins could rest content only with that wholeness.

The deeper reason for this union of contradictions, then, lies in the very nature of the God Hopkins seeks to describe. Here and throughout the poem, God's making and unmaking become, through the persistent parallelisms, one providential act. This series is not a Whitmanesque, cumulative catalogue, precisely because one cannot list separate attributes of God, the wholly simple. Neither does one break up God's activity into temporal sequences. Like the eternal ebb and flow of the sea, the act of "I Am" *is*; there is no before and after, no this and that. For this reason, conjunctions have been replaced by the more interlocking semicolons of asyndeton. The underthought of this passage conveys God's oneness and atemporality, though that simplicity may break up for us into what seem the separate realities of life and death, distance and intimacy. God's oneness is hidden in the Heraclitean blur of events ("under the world's splendour and wonder," st. 5), just as unity is hidden in the poem's structure.

After the tight parallel appositives of the first half of the stanza, the syntax of the last four lines opens and loosens into deliberately consecutive statements about the breaking in of history, both the poet's personal history and salvation history. Hopkins connects the clauses of the second half, as often

[20] As Hopkins said of convergence in an early essay: "The multiplicity of ends converges in one end. . . . Besides the multiplicity and convergence, actions must not be infinite, or in other words they really must converge," and he criticized contemporary philosophy because it "does not think of the whole." Unpublished Oxford Essays, G1 and D6.

throughout his poetry, with the coordinate conjunction "and." This "paratactic" connector, because it does not subordinate, gives each clause equal status with the others. The poet is not presuming to guess at the logical relations that underlie God's actions in his life. Parataxis, which involves the joining of clauses by simple coordinate conjunctions like "and" and "but," belongs to "simple yes and is" rather than to the hypotactic fashioning of motives, causes and defenses. Erich Auerbach shows how Augustine, so greatly imbued with the complex style of Latin rhetoric, abandoned it for the simple parataxis of biblical style to give greater urgency and drama to his writing on the inner life.[21] The "and dost thou touch me afresh" introduced by the coordinate "and" is such an urgent, dramatic moment in Hopkins' poem. To recreate *The Wreck*'s inner drama, Hopkins deliberately chose parataxis to support the grammatical parallelism he wrote so abundantly into this poetic account of his spiritual life.

It is clear from his letters that Hopkins cared about connections in poetry. He tells Bridges, "though the sequence of thought of 'But of their wanton play' is beautiful, yet the dropping the connection is more austere and pathetic."[22] And in his essay, "On the Origin of Beauty," he commented that "the absence of *and* gives more antithesis."[23] He looked on all "modulation as a corruption, the undoing of the diatonic style," a synonym for parallelism, and admired the "infinite expressiveness" of plain chant.[24] Presumably, the "modulation" that would corrupt the diatonic, parallelistic style of his own poetry is hypotaxis. Hopkins was clearly aware of the power of the paratactic style and exploited it in his poetry. Intuitively, he practiced what Auerbach finds in Gen. 1:3: "It is precisely the absence of causal connectives, the naked state-

[21] Auerbach, *Mimesis*, pp. 71ff.

[22] *Letters to Bridges*, p. 70.

[23] *Journals*, p. 114. He was therefore equally aware of the effects of asyndeton.

[24] Letters to Bridges, p. 213.

ment of what happens—the statement which replaces deduction and comprehension by an amazed beholding that does not even seek to comprehend—which gives the sentence its grandeur."[25] In telling of awesome deeds and of the awesomeness of the Creator God, Hopkins here as elsewhere uses parataxis to suppress his own comprehension and, as we shall see, to increase the surprise, the instressing of the reader.[26]

The movement in these lines, from Creation (line 5) to Fall (line 6) to the possibility of Redemption (line 7), is the movement of the entire first part of the poem and the recapitulation of salvation history. Only, where William Blake, following Boehme, had seen the Creation as a Fall, Hopkins, following Paul, sees the Fall as Redemption and the Redemption as a new Creation. In the section of his commentary on Ignatius' *Spiritual Exercises* titled "Creation and Redemption: The Great Sacrifice," Hopkins makes this identification explicit: "[humankind's] correspondence with grace and seconding of God's designs is like a taking part in their own creation, the creation of their best selves."[27] Both the poet in Part I and the nun in Part II, in corresponding with grace from "the dark side of the bay of [God's] blessing," seconding even God's dark designs, assist in "the creation of their best selves."

> I did say yes
> O at lightning and lashed rod;
> Thou heardst me truer than tongue confess
> Thy terror, O Christ, O God;
> Thou knowest the walls, altar and hour and night:
> The swoon of a heart that the sweep and the hurl of thee
> trod

[25] Auerbach, *Mimesis*, p. 110.

[26] Hopkins suppresses conjunctions as often as he uses them, making for a logical ambiguity—both difference and sameness are implied. James Milroy in *The Language of Gerard Manley Hopkins* (London: André Deutsch, 1977) sees the parataxis in Hopkins as an imitation of ordinary speech, useful in narrative.

[27] *Sermons*, p. 197.

Hard down with a horror of height:
And the midriff astrain with leaning of, laced with fire of
    stress.

Hopkins' response to the first stanza, given at the outset of
the second, is well illustrated by his definition of elevating
grace in his commentary on the *Spiritual Exercises*: "this is
truly God's finger touching the very vein of personality which
. . . man can respond to by no play whatever, by bare ac-
knowledgement only."[28] Hopkins' "bare acknowledge-
ment"—the "I did say yes"—is recorded in a bare, brief first
line that is more like a whisper. This "yes," the only response
one can make to the irresistible might and terror of God, is
also the "most pregnant and straightforward to the truth,"
containing all the "play" that will follow. For in this "yes" the
human being reveals its true pitch as defined in Hopkins' spir-
itual commentary:

> So also *pitch* is ultimately simple positiveness, that by
> which being differs from and is more than nothing and
> not-being, and it is with precision expressed by the Eng-
> lish *do* (the simple auxiliary), which when we employ or
> emphasise, as 'he said it, he did say it,' we do not mean
> that the fact is any more a fact but that we the more state
> it. (It is also at bottom the copula in logic and the Welsh
> *a* in 'Efe a ddywedodd.') (*Sermons*, p. 151)

Hopkins here equates the auxiliary *do* to the copula *is* of his
"Parmenides" essay and to the Welsh *a*, meaning *and*. In all
these connections, seemingly at the simplest substratum of
language, we encounter the overwhelming and fundamental

[28] "On Personality, Grace, and Free Will," *Sermons*, p. 158. Hereafter cited
in the text as *Sermons*. The poet's feeling the finger of God might be compared
to Adam's touching the finger of God in Michelangelo's Creation of Man in
the Sistine Chapel. Hopkins also calls the Holy Spirit "the finger of God's
right hand." *Sermons*, p. 98.

fact of relation.[29] The "did" of this line expresses the "simple positiveness" or being of the person who is ready to correspond to the simplicity and overwhelming Being of God. With this line, Hopkins creates a "pitch" of vertical relation to a God who finds expression in "play" in the world.

The parataxis of these first four parallel lines of stanza 2 (lines 1 and 2 parallel to lines 3 and 4) also expresses the "simple positiveness" of this bare but pregnant statement. Yet, lines 3 and 4 go beyond and instress lines 1 and 2 by saying that this "yes" was actually silent ("truer than tongue") but truer than language's "yes," this "lightning" was actually God. Lines 3 and 4 ("Thou heardst me truer than tongue confess/ Thy terror, O Christ, O God") present on the one hand a deeper and on the other hand a more exalted version of lines 1 and 2. Here is one of several places in Part I of this poem where Hopkins opposes language's "known" to the unknown and the extralinguistic. His bare acknowledgment is an assent of the heart like Newman's "real" rather than "notional" assent.

Lines 5 and 6 particularize and externalize the cryptic interior event of the first four lines. Here again history, both as physical place and as time, is seen to emerge from and incarnate the timeless inner realm of the spirit. The pitch of assent that is "truer than tongue" does not remain inarticulate and without "play"; the passive being "instressed" of the last half of this stanza is paralleled by stanza 5's "stressing" of God's grace. The aspirate "h," repeated in "hour," "heart," "hurl," "Hard," "horror," and "height," like the sound of a voiceless cringing shudder, conveys further human aspiration or pitch, a leaning after and responding to God's inspiration. Does the sound of the alliterated "h" suggest the heavy breathing of one in steady retreat, or of one rising up to the challenge with mingled fear and fascination? Both, I think, are part of the under-

---

[29] Hopkins anticipates Heidegger in this, for Heidegger was to speak of language as the "relation of relations."

thought counterpointing the overthought of this passage. For, as Hopkins says in his spiritual notes, "The sigh of correspondence links the present, with its imperfect or faulty pitch of will, to the future . . . it *begins* to link it, . . . And even the sigh or aspiration itself is in answer to an inspiration of God's spirit" (*Sermons*, p. 156). Thus, human aspiration, a breathing in and sighing out in response to God's inspiration, is a response to the mystery as *fascinans* as well as *tremendum*.

In the next stanza, the oscillation between these two responses, the swoon of terror and the "sigh of correspondence," continues until the poet gives a complete yes to the irresistible attraction of God. Throughout Part I, even the irregular line lengths express this oscillation between fear and fascination. Bare, tremulous first lines build in the second and third, subside in the fourth, open out more in the fifth and sixth, contract in the seventh, and yield to the longest line at the end.[30] While the first line, especially in the first four stanzas, often indicates the fear and powerlessness of the poet, the final line with its fullness expresses a plenitude of power (st. 2), of grace (sts. 3 and 4), or of fulfillment (st. 5). The lines mirror the rhythm of a spiritual life where every growth depends on cutting away, every fullness on emptying. The movement of the stanzas, then, from anxiety to awe, from loss to completion, from self to God, illustrates, as does the parallelism, Hopkins' belief that form is meaning, that it is, as he put it in "Henry Purcell," "meaning motion."

> The frown of his face
> Before me, the hurtle of hell
> Behind, where, where was a, where was a place?
> I whirled out wings that spell

---

[30] Gardner has shown that the stress pattern of each stanza remains a constant 6–3–4–5–4–6–6–4–7. John Keating calls attention to the separability of each stanza into halves, relating this to the antiphonal style of a dialogue between God and man. "A Continuous Structural Parallelism": Stanzaic Pattern in *The Wreck*," in *Readings of the Wreck*, pp. 155–161.

And fled with a fling of the heart to the heart of the
    Host.
My heart, but you were dovewinged, I can tell,
    Carrier-witted, I am bold to boast,
To flash from the flame to the flame then, tower from the
    grace to the grace.

The poet's experience in the second stanza has been that of
the numinous overpowering of God, like that described by
Rudolf Otto in *The Idea of the Holy*.[31] Mingled with God's
power is wrath (ὀργή), which Otto says is "like a hidden force
of nature, like stored-up electricity."[32] The charges from
God's lightning wrath, "electrical horror" (st. 27) and "all-fire
glances" (st. 23), are felt throughout the poem. Far from being
a tame apologetic treatment of his conversion, Hopkins' im-
ages reveal what it is like "to fall into the hands of the living
God." The proximity of the images in the first two lines of
this stanza, "frown of his face" and "hurtle of hell," gives God
a demonic quality, a near blasphemy that only a truth-seeker
would risk.[33] The nearly identical rhythm of these lines (iambs
followed by anapests), along with the parallelism of "Before
. . . / Behind . . . " at the beginning, contributes to the effect
of a steady beat and relentless tread of pursuit, perhaps paral-
leling the steady retreat of the poet in the stanza before. Con-
trasted with that doggedness is the frantic incoherence of the
pursued, conveyed in the broken and incremental repetition
of the question.

Hopkins' lines 4 and 5 ("I whirled out wings that spell/ And
fled with a fling of the heart to the heart of the Host"), full of
syntactic parallelism and enjambment, seem to arise unpre-

---

[31] Rudolf Otto, *The Idea of the Holy*, trans. John W. Harvey (London: Ox-
ford Univ. Press, 1950), pp. 19ff.

[32] Ibid., p. 18.

[33] Cf. Otto, *Idea of the Holy*, p. 13: "Specially noticeable is the *emah* of Yah-
weh ("fear of God") which Yahweh can pour forth, dispatching almost like a
demon, and which seizes a man with paralyzing effect."

pared for out of the panic of those first three lines. Instinctively, Hopkins is practicing what he describes to Bridges as the method of the fugue in music: "the answer in Bach and Handel enters, that is that the counterpoint begins, freely on an unprepared discord."[34] This kind of paratactic suddenness, without explanations, derives both from Hopkins' theology and from his understanding of counterpoint in music and poetry. The aspiration begun in the previous stanza reaches its fulfillment here; the poet, left utterly defenseless and without recourse in line 3, suddenly finds himself able to act in lines 4 and 5. Line 5's formal completeness and its massing of parallel elements ("And fled with a fling of the heart to the heart of the Host") indicate a sense of resolution and repose.

In the phrase "wings that spell," some critics, like Gardner, have seen the words "that spell" as referring to a period of time, while others have connected them to a statement Hopkins makes in his commentary on the *Spiritual Exercises'* "Contemplation for Obtaining Love": "This too brings out the nature of the man himself, as the lettering on a sail or device upon a flag are best seen when it fills" (*Sermons*, p. 195). As the man begins to experience the fullness of God, like a sail billowing in the wind of God's *ruah*, the "lettering" of the man's own nature or distinctive inscape becomes evident. His true individuality, then, is discovered in the Self of God, not in his own personality.[35] His true and best self is Christ, while the maker of this new creation is the Holy Spirit (*Sermons*, p. 100). In addition to these meanings of the words "that spell" I would add, given the other structural characteristics of the lines, that the poet's "wings," his fully acknowledged aspiration toward God, give a rest or relief, a "spell," to his frantic fear of God.

---

[34] *Letters to Bridges* (January 12, 1888), p. 271.

[35] Hopkins copied the following quotation from the *Rig Veda*, found in Max Müller's *Chips from a German Workshop*, into his notebook (D7): "Self is the Lord of all things, Self is the King of all things . . . all selves are contained in this Self. Brahman itself is the Self."

Line 5 means further, as most critics have agreed, that the poet has fled from his own heart to that of the Eucharist, the Real Presence. The finality of this movement as an answer to the poet's dilemma is brought out by the symmetry of these last four lines: lines 5 and 8, semantically, grammatically, and phonetically parallel each other, as do lines 6 and 7. Hopkins will achieve and surpass this degree of symmetry only in the very last line of the poem: "Our hearts' charity's hearth's fire, our thoughts' chivalry's throng's Lord." Here he nearly stops the poem with the repetitions in imagery, words, and syntax in order to indicate, paradoxically, the repose in this movement to "the heart of the Host." This is the hospitable *place*, provided by the eternal "Host," Christ, where the poet can rest. The nearly identical images, "dovewinged and Carrier-witted," of lines 6 and 7 express the sure, peaceful return of one who is coming home,[36] all the while being inspired ("witted") to this return by the Holy Spirit.

It seems clear that the phrases "heart to the heart," "flame to the flame," and "grace to the grace" are meant to parallel each other both in form and in meaning. Yet, although Cotter recognizes this parallelism, he says, "the poet fled to the Sacred Heart and, homing there, mounts from Christ's flame of love to that flame of love in himself, from grace in Christ to that grace in himself."[37] In other words, he sees a movement to Christ and then away from Christ and back to the self. I do not see how this interpretation is justified. Rather, the identical parallel structure of each phrase engenders "parallelism of thought," as Hopkins said it would. That is, the movement from the poet's heart to the heart of the Host in line 5 is paralleled by the movement from the "flame" of self ("laced with

[36] Hopkins used the language of coming home in his observations of stars: "As we drove home the stars came out thick: I leant back to look at them and my heart opening more than usual praised our Lord to and in whom all that beauty comes home." *Journals*, p. 254. He also translated a passage of Parmenides, "Being draws-home to Being." *Journals*, p. 128.

[37] Cotter, *Inscape*, p. 28.

fire of stress" in st. 2) to the "flame" of God's burning love, and from the "grace" of correction to the "grace" of elevation to Christ.

For this last interpretation we must turn to Hopkins' spiritual notes, "On Personality, Grace, and Free Will." There he distinguishes between "corrective [grace], turning the will from one direction or pitting into another" and "elevating" grace, which lifts the will to a "parallel and higher" plane, "from one cleave of being to another and to a vital act in Christ" (*Sermons*, p. 158). Hopkins even says God moves the creature from one possible world to another (*Sermons*, p. 154). This movement from the old self to the new self, in Christ, matched and sustained by the parallelism, is also a Creation in Redemption. The poet finds his resting place and his complete identity not in himself but in the "Host," Christ. Self-abandonment, both for him and for the nun in Part II, brings about the creation of their "best selves," their Christ selves. But only their figurative and literal shipwrecks make this turn to and into Christ possible. The very terror of God at the beginning of the stanza hurls the poet into the arms of God by the end.

Yet another parallelism of lines 6 and 7 consists of the phrases "I can tell" and "I am bold to boast": the inarticulate poet of stanza 2 now has the freedom not only to move but to speak of it; he "*can* tell." The movement in the last four lines of stanza 3, however, is not simply a "parallelism," a synonymity or equivalence. That is its first moment, one that creates likeness in unlikeness or metaphor. But there is also a second moment that occurs when the second parallel word or phrase "afters" and alters by surpassing its counterpart. Thus, the "Carrier-witted" poet is not only peaceful, "dovewinged," but homeward bound; he cannot only "tell" but "boast" of it; he moves not only from his heart to the Host's but from the flame of his subjective self to the greater "flame" of God's love in the Eucharist, and, most significantly of all, from the grace of God's corrective action in his particular life, recounted in stanza 2, to the universal grace embodied in Christ.

We know how large a part belief in the Real Presence played in Hopkins' conversion to Catholicism;[38] these lines, with their sixfold iteration of the movement from the self to the Reality of the altar, celebrate that conversion. In this, as in his poetic theory, Hopkins is anti-Romantic, rejecting subjectivity and personality, and choosing reality in all its concreteness and otherness. The increased parallelism of this half of stanza 3 conveys not only stasis in movement, not only starriness in the vagueness of the abyss, but an elevated, consecrated thought. Like the elevation of the Host at the consecration of the Mass, the poet's heart is carried "to or towards the end of its being, which is its self-sacrifice to God and its salvation" (*Sermons*, p. 154).

> I am soft sift
> In an hourglass—at the wall
> Fast, but mined with a motion, a drift,
> And it crowds and it combs to the fall;
> I steady as a water in a well, to a poise, to a pane,
> But roped with, always, all the way down from the tall
> Fells or flanks of the voel, a vein
> Of the gospel proffer, a pressure, a principle, Christ's gift.

In stanza 4 (above), instead of moving on in a narrative order, the poet parallels the movement of stanza 3 with an image of desperation and no resort followed unexpectedly by an answer. Where the poet in stanza 3 had frantically sought a "place," in stanza 4 he is all too arrested in an hourglass place where, however, his life seeps out without hope of abiding. Hopkins knew this experience personally; to his sister he once said, "I have prescribed myself twenty-four hourglasses a day . . . even this does not stop the ravages of time."[39] The poet, "at the wall/ Fast," makes a futile attempt to cling to his hour-

---

[38] One of the great attractions of the Catholic religion for Hopkins was the doctrine of the Real Presence.

[39] *Further Letters* (April 25, 1871), pp. 114–115.

glass prison but finds his life running inexorably on as with
the motion of sand sifting through an hourglass or rapids
moving to a waterfall. The first three enjambed lines, fol-
lowed by the quick anapests and parallel syntax of line 4, head
rapidly to a full stop on the word "fall." This poet, who would
call himself "Time's eunuch," finds his life ravaged by time at
the point of complete defeat. On this note the answer arises,
offering stasis in the flux, elevation from the "fall." This fall
too is a grace and a new creation. The quick anapests of line 4
give way to the slow spondee, "I steady." The dry sand of the
hourglass, seemingly spent, has become the serene, ever re-
plenished water of a well. Despair over the falling away of life
has quietly turned to grace.

It is part of the poet's purpose to juxtapose these contrary
images of hourglass and well without hypotactic cause-and-
effect or sequential connections. No available logic could es-
tablish such connections. "Christ's gift" is free, not a reaction
to the poet's efforts. His efforts to save himself in lines 2 and
3 ("at the wall/ Fast") came to nought, undone by the anti-
thetical "but" of line 3. The parallel "But," however, promi-
nently placed at the beginning of line 7, supersedes that min-
ing motion to the fall (Fall) and establishes the "something
more" of the whole stanza. The paratactic structure of the two
halves of this stanza, rather than indicating that the poet has
fallen and *then* finds himself in a steady, life-giving well, im-
plies that both conditions are simultaneously present—espe-
cially from the standpoint of eternity. Even at the moment of
seeming dryness the ever-living water wells up unseen. This
"fall" too "galls [itself], breaks open, and "gash[es] gold-ver-
milion." The poet's life is held "Fast" (line 3) and "steady"
(line 5) not by his holding on to it but by his letting it go at the
same time that he discovers a "rope" to the vertical (cf.
"strand" of st. 1), an ascent or pitch as well as a deterioration.
This *kenosis* or emptying out of life has become a fullness.

The conversion of stanzas 2 and 3 has not been a once-and-
for-all salvation but must be continually renewed. The gospel

of Christ, constantly anchoring his descent, is the source of continued, steadying grace for the poet, just as the Eucharist was the "momentary" means of his answering the call of God. Hopkins spoke of these two kinds of grace, the "momentary" and the "continued," in his writings, "On Personality, Grace, and Free Will":

> a momentary shift from a worse, ungracious/ to a better, a gracious self, is a grace . . . bestowed for the moment and offered for a continuance. But the continued and unconstrained correspondence is a greater blessing and therefore still more a grace and as it was only possible through the first or constrained one (the "forestall"), the second multiples the first and is a grace upon a grace . . . what will be most strongly experienced when the after-consent is most perfect, is a condition, an "install" of ourselves in which we have consented to do, are doing, or have done that thing to which we feel God to be inviting us. (*Sermons*, pp. 154–155)

Grace is present not only in lightning-charged events but in the ordinariness of the everyday. In the last half of stanza 3, parallelism tightened up the discourse, "constrained" it; here the discourse is freer, unconstrained. The sacred moment of consecration gives way to the steady "install" of a life sustained by God. The stanza ends with four parallel appositives, "proffer," "pressure," "principle," "gift," a strong hint of the steadying sacred that "heeds but hides, bodes but abides" (st. 32).

> I kiss my hand
>   To the stars, lovely-asunder
>   Starlight, wafting him out of it; and
>   Glow, glory in thunder;
> Kiss my hand to the dappled-with-damson west:
> Since, tho' he is under the world's splendour and wonder,
>   His mystery must be instressed, stressed;

For I greet him the days I meet him, and bless when I under-
stand.

Out of this continued correspondence with God's grace
arises the poet's chivalric acknowledgment of God's manifes-
tations in nature, his free act of praise in kissing his hand to
the stars. This stanza, a hymn of praise, sets in motion much
that follows in Part I. Hopkins had reflected on the words that
stand at the beginning of St. Ignatius' *Spiritual Exercises*: "Man
is created to praise, reverence, and serve God our Lord, and
by this means to save his soul."[40] In his notes on the "First
Principle or Foundation" from which Ignatius' words are
taken, Hopkins defines praise as "the joyfully welcoming
God's manifestations of himself, with hope" (*Sermons*, p.
129). The terror and despair that formed parts of the last three
stanzas suddenly yield to an entire stanza of joyful confidence
in God. Sustained by the abiding, steadying grace of the last
stanza, the poet can now "look" to the stars as he bids others
do in his poem, "The Starlight Night." The stars had a special
symbolism for Hopkins; perhaps because they shine amid
darkness, they seem guarantees of light under all conditions. I
have already called attention to Hopkins' seeing the parallel-
isms of a poem as its "starriness." Here it is the fact that they
are "lovely-asunder," their Heraclitean quality, that is signifi-
cant and even purposeful. Hopkins once said, echoing Hera-
clitus, "All the world is full of inscape and chance left free to
act falls into an order as well as purpose."[41] Much of the beauty
of the poem's parallelisms is, in the same way, their apparent
randomness: they are "lovely-asunder" in the poem. The stars
"waft" God out of themselves, that is, carry him to man
lightly and faintly, without "doomsday dazzle" (st. 34) or
apocalyptic revelation. Yet, even this dim perception of God

---

[40] St. Ignatius Loyola, *The Spiritual Exercises of St. Ignatius*, trans. Anthony
Mottola (New York: Image Books, 1964), p. 47.

[41] *Journals*, p. 230. This comment was added as a footnote in Hopkins' man-
uscript.

can cause the poet to "Glow, Glory in thunder," to catch fire
from these stars as he did in the second stanza. This ability to
see God in the everyday and to be changed by God's presence
is the property of continued grace, and specifically of contem-
plation. Like the nun in Part II, the poet can, with God's
grace, know the Word that "Heaven and earth are word of,
worded by" (st. 29). The image in line 5, "the dappled-with-
damson west," like that in line 3, also represents light in dark-
ness, but now it is the waning light of sunset. That too must
be acknowledged, as it is again at the end of "God's Gran-
deur."

Lines 6 and 7 of stanza 5 express Hopkins' poetic task as
well as his theology. His task as a man of God and as a poet is
to be instressed by the mystery, to receive it in contemplative
receptivity and awe, then to *stress* it in the poem itself. The
poem can be seen as the praxis that follows θεωρία, the stress
that follows instress. Though inscape manifests God's pres-
ence in nature, as it manifests unity in the poem, it must first
be experienced by the poet and the reader and then stressed.
"Stress," Hopkins said in a letter to Patmore, "is the making a
thing more, or making it markedly, what it already is; it is the
bringing out its nature."[42] The stress that is the poem, then,
brings out the nature of the experience of God. In the final line
of the stanza, Hopkins' greetings turn to blessings; faith seeks
and finds understanding like that which is to follow in the
poem. Each word of the poem is a kissing of the hand to
Being, "one way of acknowledging Being," and each sentence
by its copula *is*, each full syntactic statement, is a blessing,
"the utterance and assertion of it" (*Journals*, p. 129). Thus, the
poem is actually strewn with such utterances of Being, such
blessings.[43] These blessings with their "simple positiveness"
deliver us from the night of incomprehension and terror.

[42] *Further Letters* (November 7, 1883), p. 327.

[43] In an unfinished poem, Hopkins was to say: "What I know of thee I
bless,/ As acknowledging thy stress/ On my being and as seeing/ Something
of thy holiness." *Poems*, p. 194.

Not out of his bliss
    Springs the stress felt
Nor first from heaven (and few know this)
    Swings the stroke dealt—
Stroke and a stress that stars and storms deliver,
    That guilt is hushed by, hearts are flushed by and melt—
    But it rides time like riding a river
(And here the faithful waver, the faithless fable and miss).

Stanza 6, continuing the theme of the poet's stress, consists structurally of two parallel negations (lines 1 and 2 parallel to lines 3 and 4), a long appositive between dashes, and a final affirmation introduced by the antithetical "But." The highly symmetrical physical properties of the first four lines, nearly complete parallelism reinforced by double rhymes and consonant chime, beget an equivalence in the two parallel pairs, "stroke and stress, stars and storms," of the fifth line. The alliteration of the *str* consonants, culminating in a line of four such alliterations (line 5), imitates the pulsating rhythm of God's constant stress on human life. Already we have seen the storms of the spiritual life, with their lightning strokes, as both crushing (st. 2) and glorifying (st. 5). We have seen the starlight gently instress the poet, bringing about his stress and blessing (st. 5), but we have also seen stress consume him (st. 2). God's terrifying strokes are as saving as the gentle stresses, the purgations as healing as the illuminations. As in stanza 1, parallelism unites seemingly contradictory aspects of the one, simple God. God's power and love are really one and the same.

We have seen throughout the poem thus far that the second half of each stanza reveals God's *presence* in Creation (st. 1), the poet's life (st. 2), the Eucharist (st. 3), the grace of continuance (st. 4), and nature (st. 5). The second half, expressing God's immanence, parallels the first, expressing God's transcendence. In the parallelism between parts of each stanza, Hopkins conveys a sacramental view of the universe, indicating that transcendence is present in immanence. It is divine concern with human life, in spite of God's awful majesty, that hushes the guilt and terror of stanzas 2 and 3 and flushes and instresses hearts. Hopkins often used the word "flush" for instress (*Journals*, p. 127) and for what he called prepossession of feeling (*Journals*, p. 125). In Chapter 1, we spoke about prepossession as an intuition of the unity of the whole that retires behind a complex work of art. *The Wreck of the Deutschland* is such a complex work whose unity, the prepossession of the poet, must be recovered by the reader in a contemplative synthesis of its parallel structure. The parallel structure of both halves of each stanza, often reinforced by strict repetition of words ("kiss my hand . . . Kiss my hand," "but mined with . . . But roped with," "stress . . . stroke . . . Stroke and a stress") drives each stanza and the whole of Part I toward unity.

All the negation and appositive explanation of the preceding lines has been in the service of the single affirmation of line 7, "But it rides time like riding a river." The point of the negations ("Not out of his bliss" and "Nor first from heaven") is to reject a dualistic, Manichean view of the world. In his commentary on "Creation and Redemption: The Great Sacrifice," Hopkins gives what might be considered a gloss on this line:

> Time has 3 dimensions and one positive pitch or direction. It is therefore not so much like any river or any sea as like the Sea of Galilee, which has the Jordan running through it and giving a current to the whole.
>
> Though this one direction of time if prolonged for ever might be considered to be parallel to or included in the duration of God . . . it is truer to say that there is no relation between any duration of time and the duration of God. (*Sermons*, p. 196)

Hopkins' sacramentalism means to avoid any pantheistic equation of the eternity of God with time. It does not allow for a mere baptizing of circumstances as in Hegel's philosophy but preserves a transcendence that is "wholly other," "past all/ grasp God" (st. 32). The positive pitch of time is its teleological convergence, not its running down like the sand of the hourglass. Further, a three-dimensional time that is more like a sea than a river has the fullness of *kairos* rather than the one-dimensionality of *chronos*. Yet, since it merely "rides" time, Hopkins avoids, as did the Hebrew psalmists and prophets, the closed world of mythology.[44] His stars and storms, like the nature imagery of Ps. 19, are only "word, expression, news of God" (*Sermons*, p. 129), which still maintain a distance from their Creator.

The "it" of line 7, reiterated five times in stanza 7 and carried to stanza 8, has its antecedent, I believe, in the word "mystery" of stanza 5 rather than in the word "stress," as some critics have suggested. This "it" that rides time parallels the mystery under the world's splendor, which delivers *both* stress and strokes. The mystery has been ambivalent all along, filled with lashing strokes and gentle stress, just as each of these effects is itself ambivalent: in stanza 2, "stress" is a consuming fire, while in stanza 6 it is the marking of the mystery, and strokes are similarly both terrifying and comforting.

Both parenthetical statements ("and few know this," "And here the faithful waver, the faithless fable and miss") parallel and contrast with one another, as references to the common views of eternity in time. Within the last parenthetical statement is an antithetical parallelism, of the kind we will take up in Chapter 3. Few, perhaps the faithful who seek God only in heaven and in peak experiences, know that God's mystery is present in nature, is also immanent, while the faithless confine God to mythological fables, enclosing the mystery in nature

[44] Herbert N. Schneidau makes the point that the prophets demythologized older, closed systems of mythology, radically opening the world to God's action in history. "So perhaps the fundamental message [of the Hebrew Bible] . . . is that of a need for change which derives from ambivalence toward culture of any kind, but particularly one's own." *Sacred Discontent: The Bible and Western Tradition* (Baton Rouge: Louisiana State Univ. Press, 1976), p. 3.

and therefore missing God's utter transcendence of that nature. Hopkins once said of mythology that it was "man setting up the work of his own hands, of that hand within the mind the imagination, for God Almighty who made heaven and earth."[45] Neither the faithful nor the faithless can, as can the nun in the second half of the poem, "read the unshapeable shock night" (st. 29), find the mystery riding the river as the Incarnation rides it. The faithful waver over God immanent in stars and storms, while the faithless miss God transcendent of them.

That the mystery of God's relation with humanity is manifested most clearly by the Incarnation is evident from the content of stanza 7. To Bridges Hopkins explained that mystery for a Catholic was not a matter of interest or curiosity but an "incomprehensible certainty."[46] He explains further that for the Catholic the Incarnation does not mean that Christ is in some sense divine and in some sense human but that "Christ is in every sense God and in every sense man, and the interest is in the locked and inseparable combination."[47] Our interest in such a mystery, he says, might be called "the ecstasy of interest," which leaves the mind "swinging; poised but on the quiver."[48] Much of this first part of *The Wreck of the Deutschland* attempts to leave the reader's mind in just this ecstatic state, swinging and poised between the paralleled opposites, but "on the quiver," not at rest.

> It dates from day
> Of his going in Galilee;
> Warm-laid grave of a womb-life grey;
> Manger, maiden's knee;
> The dense and the driven Passion, and frightful sweat:

---

[45] *Correspondence* (October 23, 1886), p. 146. In that sense he agreed with the biblical view of imagination as an evil *yeser*. See Gen. 6:5.

[46] *Letters to Bridges* (October 24, 1883), p. 187.

[47] Ibid., p. 188.

[48] Ibid.

Thence the discharge of it, there its swelling to be,
  Though felt before, though in high flood yet—
What none would have known of it, only the heart, being hard
    at bay.

Hopkins' Christology has thus far been "high"; Christ
shares the terror of God (st. 2), sustains the poet through Eu-
charist (st. 3) and Gospel (st. 4), and, more subtly, is the mys-
tery under the world's splendor (sts. 5–6) made manifest in his
life and Passion (st. 7). From this cosmic Christ we now pass
abruptly to the earthly Jesus. The sequence of details from Je-
sus' life—womb, manger, Mary's knee, the Passion—empha-
sizes his humanity, his being "in every sense man." His
"grave" in the womb, his death in the beginning of life, is in
some sense to his Godhead. In his famous exegesis of the
"kenosis" passage of Phil. 2:6–11, Hopkins explained to
Bridges that Christ Jesus "could not but see what he was,
God, but he would see it as if he did not see it . . . he emptied
or exhausted himself so far as that was possible, of godhead
. . . and then being in the guise of man humbled himself to
death, the death of the cross."[49] This "emptying" of himself is
for Hopkins the root of all Christ's holiness and its imitation
the source of good in human beings.[50] Hopkins does imitate
Christ's kenosis, in the religious content of the poem and in
the paratactic suppression of his own reasoning. Yet that ke-
nosis yields again and again to the fullness of grace.

Although he is, like Scotus, a "supralapsarian," that is, one
who sees the Incarnation as destined from all eternity rather
than as atonement to an avenging God, Christ's Passion still
has its place in the divine scheme. The last words of line 5,
"And frightful sweat," dislodged from their normal order in
the line and followed by the colon, are given added emphasis
by following the caesura after "Passion." This sweat of Christ

[49] *Letters to Bridges*, p. 175.
[50] "It was only through Christ and the great sacrifice that God had meant
any being to come to him at all." *Sermons*, pp. 137–138.

may provide another possible antecedent for the third-person-singular pronouns that follow. It may also be the sweat of God actually creating the world: "It is as if the blissful agony or stress of selving in God had forced out drops of sweat or blood, which drops were the world" (*Sermons*, p. 197). Selving is also kenosis in God; God's stress is necessary for the stress on human life. In this mystery of Redemption we encounter Creation of the world, and in sacrifice new being. "Thence," that is in the Passion, the mystery of Christ was "discharged," which can mean "sent forth," "paid," "acquitted," or even "emitted" like a charge of electricity or lightning (cf. st. 2). The images of lines 6 and 7 intricately parallel one another.[51] Hopkins has used such interwoven parallelism before, as in the first four lines of stanza 6. Besides the images, the time elements "Thence . . . there" and "before . . . yet" are paralleled and contrasted within the lines. The effect is to parallel the once-and-for-all nature of the Passion with its eternal efficacy.

The last line of this stanza is the only one to find its completion in the following stanza. We are left with the "heart, being hard at bay" in a moment of hesitation that duplicates its pursuit and search. The pursuer, however, is now no longer God as in stanza 3 but is the heart in search of "it," the elusive and mysterious "it" that waits for another stanza to join, by means of the copula "Is," with that heart. There is a simple positiveness in the heart that "*Is* out with it" as there was in "I did say yes" and as there is in every paratactic "and." Again Hopkins

[51] If it means a charge of electricity, then the first part of line 7 ("Though felt before") parallels the first part of line 6, and the second part of line 7 ("Though in high flood yet—"), a change to sea imagery, parallels the "swelling" of the last part of line 6. One technical meaning of "discharge" is "the equalization of a difference of potential, as between two terminals" (*Random House College Dictionary*). Hopkins was clearly aware of such meanings, as various notes in his journals and spiritual writings show. He may have meant, though it is highly technical, that Christ's Passion equalizes our potential with that of the other "terminal," God.

juxtaposes "what none would have *known* of it," received in neat intellectual propositions, to the heart's pursuit.[52] The heart holds the mystery that none, neither faithful nor faithless, can know, as the maiden's womb and knee held, just as mysteriously, the Son of God.

> Is out with it! oh,
> We lash with the best or worst
> Word last! How a lush-kept plush-capped sloe
> Will, mouthed to flesh-burst,
> Gush!—flush the man, the being with it, sour or sweet,
> Brim, in a flash, full!—Hither then, last or first,
> To hero of Calvary, Christ's feet—
> Never ask if meaning it, wanting it, warned of it—men go.

The heart "*Is* out with it," just as the mystery is stressed by the Incarnation and by the poem's stresses on it. Stanza 8, like Hopkins' poem, "Pied Beauty," is laced with three pairs of opposites, "best or worst," "sour or sweet," and "last or first." This stanza continues the discussion of the Passion, the "great sacrifice," and of our responses to it. The rather odd image of the "sloe," fruit of the blackthorn bush, could be associated with the "fruit of the Tree of the Cross," a reference to Christ common in liturgical and devotional usage. The fruit of the Cross can, as can no other, flush and instress us both with its sourness and sweetness.[53] I believe these pairs of opposites should have parallel force, so that as we read the pair, "last or first," keeping in mind the parable of the Workers in the Vine-

---

[52] Cf. the famous saying by Lessing that if God held all truth in His right hand and in His left hand the lifelong pursuit of it, he would choose the left hand. Cited in Soren Kierkegaard, *Concluding Unscientific Postscript*, trans. David F. Swenson and Walter Lowrie (Princeton: Princeton Univ. Press, 1974), p. 97.

[53] Nikos Kazantzakis says of his writing *The Last Temptation of Christ*, "I had never felt the blood of Christ fall drop by drop into my heart with so much sweetness, so much pain" [trans. P. A. Bien (New York: Simon and Schuster, 1960), p. 2].

yard and the miracle at Cana of saving the best wine till last, by a process of "retrospective patterning"[54] we apply the same thought—it matters not which—to each of the other pairs. Just as it matters not if we seek Christ by deathbed conversion or lifelong fidelity, so it matters not whether the taste of this fruit is sour or sweet (like strokes and stresses), and it matters not whether the heart's choice brings "best or worst" into one's life.

This last reading, which differs from that given by most critics, can be justified by seeing that the parallelism of these pairs creates parity where disparity is usually seen. Hopkins had before him the model of the Ignatian "First Principle and Foundation": "Therefore we must make ourselves indifferent to all created things, insofar as it is left to the choice of our free will and is not forbidden. Accordingly, for our part, we should not prefer health to sickness, riches to poverty, honor to dishonor, a long life to a short one."[55] Knowing well that the choice of Christ in his Passion and humiliation could have the worst consequences in terms of worldly success, Hopkins told Canon Dixon that Christ "would have wished to succeed by success" but was "doomed to succeed by failure."[56] On this reading, the "Word" of line 3, because of its prominence and capital, cannot but be associated with the Eternal Word, Christ. When the heart is finally ("last") out with this Word, it makes all the difference in the life; it is *the* "best or worst" ever uttered, but it matters not which. The nun in Part II, who by the choice of Christ "christens her wild-worst Best" (st.

---

[54] Barbara Herrnstein Smith discusses this process of reading poetry in her book, *Poetic Closure: A Study of How Poetry Ends* (Chicago: Univ. of Chicago Press, 1968), pp. 10ff.

[55] St. Ignatius, *Spiritual Exercises*, pp. 47–48.

[56] *Correspondence*, pp. 137–138. The letter continues: "his plans were baffled, his hopes dashed, and his work was done by being broken off undone. However much as he understood all this, he found it an intolerable grief to submit to it. He left the example: it is very strengthening, but except in that sense it is not consoling."

24), is also out with this Word. In their baptisms by fire, it is the "christening" of their terrible moments that makes them for both nun and poet a grace.

The "lush-kept plush-capped *sloe/ will*," a pampered, slug-gish will, when nourished with Christ's sweet and sour Pas-sion, suddenly charges the whole person with energy. A con-version to Christ in the face of the Passion, not one based on naive notions of heavenly comfort, can transform one's being so that one is brimfull with Christ. In the last chapter of this study, we will return to the idea of a transformation attendant on kenosis and assent. Here momentary and continued grace effect an elevation to new being in Christ. "Hither" we go just as Hopkins found his "place" in fleeing to the heart of the Eu-charist. The parallel series of participles in the last line, "mean-ing it, wanting it, warned of it," indicates with increasing em-phasis that we approach this "hero of Calvary" without knowing the danger as the poet has known the danger of being close to God. Christ is, as Hopkins says in "The Windhover," a billion times "more dangerous" than any natural thing. Yet, that more dangerous choice is the way to new creation, to Paul's "I live, now not I, but Christ lives in me."

> Be adored among men,
> God, three-numberèd form;
> Wring thy rebel, dogged in den,
> Man's malice, with wrecking and storm,
> Beyond saying sweet, past telling of tongue,
> Thou art lightning and love, I found it, a winter and warm;
> Father and fondler of heart thou hast wrung:
> Hast thy dark descending and most art merciful then.

> With an anvil-ding
> And with fire in him forge thy will
> Or rather, rather then, stealing as Spring
> Through him, melt him but master him still:
> Whether at once, as once at a crash Paul,
> Or as Austin, a lingering-out swéet skíll,

Make mercy in all of us, out of us all
Mastery, but be adored, but be adored King.

Stanzas 9 and 10 form a prayer framed by a kind of doxology.
Like the first two stanzas, they are addressed exclusively to
God and therefore complete the frame or envelope of the en-
tire first part of the poem. The prayers remind us that Hop-
kins considered *The Wreck of the Deutschland* an ode rather than
a narrative poem[57] and that its ultimate unifying subject is
"God, three-numberèd form." Unity, of sounds, phrases, and
meanings, is the keynote of these two stanzas. The semantic
parallelisms running through and binding them (st. 9's lines 3
and 4 paralleled by st. 10's lines 1 and 2; st. 10's lines 3 and 4
paralleled by line 7) create the effect of hymnal refrains.

The rebel, whom Hopkins asks God to "Wring," is de-
picted as a kind of Grendel figure "dogged in den," reminis-
cent of the first halves of stanzas 3 and 4 and then reduced to
an abstraction, "Man's malice," a far cry from the self whose
whole being was flushed with God. As in many of the nature
poems like "Ribblesdale," it is "dear and dogged" man who,
"To his selfbent so bound," cannot join in the litanies of praise
offered by a selfless nature. As Hopkins offers such a litany in
these last two stanzas, and indeed in the entire ode, he is con-
cerned that we join with the whole universe in praising God.

Abruptly, Hopkins turns from his pleas for mastery to the
ineffable sweetness of being mastered by God. The last half of
stanza 9 is an attempt to use language to say what is "Beyond
saying" and, like Hopkins' confession of faith in stanza 2,
"Past telling of tongue." Yet, the poet finds words; the "I
found it" can refer both to the end of the search of the heart
"hard at bay" and to the poet's discovery of expressions for
the inexpressible. In line 6, Hopkins exploits and foregrounds
the pairing of opposites in blatant violation of the principles

[57] *Letters to Bridges*, p. 49. "The Deutschland would be more generally in-
teresting if there were more wreck and less discourse, I know, but still it is an
ode and not primarily a narrative."

of noncontradiction and identity that hold in ordinary speech. As suggested, the nature of the subject, the simplicity and unity of God, calls forth this apparent contradiction. The mystics of every tradition have played with the opposites to express this ineffability. With line 7 we can compare the prophet Hosea's "he has torn, that he may heal us; he has stricken and he will bind us up" (6:1). We know from Hopkins' early essays that he used parallelism because he wanted comparison, the mind's unifying energies. Still, he wanted each *and* to conceal an *and yet* so that it would surprise and arrest us by its incongruity in the pair. In lines 6 and 8 that is in fact the case. We really say "lightning *and yet* love," "winter *and yet* warm." It has taken much of the poem to make the pairing of God's lightning terror and God's more hidden love possible. Because of stanzas 2, 3, and 7, we know Hopkins is making no easy, sentimental statement. God is most merciful in fact in the dark descending and unmaking of the poet. The parallelisms, along with the end-stopped, epigrammatic lines of stanza 9, elevate the language, making it serve a supralogical, supratemporal purpose.

Stanza 10, however, which deals with divine action in human life, pulls the opposites of God's nature apart, suggesting an either–or contained within a both–and. Offering the two models of Paul's lightning-quick conversion, or Augustine's gradual one, the poet pleads for the more merciful "melt him," an image to be compared with the "Glow" of stanza 5 and the "Gush!" of stanza 8, a principle that runs through the man's whole being "as Spring" (a contrast at first sight but actually a natural consequence of the God who is "winter and warm"). This contrast between the Pauline and the Augustinian conversions harkens back to the contrast in Hopkins' life between momentary grace and the grace of continuance and to the "last or first" choices of stanza 8.

Hopkins makes word music with chiastic prepositional phrases in lines 5 and 7: "at once, as once at" and "in all of us, out of us all," background harmonies that prepare for his final crescendo, the repetition of the passive imperative "but be adored." It is introduced by the paratactic "but," which does no more than hint at the enormity of the conversion necessary for God's "rebel" to bow before him. Part I ends, then, on an almost incantatory note, as is fitting to the hymnal context and to the "canons and repetitions" that have formed the underthought throughout these ten stanzas.

Hopkins uses myriad parallelism in *The Wreck*, of sound, of syntax, and of meaning, to create parity amid disparity and then, as in stanzas 9 and 10, to create tensions in what has been joined. He intends both equivalence and surprise, for even within the equivalence created by parallelism's form, there is distinction or contrast. No repetition is really pure, for, while it "afters" the inscape of the first, it also instresses or intensifies it. What James Kugel has found to be the true nature of Hebrew parallelism, its going beyond and intensifying the thought it "parallels," Hopkins instinctively employed in his great poem. Every parallel structure, while it repeats the syntactic rhythm, at the same time causes semantic difference. Every *and* conceals an *and yet*. Two movements can thus be discerned in the parallelism: the aesthetic, the "over-and-over-ing" of the inscape, and the cognitive, the instressing by surprise and asymmetry. Parallelism gives, then, both beauty and truth.

Parallelisms further elevate or sacralize the thought beyond ordinary thinking and speaking and provide order or inscape to the poem. Yet, it is an order and a unity like that which Hopkins found in nature, where irregularity and asymmetry seem to triumph, and only the repetitions of the parallelism give a hint of stability.

Hopkins wishes to show in Part I of his poem that if grace, the ambiguous gift of the Divine, has operated in the dark, nearly unspeakable events of his own spiritual life, so too it is at work in the seemingly absurd drowning of the German nuns at England's shore. For each of the interior events that brought him to a desperate Fall and an unmaking also brought him to God's grace. And that grace brought him each time not only into relationship but into identification with Christ. This ritual process of loss of self and assent to God, leading to transformation and re-creation into Christ, is mirrored, Hopkins means to say, in the nuns' baptismal descent into the dark waters of the sea. Each Fall is hidden Creation, each shipwreck a grace. The background harmonies of this poem, orchestrated in parallelisms, offer the swelling, if hidden, conviction that creative grace is present even in the darkest moments of existence.

3

"Thoughts Against Thoughts": Antithesis in Hopkins' Sonnets

*T*HE NOTION OF antithesis pervades the thought of Gerard Manley Hopkins. If we are to understand him fully, we must recognize the antithetical character of his anthropology, his cosmology, and his poetics. His vision of human nature and even of the perfect human, Christ, is marked by this antithesis. In an 1865 essay, speaking of Wordsworth as a contradiction to the spirit of the age rather than its representative, he states:

> It is these contrasts and disparities which give complexity and interest to the lives or writings of great thinkers so clearly beyond what they would otherwise have had, making for instance their enthusiasm not free from pathos or, if the proportions be the other way, their denunciations from hope. What can be a better case of this than the position of Plato? As his writings are found to be full of thoughts which are not reconciled and have since acquired definiteness in opposite systems, so his philosophy and mind as compared with the Greek contemporary world seem to offer opportunities for endless balancing, antithesis as well as parallel. ("The Position of Plato to the Greek World," *Journals*, p. 115)

In describing Plato, Hopkins might in fact be writing his own proleptic autobiographical sketch. His sonnets of 1877 express an enthusiasm often at the point of ecstasy, while his Dublin sonnets of the last four years indeed convey what Dixon called a "terrible pathos."[1] Enthusiasm and pathos might well be considered the emotional poles of Hopkins' nature, just as beauty and holiness can be considered its antithetical goals. Even more prophetically, we can see that what Hopkins says of Plato is also true of Hopkins himself: he too is "full of thoughts which are not reconciled." The question of his character and of whether the priesthood made him the God-inebriated lover of nature of his Welsh sonnets or led him to the pathos and sterility of his last years will remain as unresolved among critics as it was in his own life. For this antithesis was tolerated in his nature and cultivated in its dual goals as if by design, offering him "opportunities for endless balancing." In unpublished notes on "Plato's Philosophy," he remarks on the impossibility of reconciling the opposites logically: "Wherever you have an antithetic dualism you must always have this discontinuity point. [A]nd there is no log[ical] account to be given of the bridging over the gulf" (Unpublished Oxford Notes, D8). One wonders if Hopkins was aware of the self-description he was giving in his view of Plato: "His own ideas could not be felt to be not satisfying and contained incompatibilities which while they prove the comprehensiveness of his mind made the ideals themselves less credible; so that we hear of his habitual melancholy" (*Journals*, p. 116).

Hopkins' Parmenidean ideal of unity both for art and for his own nature had to compete with a Heraclitean vision of particulars that refused abstraction and universality. Like Plato, he too felt "despair at the multiplicity of phenomena unexplained and unconnected" along with "enthusiasm for the . . . one" (*Journals*, p. 116). Hopkins' Parmenidean ideal of Being could not be satisfying as long as it denied the rich-

---

[1] *Correspondence*, p. 80.

ness and complexity of life. He even criticized Plato for divesting the universal Forms of the sensory: "the defect of the Platonic as of all transcendental theories is that it confines itself to the upper world without caring at all ab[ou]t the sensible as if the abstraction were truer than the thing it was meant to explain" (Unpublished Oxford Notes, D8). Yet, Plato probably came closer to resolution of these opposites by denying one of them, the *aisthesis*, or sights and sounds of the world, than did Hopkins. For, as Hopkins says elsewhere, for Plato "nature has retired into unimportance."[2] With Hopkins, it is instead the unity that "retires, is less important, serves rather for the framework of that of the parts" (*Journals*, p. 126). Calling the "always recurring coexistence of contraries . . . highly exciting to thought" (Unpublished Oxford Notes, D6, no. 6), he seemed to like the challenge, in life as well as in art, of living out an antithesis that might never, at least in this life, be resolved or restored to unity.

Indeed, Hopkins described the life of his model of holiness, Christ: "It leads one naturally to rhetorical antithesis to think for instance that after making the world He sh[oul]d consent to be taught carpentering."[3] Antithesis, then, is the new ideal or goal for a life in the world rather than among the Platonic Forms. A unified sensibility may no longer be possible "when the old unity of belief which gives meaning to every subordination of thought and action" (*Journals*, p. 116) is gone. For Hopkins this means both spirit and sense must have their due. He must accept the dualism of his nature as Christ accepted manhood and the Crucifixion. Hopkins is in fact a composite—of Oxford sophistication and Catholic piety, of aesthetic sensitivity and ascetic self-denial, of Pater and Newman. It is probably to his credit that he did not deny or extirpate one side of his nature for the other but lived in the tension of a "both/and."

---

[2] "The Connection of Mythology and Philosophy," Unpublished Oxford Essay, D6, no. 5; published in Cotter, *Inscape*, pp. 307–309.

[3] *Further Letters* (Letter to E. H. Coleridge, January 22, 1866), p. 20.

Hopkins' division between the affective and elective wills, explained in his spiritual writings, reflects a kind of Kantian split between inclination and duty. In Christopher Devlin's view, this "exaggerated" distinction between desire and choice does not derive either from the Scotist or Ignatian influences on Hopkins, though the terms of that distinction are laid down in both systems.[4] As Devlin sees it, although there are similes in Ignatius about the subject making his natural self "like a corpse," Ignatius actually counseled that the sympathies of the understanding, the "affective will" in Hopkins' terms, be joined to choice, the "elective will." I do not, however, think the strong influence of St. John of the Cross's "night of the understanding" on Ignatius himself and on the entire Jesuit tradition should be understated. St. John of the Cross's night strips and obliterates the affections, "leaving the understanding dark, the will dry, the memory empty and the affections in the deepest affliction."[5] Since, for St. John of the Cross, "two contraries cannot coexist in one subject," namely the divine and the human, the "annihilation" and "undoing" of the soul are "in a certain manner" necessary.[6]

This language of "annihilation" and "undoing" we have met with in Hopkins himself, in his exegesis of Phil. 2:6–11 for Bridges ("he thought it no snatching-matter for him to be equal with God, but annihilated himself") and in stanza 1 of *The Wreck of the Deutschland* ("And after it almost unmade, what with dread,/ Thy doing"). His interpretation of virtue in Plato reveals the same extreme language: "If all bodily desires etc. bad it is not enough to reduce them to a *minimum*; they must be crushed altogether. Therefore he is inconsistent" (Unpublished Oxford Notes, D8). This opposition between the affective and elective wills, with its tremendous consequences in Hopkins' personal life, could in part stem from the

---

[4] Devlin, "Introduction to Spiritual Writings," *Sermons*, pp. 116–121.

[5] St. John of the Cross, *Dark Night of the Soul*, trans. and ed. E. Allison Peers (New York: Image Books, 1959), p. 97.

[6] Ibid., pp. 101–107.

Carmelite strain in the Jesuit tradition. Hopkins' tendency toward the total extirpation of one contrary in his nature, based as it is in his reading of the kenosis passage of Philippians as an annihilation, was only a tendency that was itself at war with his tendency toward counterpoise. I believe he sensed that his ideal of "the great sacrifice" was better fulfilled, not by the annihilation of his natural capacities, but by his oblation of the total self to God. He said, for example, in an exchange centering on this subject with Dixon, "a very spiritual man once told me that with things like composition the best sacrifice was not to destroy one's work but to leave it entirely to be disposed of by obedience."[7] I think Hopkins knew that a sacrifice to God would yield, not the end of the self, but its true actualization in and of God, just as Christ's sacrifice yielded new being (*Sermons*, p. 138) and as John of the Cross's darkness yielded true illumination.

It makes an interesting historical note to compare with Hopkins a man born the same year who passed into the oblivion of insanity the year of Hopkins' death. This man was Friedrich Nietzsche. Nietzsche too stressed antithesis and wished to suffer the opposites—of body and spirit, passion and reason, good and evil—rather than destroy one and live out of a false onesidedness. Nietzsche perfectly exemplifies the kind of thinker whose denunciations were not free from hope (*Journals*, p. 115). But Nietzsche increasingly chose body over spirit, rather than live out his ideal of "wholeness in manifoldness,"[8] just as Hopkins increasingly chose spirit over body, rather than live out his ideal of counterpoise.

It is also important to note that for Hopkins the antithesis is *within* the self or *within* the world, rather than between self and world, as it was for some of the Romantics. This latter stance would result in *irony*, in the posings of a *flâneur* like Baude-

---

[7] *Correspondence*, p. 88.

[8] Friedrich Nietzsche, *Beyond Good and Evil*, trans. Walter Kaufmann (New York: Vintage Books, 1966), p. 137.

laire. Hopkins' "simple *yes* and *is*," his acknowledgment and affirmation of Being, purchased at the expense of his "no" to self, break with an irony that is "conscious dissimulation."[9]

It may be that Hopkins allowed himself to suffer the contradictions of his own nature because he saw such contradiction in nature. In 1879, commenting to Bridges on his poem "A Voice of Nature," Hopkins remarks, "the leading thought is that nature has two different, two opposite aspects, teaching opposite lessons of life—that one is between two stools with the two of them."[10] Commenting on a poem of Dixon's two years later, he specifies nature's antithetical aspects: "In Nature is something that makes, builds up, and breeds, as vegetation, life in fact; and over against this, also in Nature, something that unmakes or pulls to pieces, what in another place is called Death and Strife. This latter power must be utterly unconscious, blind, and the other not; for if it were otherwise this scene of havoc, strife, and defacement could not go on."[11] We of the twentieth century are reminded here of the conflict between Eros and Thanatos, the life and death principles in Freud, and in the latter part of the quotation, of Hardy's Immanent Will "Apprehending not how fare the sentient subjects of its scheme" (*The Dynasts*). Hopkins had a sympathy with Hardy, whom he called a man "of pure and direct genius."[12] Although the above quotations describing two opposite aspects of nature are comments on others' poems, Hopkins wrote this Heraclitean opposition into his own poetry. In the early stanzas of *The Wreck of the Deutschland*, as we have seen, nature is present both as "lovely-asunder/ Starlight" and

---

[9] Friedrich Schlegel uses this definition and discusses irony at length in his *Literary Aphorisms*, trans. Ernst Behler and Rouan Strae (University Park: Pennsylvania State Univ. Press, 1968), Aphorism 108. See also Paul de Man, "The Rhetoric of Temporality," *Interpretation: Theory and Practice*, ed. Charles S. Singleton (Baltimore: Johns Hopkins Univ. Press, 1969).

[10] *Letters to Bridges*, p. 82.

[11] *Correspondence*, p. 53.

[12] *Letters to Bridges*, p. 251. See also p. 239.

as the "stroke" of storms and lightning. There are also "the jay-blue heavens appearing/ of pied and peeled May" in stanza 26 and "wind's burly and beat of endragonèd seas" of the following stanza. In the beginning were the "cheer and charm" of "The Sea and the Skylark's" Eden, but antedating that *order*, reflected in the alliteration and parallel syntax of "cheer and charm," was "man's first slime," the chaos of the *tehom* in Genesis, chapter 1. Hopkins' love of nature is no naive, sentimental one like that of the Enlightenment; he knew its demonic, trickster elements. But nature is for Hopkins always creation, the ongoing act of God, rather than as for the Romantics mere nature.

Even Hopkins' theology of creative and corrective grace polarizes the activity of God, making God into a kind of Shiva and Krishna, Destroyer and Creator. God the Father's grace is creative grace, "the grace which destined the victim for the sacrifice," while Christ's grace is " 'medicinal,' corrective, redeeming" grace, "bringing the victim to the altar and sacrificing it" (*Sermons*, p. 158). In the poetry, however, these roles seem reversed, for it is God the Father who almost unmakes his creation (st. 1) and treads the victim "Hard down" (st. 2) while Christ offers a rope of support to the mountain–climber (st. 4) and is the humble figure of "Manger, maiden's knee" (st. 7). In "The Blessed Virgin Compared to the Air We Breathe," it is the blue sky, metaphor for Mary's mediation, that slakes the fire of the sun, "A blear and blinding ball," representing the terror of God. Yet, no matter how the attributes are divided (and surely Hopkins was careful to avoid a Marcion-like identification of God the Father as a God of wrath), the polarity in the deity seems to remain.

God is not just duality and trinity, however; God is One, and Hopkins never forgets God's unity and simplicity. That is, after all, the true basis of his hope. For, as Hopkins says in his sermon on God's Kingdom, on January 11, 1880: "He brings together things thought opposite and incompatible, strict justice and mere mercy, free grace and binding duty"

(*Sermons*, p. 57). Further, in an unpublished lecture discovered by Norman MacKenzie in 1975,[13] composed by Hopkins about 1885, he says, commenting on Cicero's "On Duty": "for a weight which outweighs all possible counterpoise, a force which resists all possible counter-effort, is infinite; and there is no infinite but God."[14] God's reconciling of opposites, the *coincidentia oppositorum*, is the mark of the divine Kingdom, the last word, so to speak, of Hopkins' sermon, for he ends: "This was the first kingdom of God and his justice, and to it every other boon and blessing was added. And all fell, all is gone: it was divided against itself, the subject against the sovereign, man against God, and every kingdom, said the Son of God, even God's kingdom divided against itself must come to desolation" (*Sermons*, p. 58). This Heraclitean vision of discord and division at the heart of the world prevails over the more inchoate and receding notion of a Parmenidean unity and of God as the great reconciler. Hopkins' last word about reality remains as largely unspoken in his anthropology, his cosmology, and his poetry as in his life. Reconciliation is not so cheaply won as it was for Hegel.

Antithesis occurs in Hopkins not only as an ontological principle bound into the world and human life, but also, and therefore, as a primary element of Hopkins' poetics. As we recall from his essay "On the Origin of Beauty," Hopkins said that likenesses and unlikenesses, when found together, "make of each resemblance a reason for surprise in the next difference and of each difference a reason for surprise in the next resemblance; *and yet* or such words run before each new point of comparison, and resemblances and antitheses themselves are made to make up a wider antithesis" (*Journals*, p. 105). Antithesis has the last word in this poetics just as division had in his sermon. In this essay's discussion of Shelley's line, "-thy

[13] Norman MacKenzie, "The Imperative Voice—An Unpublished Lecture by Hopkins," *Hopkins Quarterly* 2 (October 1975): 101–117.

[14] Ibid., p. 112.

thoughts, when thou art gone," Hopkins' Professor considers the two possibilities, either that the idea arose in Shelley's mind first and that he chose an antithetical expression for it, or more likely, "that his thought rose at once into his mind in that form" proving that the antithesis is essential to the beauty and that "the pathos" is destroyed if the last part is left out (*Journals*, p. 110). In his incarnational aesthetics, antithesis witnesses to the pathos of Hopkins' vision of nature, just as parallelisms of resemblance witness to his enthusiasm for inscape.

As we concluded in Chapter 2, for Hopkins as for Kugel, no parallelism, of grammar or of sound, merely repeats. It goes beyond and alters the inscape of the first, so that the whole encompasses variety as well as unity. Antithesis is the extreme instance of this instressing of one word by another. Where parallelism of resemblance, involving nuanced difference, achieves surprise, parallelism of antithesis, yet still involving sameness, might be expected to achieve not just surprise but shock. As Gadamer put it in this century, the element of surprise is based on the eclipsing of the familiar in the experience of art.[15] But "in a joyous and frightening shock," it is not only the "This art thou!" but the "Thou must alter thy life!"[16] The "This art thou!" of the Upanishads might be compared to Hopkins' experience of inscape, and the "Thou must alter thy life!" to instress.

Alison Sulloway too sees "fiercely polarized" antitheses in Hopkins, attributing them to the Ruskinian "antitheses between likeness and difference, smoothness and ruggedness, unity and diversity, restraint and liberty, dominion and subordination."[17] Yet, in her zeal to connect Hopkins with Rus-

[15] Hans-Georg Gadamer, "Aesthetics and Hermeneutics," in *Philosophical Hermeneutics*, trans. David E. Linge (Berkeley: Univ. of California Press, 1976), p. 101.

[16] Ibid., p. 104.

[17] Alison G. Sulloway, *Gerard Manley Hopkins and the Victorian Temper* (London: Routledge and Kegan Paul, 1972), p. 75.

kin, she may be overlooking Hopkins' own derivation of antithesis as a formal principle from its origins in Hebrew poetry. "Hebrew poetry," he says in "On the Origin of Beauty," "is structurally only distinguished from prose by its being paired off in parallelisms, subdivided of course often into lower parallelisms. This is well known" (*Journals*, p. 106). Hopkins' continual pointing to the example of Hebrew poetry[18] makes it clear that he derives the terminology and the concept of antithesis in poetry from Robert Lowth, who inaugurated the dubious taxonomy of synonymous, antithetical, and synthetic parallelisms. Hopkins accepted the first two members of Lowth's classification, although he realized that antithesis is still subsumed under parallelism or comparison.[19]

Recently, Kugel has called Lowth's antithetical parallelism "a distinction without a difference," for the supposedly "antithetical" idea of the second half of a Hebrew line really completes the first half, forming a single statement.[20] In other words, both Lowth's categories, the "synonymous" and the "antithetical," really accomplish the same thing; both complete, yet go beyond, the first half of a parallelism. Kugel takes a typically antithetical verse, one of Lowth's examples, from the Book of Proverbs' Solomonic collections, that abound in "antithetic" parallelisms. In the RSV translation it reads:

[18] Besides the instances found in the essays and notes printed in the *Journals*, in an unpublished manuscript titled "Notes on Antiquities," Hopkins says, "Poetry is the art of utterance in verse, or, to include Hebrew poetry, in which the figure of Parallelism is used, and other possible kinds, of utterance in some figure or pattern of language independent of the matter; so that where there is no such pattern there is no poetry, though there may be eloquence." Unpublished Oxford Notes, G3.

[19] Hopkins said, "Now any two things, however unlike, have something in common, if only we take a wide enough basis of comparison: one knows that from Logic." *Journals*, p. 104. Similarly, in *The Prose Style of Samuel Johnson*, W. K. Wimsatt defines antithesis as the "equal relation of two opposites to a third notion" (New Haven: Yale Univ. Press, 1941), p. 23.

[20] Kugel, *The Idea of Biblical Poetry*, p. 13.

> Faithful are the wounds of a friend;
> profuse are the kisses of the enemy. (Prov. 27:6)

But Kugel translates the relationship between the verse halves as:

> *Just as* a friend's barbs are sincere/ *so* are an
> enemy's kisses false.//

Whatever opposition there is, between the word-pairs "friend's/enemy's" and "barbs/kisses," is subsumed under agreement, under the comparison set up between the "Just as" clause and the one that follows. The opposition, we might say, is merely lexical, in the word-pairs, while the agreement is syntactic-semantic. It should be noted, however, that Kugel's reading and translation remove the *paratactic* quality of the verse and replace it with a more *hypotactic* reading. In a reading of the actual paratactic Hebrew verse, the reader is surprised not only by the opposition but by the comparison implicit in the formal similarities.

Auerbach notes in his analysis of the paratactic Augustinian style that antithesis served Augustine in his exploration of the conflicting inner forces of the Christian life.[21] I believe Hopkins understood the force of a *paratactic* antithesis, one that effaces and conceals the comparison between the terms, letting the form itself carry this element to the reader. He says at the end of his essay "On the Origin of Beauty," "the absence of *and* gives more antithesis" (*Journals*, p. 114). In an 1879 letter to Bridges, he says of the line "But never of their wanton play they tire/" in Bridges' poem "Covetousness," "though the sequence of thought of 'But of their wanton play' is beautiful, yet the dropping the connection is more austere and pathetic."[22] In other words, he is urging Bridges to consider the austerity and pathos of the paratactic style. Hopkins has chas-

---

[21] Auerbach, *Mimesis*, p. 71.

[22] *Letters to Bridges*, p. 70. The original version of Bridges' poem is printed as Note J of the Appendix.

tened his style in its connections rather than in its images or grammar. It is, as Peters called it, a "language of coordination."[23] It is also a language of asyndeton, where "the absence of *and* gives more antithesis," making it tense, taut, gathered. With its parataxis and asyndeton, the poet's interpretive voice recedes, and the world is "let be" to speak for itself—the hallmark of a contemplative rather than a Romantic vision of the world. Hopkins' "innocence of eye" becomes his innocence of mind, or as he calls it elsewhere, "chastity of mind."[24]

The hypotactic style, one that explains the relationships between its phrases and images, would appeal to the conscious intellect, to what Hopkins called the "transitional energy" of the mind. But the paratactic style, lacking most causal connectives, appeals to what Hopkins called the "abiding energy" of the mind (*Journals*, pp. 125–126). Synthesis, the recapturing of unity, is accomplished by a reader's exercise of the power of comparison. This "exercise" of comparison might be compared with the exercise of the faculties in reaching the hidden spiritual or allegorical sense of Scripture in Augustine's *De Doctrina Christiana*. The hidden sense recedes, the unity retires, and the reader must recover it through the mind's abiding energy, that of contemplation. Explaining the connections through a hypotactic rendering of the verse, therefore, robs the reader of the contemplative exercise. It also decreases the reader's surprise and shock. Consequently, though the unity and agreement of any antithesis must be maintained, they are best maintained, for maximum poetic effect, by the reader who recovers them. Hopkins must have felt, in writing his poetry so full of antitheses without connections, that he could entrust this recovery to his reader. I believe he wanted his verse to be experienced as he experienced leaf, cloud, and wave, with a sudden burst of the experience of inscape or pat-

[23] W.A.M. Peters, S.J., *Gerard Manley Hopkins: A Critical Essay Towards the Understanding of His Poetry* (London: Oxford Univ. Press, 1948), p. 112.

[24] *Letters to Bridges*, p. 174.

tern from out of the seemingly meaningless detail. As stated before, Hopkins so sympathized with Heraclitus, who fully underwent the incoherence and flux of the world, and yet somehow found a "rhythm." Hopkins repeatedly spoke of unity as difficult to attain;[25] with antithesis he made it most difficult. Like Spinoza, he probably knew that "all things excellent are as difficult as they are rare."

We turn now to an examination of antitheses in several of Hopkins' sonnets. Antitheses become especially evident in the sonnet form because of the sonnet's inherently symmetrical and asymmetrical character. Hopkins saw the morphology of the sonnet this way, as he explained to his former teacher, Canon Dixon:

> The equation of the best sonnet is
> $(4 + 4) + (3 + 3) = 2.4 + 2.3 = 2(4 + 3) = 2.7 = 14.$
> This means several things—(A) that the sonnet is one of the works of art of which the equation or construction is unsymmetrical in the shape $x + y = a$, where x and y are unequal in some simple ratio, as 2:1, 3:2, 4:3. . . . Neither would 4:2 do, for it would return to 2:1, which is too simple. (B) It is divided symmetrically too in multiples of two, as all effects taking place in time tend to be, and all very regular musical composition is: this raises the 7 to 14. (C) It pairs off even or symmetrical members with symmetrical (the quatrains) and uneven or unsymmetrical with uneven (the tercets).[26]

In this 1881 letter, Hopkins preserves his need for both symmetry and asymmetry as reflected in the Oxford essays written fifteen years earlier. With his quasi-mathematical formula of a 4:3 ratio, rather than a "too simple" 4:2, he is still thinking in terms of a golden mean proportion. As he remarks in the

[25] He says, for instance, in "Rhythm and Other Structural Parts of Rhetoric—Verse": "And in everything the more remote the ratio of the parts to one another or the whole the greater the unity if felt at all." *Journals*, p. 283.

[26] *Correspondence*, pp. 71–72; see also p. 85.

letter, the sonnet ratio is "founded on a principle of nature." By that he means that very golden mean proportion discovered by the Greeks, which we alluded to in Chapter 1. The sonnet provides this proportion; within the larger, all-encompassing asymmetry of the octet to sextet form, it contains symmetries. Thus, Hopkins' conception of the sonnet wins the opportunity for parallelisms and antitheses within its symmetries, at the same time as it throws the whole into an inequality or asymmetry. I believe this account of the sonnet reinforces Hopkins' saying in the earlier essay, "resemblances and antitheses themselves are made to make up a wider antithesis" (*Journals*, p. 105).

In an article published in the October 1972 issue of *Hopkins Quarterly*, Sr. Marcella Holloway examines "Hopkins' Theory of 'Antithetical Parallelisms' " and concludes that his own theories of parallelism and antithesis are not only a guide to the poems but can prevent their being misread.[27] She states, "So marked are the antithetical parallelisms in Hopkins' curtal sonnet, 'Pied Beauty,' that the application of his theory is child-play."[28] It is in this "child-play" that we will now engage, turning to Hopkins' sonnet "Pied Beauty."

> Glory be to God for dappled things—
>   For skies of couple-colour as a brinded cow;
>   For rose-moles all in stipple upon trout that swim;
> Fresh-firecoal chestnut-falls; finches' wings;
>   Landscape plotted and pieced—fold, fallow, and plough;
>   And all trades, their gear and tackle and trim.
>
> All things counter, original, spare, strange;
>   Whatever is fickle, freckled (who knows how?)
>   With swift, slow; sweet, sour; adazzle, dim;
> He fathers-forth whose beauty is past change:
>   Praise him.

[27] Sr. Marcella Holloway, "Hopkins' Theory of 'Antithetical Parallelisms,' " *Hopkins' Quarterly* 1 (October 1974): 132.

[28] Ibid., p. 130.

I read "Pied Beauty" as one large antithetical parallelism. It consists of three tercets, followed by a coda of two lines, for a total of eleven lines. Following Hopkins' analysis of the sonnet in his letter to Dixon, we could say Hopkins has set up an overall asymmetrical piece, within which are symmetrical lines, the first and last, the second and third, and asymmetrical lines. Lines can seem asymmetrical because they do not have doubles in meaning or syntax. Succeeding lines of each tercet are indented and extended beyond the last, so that the lines seem to "grow" or reach out. Each line is end-stopped, except for line 8, which is slowed by the parenthetical remark, giving the effect of a series of discrete elements, each with its own integrity. The first two tercets consist almost entirely of images, while the last consists almost entirely of a series of descriptive words. Thus, the movement within the poem is from substantives to attributes and from the universal "dappled things" to the particulars of skies, trout, chestnuts, and finches' wings, to the subuniversal "all trades" to the global universal "All things."

This entire movement and display of inscape is bound within the parallel instressing exhortations: "Glory be to God for dappled things—" and "Praise him." The diversity of "dappled things" celebrated in the imagery of the first two tercets is made explicitly antithetical, "counter" in the final tercet, which ends with its series of opposites, "swift, slow; sweet, sour; adazzle, dim." As the poem moves toward greater abstraction, it also moves toward more and more opposition.[29] What makes this poem a "wider antithesis" is the way

---

[29] As Wimsatt points out, "abstraction and generality favor antithesis. Not things but apsects of them can be contrasted in words" (*The Prose Style of Samuel Johnson*, p. 43). Written sideways in one of Hopkins' Oxford notebooks is the statement "Now ab[ou]t contradiction. Can a contradiction in terms be true? In one sense yes, in one sense no: Of facts no contradiction is true, e.g., That we are both in and out of this room. And those who make fun of contradictions in terms confuse contradictions of the abstract with

the final indicative "He fathers-forth whose beauty is past change" paratactically follows the set of explicit opposites. We are asked to accept this indicative not "because" but somehow—("who knows how?"). Again, as in *The Wreck of the Deutschland*, Hopkins subordinates notional assent, one that would be replete with hypotactic rationalizations, to real assent, one based on the heart's reasons. In Chapter 4, we shall return to Newman's distinction between real and notional assent and its effect on Hopkins' poetics. To read the final coda of this poem independently, which is certainly one of its possible readings, is to assent to the imperative "Praise him" on the basis of an indicative that is itself "counter" and "strange."

The polysyndeton of lines 5–6 contrasts with the rest of the poem: Hopkins uses semicolons to lock together the images from nature, while those of husbandry and mercantilism in lines 5–6 are loosely joined with five "and's." This syntax contrasts the intimacy and harmony of nature with the more clumsily additive ways of human life. Both are paratactic connectors, leaving the logic of these relations underground. Each word that follows the dash in line 5 can be read as an adjective describing three stages of the land's use: "fold, fallow, and plough." As a noun, "fold" can be read as "enclosure" or as a suffix of multiplication; as a verb, it can be read as "clasp" or "break down, collapse." Thus, the nominal and verbal meanings contain antitheses. The movement in lines 2–3 and within line 4 is downward—from skies to sea, "chestnut-falls" (with "falls" read as a verb or noun)—and then upward to "finches' wings." This movement is one of the inchoate ways Hopkins' poems have of enclosing heaven and earth in one continuous sweep rather than posing the dilemma of ascent or descent.

As stated above, the poem begins and ends with parallel exhortations or imperatives. From this we may conclude that the

those of the concrete. In necessity and free will we look at the same thing in contradictory aspects." Unpublished Oxford Notes, B2, dated May 23, 1862.

final "Praise him," coming as it does after the colon, can also be the indicative in the much interrupted statement "All things . . . Praise him." That Hopkins deeply felt the statement that all things praise God is shown in his commentary on the "First Principle," where he describes the world as a book God has written, "a poem of beauty," and asks "what is [the world] about? His praise, the reverence due him, the way to serve him; it tells him of his glory" (*Sermons*, p. 239). It is a sentiment like that of Ps. 19, which speaks of the revelatory quality of things, making nature seem like a censer, wafting up its praise like incense. Yet, it leaves us with the mystery of the earth's response to God and makes the final indicative even more enigmatic and antithetical.

The third tercet contains a series of what appear to be adjectives: "counter, original, spare, strange." All indicate a condition apart from the norm. Those things that are "counter," opposite, and "fickle," changeable, are yet taken up into the two possible statements we have seen this section of the poem making. As an adjective, "spare" can mean something set aside, in excess; it can also mean something sacred and consecrated. But "counter" and "spare" can also be read as verbs, with nearly antithetical meanings. ("Spare," which means to save, or care for, is the axial word of Hopkins' poem "The Leaden Echo and the Golden Echo.") "All things counter," oppose one another, *and yet* "All things spare." The "and yet," which introduces the paradoxical element, is the underlying syntactic principle of the poem's antitheses. Perhaps the interrogatory parenthetical remark of line 8 is meant to discount the adequacy of scientific explanation in the face of such an ultimate mystery of creation.

The verb "fathers-forth" of line 10 has a fruitful ambiguity to it, like the Hebrew verb *qanani* of Prov. 8:22. It establishes God's biblical role of paternal care and intimacy rather than Deistic creation and production, and it echoes with the "brooding" of God (caring, worrying, breeding) in other Hopkins poems. Further, the simple preposition, "forth," indicates relation, manifestation to and in the world. Yet, the fathering-forth of One past change, like the self-giving of Plotinus' One, the *energeia* of the Unmoved Mover, or the revelation of Eckhart's Godhead, is wrapped in mystery.

The largest contrast or antithesis of this poem, that this poem in fact *is*, is the contrast between the beauty "past change," God's beauty, and the beauty that is "counter" and fickle." Many interpreters of the poem tend to emphasize its unity and reconciling of opposites rather than its antitheses. Elizabeth Dunlap says, for example, "Each adjective alliterates with its opposite, implying some connection in meaning."[30] Alison Sulloway also states that the "alliteration and the parallel punctuation imitate nature's benign reconciliation between 'things usually thought incompatible.' "[31] While I agree that the poem's assonances and alliterations do create resemblances within and between the poem's dappled images, I believe these resemblances are only one fairly subtle element in a complex of antitheses. The truth of this poem, its unity, is not intrinsic but is "extrinsic . . . implied in the spectator" (*Journals*, p. 75) and is experienced only after great difficulty, the poem's unresolved "wider antithesis." We move through the oppositions to the indicative paratactically appended and encounter an almost parabolic reversal. After all, as New Testament scholar Rudolf Bultmann points out, the parables of the New Testament often take the form of an antithesis of two types, the two debtors, two sons, wise and foolish virgins, two servants, which require of the reader choice and judgment.[32]

Hopkins juxtaposes two visions of the world, one of the Heraclitean flux and one, in the coda, pointing toward the Parmenidean unity. It is not so much the alliterations that resolve the poem's antitheses but the parallel exhortations addressed

[30] Elizabeth Dunlap, "Sound and Sense in 'Pied Beauty,' " *Hopkins Quarterly* 3 (April 1976): 36.
[31] Sulloway, *The Victorian Temper*, p. 106.
[32] Bultmann, *History of the Synoptic Tradition*, p. 192.

to the reader as its "bidding." The way Hopkins has placed his first and last lines on the page gives a sense of an almost physical enclosing of a world full of contraries by a God simple and past change. The effect is one of surprise, of parabolic extravagance, not of clarity and resolution. It is in spite of "the distracting multiplicity of life" that the vision of a beautiful and immutable God is glimpsed. For Hopkins, "He . . . whose beauty is past change" is the great reconciler of opposites (*Sermons*, p. 57); to arrive there is to arrive beyond opposition. But that "arrival" occurs only in the silence of contemplation. Thus, the poem is not actually resolved and reconciled until the reader accepts both the dappledness *and yet* the God who fathers it forth and whom it praises. On either reading, "He fathers-forth [All things]" or "All things . . . Praise him," there is only mystery and irresolution, what Frank Kermode in *The Genesis of Secrecy* calls the *hina* reading rather than the *hoti*, which would resolve and explain.

Antitheses occur in and take up the entire structure of other sonnets written during Hopkins' most fecund year, 1877. While I hesitate to offer another interpretation to the plethora already available on "The Windhover," I would like to comment on the "AND" that so prominently displays itself in capital letters in this poem. The sextet consists of two sets of parallel clauses both connected by the coordinate conjunction "and." As Hopkins composed these lines, they take the form:

Brute beauty and valour and act, oh, air, pride, plume, here
    Buckle! AND the fire that breaks from thee then, a billion
Times told lovelier, more dangerous, O my chevalier!

No wonder of it: shéer plód makes plough down sillion
Shine, and blue-bleak embers, ah my dear,
    Fall, gall themselves, and gash gold-vermilion.

Within each set of parallel clauses connected by "and" is a parallelism of resemblance, a comparison that expresses through metaphor both likeness and difference. The "AND" of the first set of paralleled clauses conveys relation and conceals the *and yet*, the going beyond of the "chevalier's," Christ's, greater beauty. Thus, both of the most proffered interpretations of "Buckle!"—as "connection" and as "collapse"—are right on this reading of the tercet's parallelism. As stated in Chapter 1, the Lord "is at one and the same time united in comparison with the awesome bird but overriding it by his greater danger, his more awful might, his transcendence." We are using the word "but" in this paraphrase, but Hopkins used "AND," calling attention to it by its capitals. He wanted just what he spoke of in his essays and his letter to Dixon, a symmetry and an asymmetry. There is comparison, but within that comparison there is an asymmetrical tension great enough to become nearly an antithesis. The antithesis is approximate because it should not be implied that Christ's beauty cancels out the bird's beauty; the "AND" prevents that reading. The bird's beauty, we might say, is *aufgehoben* in the Lord's; that is, it is both canceled and raised up. The "AND" elevates the second part of this parallelism to a "what's more," but it does not create of the first part a "nothing but."

I say this so deliberately because one interpretation of "The Windhover" that seems to be gaining ground is that the windhover or kestrel is a diabolic figure, an imitation of Lucifer,[33] and that this and other Hopkins poems are written in a "Manichean mood."[34] Alison Sulloway argues that "since the two figures, the windhover as 'Brute beauty' and the plough-ploughman, are in grammatical as well as moral opposition to each other, the model for salvation cannot be both of them."[35] This reading, while it foregrounds the antithetical relation in the poem, ignores the "AND" that makes a *comparison* between

[33] Hopkins, "Plato's View of the Connection of Art and Education," Essays for W. H. Pater, Unpublished Oxford Notes, D3. See Alison G. Sulloway, "St. Ignatius Loyola and the Victorian Temper: Hopkins' Windhover as Symbol of 'Diabolic Gravity,' " *Hopkins Quarterly* 1 (April 1974): 43–51.

[34] Sulloway, *The Victorian Temper*, p. 95.

[35] Sulloway, "St. Ignatius," p. 44.

the bird and the "thee" to whom the poem is addressed. But, far more seriously, it creates a Manichean vision of nature as evil that is in no way consistent with Hopkins' views as expressed in poems like "God's Grandeur," throughout his journals, and in his experience of inscape. Hopkins' inscape is a moment of grace, a fleeting vision of the world transfigured. As he says to Patmore, "It is certain that in nature outward beauty is the proof of inward beauty, outward good of inward good. Fineness, proportion, of feature comes from a moulding force which succeeds in asserting itself over the resistance of cumbersome or restraining matter."[36] In asserting the interrelation of matter and spirit and refusing a Victorian disparagement of body, he is exceedingly modern and at the same time contemplative. In this poem, even common dirt has become luminous, just as for the mystic, Eckhart, God shines out of *every* creature. Hopkins' "catching" of the windhover's flight is a holy moment almost out of time, which can be compared with Ramakrishnan's enlightenment by the sight of a flight of birds. It is in no way an evil vision that must be rejected by the humble ploughman[37] (whom I do not find in the poem at all). In the parallel clauses of this tercet, Hopkins is again, as in *The Wreck*, "flash[ing] from the flame to the flame, tower[ing] from the grace to the grace." In this, he is imitating the movement in the Franciscan Bonaventure's *Itinerarium Mentis ad Deum*, where the soul passes from the reflection of God in his traces in the sensible world to his perfect image in Christ.[38]

Yet, what Sulloway's reading does point up is the danger of idolatry of any earthly thing, of being satisfied with it rather than referring it to God. Hopkins was well aware of these dangers. As he told Bridges: "I think then no one can admire beauty of the body more than I do, and it is of course a com-

---

[36] *Further Letters*, p. 306.

[37] Sulloway, "St. Ignatius," p. 51.

[38] Saint Bonaventure, *The Mind's Road to God*, trans. George Boas (Indianapolis: Bobbs-Merrill Co., 1953).

fort to find beauty in a friend or a friend in beauty. But this kind of beauty is dangerous. Then comes the beauty of the mind. . . . And more beautiful than the beauty of the mind is beauty of character, the 'handsome heart.' "[39] Hopkins knew the temptation to stop at "Brute beauty" and continually countered that temptation. When he says in "To what serves Mortal Beauty?"

> To man, that needs would worship | block or barren
> > stone,
> Our law says: Love what are | love's worthiest, were all
> > known;

he is reviving the Hebraic prohibition against idolatry. In that sense, Hopkins' tercet is an antithesis, but not an either-or that excludes one of the alternatives. The inclusive nature of the relation between the bird's beauty and danger and Christ's beauty and danger is marked by the "AND." But the difference between the two is so great and so tensive that an even more powerful connective must be used to join them. As in "Pied Beauty," which offers a Parmenidean framework to its Heraclitean opposites, both earthly and unearthly beauty must be accepted and reconciled by the reader.

The relation between the parallel clauses of "The Windhover's" first tercet is duplicated by that between the parallel clauses of the final tercet. In fact, this relation is emphasized by the words "No wonder of it," which introduce this tercet as a kind of illustration or proof of the first. Thus, the two tercets are parallel to one another. The same connective, "and," is used to tie the image of the sillion, ploughed with such sheer effort and plodding that it is made to shine, to the image of similarly dull ashes that all at once (but of themselves as in Mark 4:27) break apart and reveal their gold-red interior. Both these images have antithetical structures; monotonous toil and brown dirt somehow yield brilliance, just as embers

---

[39] *Letters to Bridges*, p. 95.

somehow do. Parallelism between members of these clauses has increased, making this tercet approximate to a *parallelismus membrorum*. This is consistent with Hopkins' practice of reaching near symmetry at peak moments of his verse. Parallelism of expression between these two tercets is engendering parallelism of thought, so that, as in the first tercet, we see the second part of the parallelism break away from and surpass its counterpart.

Indeed, the image of the embers becoming fiery does parallel the image of the fire that breaks from the chevalier in the second part of the first tercet, and the image of mundane effort yielding beauty in the second tercet parallels the image of the bird's earthly beauty and act. These images not only parallel but explain one another, so that the bird's seemingly effortless beauty linked to "sheer plod" makes its beauty seem less masterly. Further, the image of ploughed soil is both canceled and raised up to that of the bleak embers. The whole second part surpasses the first by a concealed "and yet," just as the last part of this parallelism, "and gash gold vermilion," conceals an "and yet" that far surpasses the first part. Hopkins ends his poem with an image of a nearly alchemical transformation from lifeless, burnt-out wood to glowing gold. The images of earth and fire paralleled in this last tercet are Parmenides' two elements, where earth, as Hopkins says in his essay on Parmenides, is "unmeaning night, thick and wedgèd body," and fire is "marvelously subtle, throughout one with itself" (*Journals*, p. 130). Hopkins' comment in this essay is that each person's inscape is made up of a mingling of these two elements, "those in which the heat-principle predominates having the finer wits" (*Journals*, p. 129). Using his notion of inscape here as a mingling, we can say that there is still connection, between body and spirit, between bird and Christ, between earth and fire. Hopkins is no Manichean. The single word "Buckle!" does not wipe out the beautiful vision detailed in the octet; it simply indicates, like the "AND" that is also an *and yet*, that this beauty is surpassed by Christ's greater beauty.

And in the final tercet, the earth's ability to be made beautiful is surpassed by the greater beauty of embers thought dead but alive and glowing. As in Plato, earthly beauty is a step on the ladder to something higher. To paraphrase another famous poem, nature's Heraclitean fire is prolegomena to the resurrection.

Beyond this fairly realistic reading of the final tercet, and for the most part I agree with Kathleen Raine that "No poet was ever less a symbolist,"[40] I believe a more symbolic reading is justified by the address to "my chevalier" and the invocation "To Christ our Lord."[41] Thus, both images of the final tercet are symbols of Christ as "the greatest rhetorical antithesis." As Hopkins says to Baillie, Christ consented to be a carpenter, to its "sheer plod," and yet was God. He points explicitly to Christ's radiance in a sermon, "Poor was his station, laborious his life, bitter his ending: through poverty, through labour, through crucifixion his majesty of nature more shines" (*Sermons*, p. 37). Further, as Hopkins' Philippians exegesis puts it, Christ humbled himself to the death of the cross: the "gall" and "gash" of the final line are reminders of that Crucifixion. Yet, this Crucifixion gashes itself open to reveal the Resurrection. Current theological interpretations of the Crucifixion as the actual exaltation of Christ are therefore anticipated in this reading of Hopkins' line. In both tercets, therefore, the paratactic connector "and" and the parallelism are essential to the expression of these antitheses as mystery.

What we see, then, in the sextet of "The Windhover" is a

[40] Kathleen Raine, "Hopkins: Nature and Human Nature," *Hopkins Society Third Annual Lecture*, Univ. of London, March 6, 1972. Reprinted by the Hopkins Society at the Stanbrook Abbey Press, Worcester. But note that Miss Raine admits that in Hopkins' realism symbolic dimensions are present (p. 3).

[41] Bridges says in his notes to this poem: "The dedication was added by Gerard Manley Hopkins only at the last revision; nevertheless it is highly probable that his motive in introducing Christ *by name* was in part, at least, to clarify the deeper symbolic implications of the sestet." *Poems*, p. 268.

complex double set of parallelisms that prospectively and ret-
rospectively instress one another. The element of antithesis is
strong within each parallelism, but the mystery is that near
opposition is contained in a greater, more inclusive compari-
son.

Several other poems of this period express an antithesis be-
tween human life and nature. "God's Grandeur," "The Sea
and the Skylark," and "Spring" are poems of this kind. Hop-
kins opposes, in "The Sea and the Skylark," two noises, the
steady, ancient tide and the lark's "rash-fresh re-winded new
skeinèd score," which never loses its "first freshness, being a
thing both new and old."[42] He further opposes the endurance
of "two noises too old to end" to the impermanence of the
city. Even the alliteration and assonance carry through the an-
tithesis, as in this line from "The Caged Skylark":[43]

> As a dare-g*a*le s*k*ylark *sc*anted in a *d*ull c*a*ge

A chiastic pattern is set up where positive words at the be-
ginning of the line, "dare-gale," alliterate with negative words
at the end, "dull cage." In the center of the line, the words
"skylark scanted" collide in meaning and sound. In many
poems, human beings, because they continually encroach on
and destroy nature ("Binsey Poplars," "God's Grandeur") in-
volve themselves in a needless antithesis; "Only the inmate
does not correspond" ("In the Valley of the Elwy"). Hopkins
even thought of this correspondence in terms of a kind of
moral parallelism or inscape, as the following excerpt from an
unpublished Oxford essay indicates: "supposing all mankind
acted on the categorical imperative they w[oul]d all be acting,
as we might compare it, in parallels, and this w[oul]d give the
look of acting by strict law . . . yet again this look w[oul]d

---

[42] *Letters to Bridges*, p. 164.

[43] Von Christoph Kuper, *Wälische Traditionen in der Dichtung von Gerard
Manley Hopkins* (Bonn: Bouvier Verlag, 1973), p. 152.

come fr[om] the freedom and not the constrainment of their action, and thus law and freedom w[oul]d be reconciled." [44]

In poems of 1882, like "Ribblesdale," there is still friction between "sweet earth" and a human being "to his own self-bent so bound." In "As kingfishers catch fire," the surpassing of self by the just person who "Acts . . . Christ" resembles the movement of "The Windhover." "The Leaden Echo and the Golden Echo" embodies in form and theme a near fission between earthly beauty, "death's worst," and beauty given to God that becomes the "hundredfold." But nowhere is the fissure more pronounced, and the tension between Parmenidean unity and Heraclitean entropy more strained, than in the poem written less than a year before Hopkins' death—"That Nature is a Heraclitean Fire and of the comfort of the Resurrection."

That Nature is a Heraclitean Fire and of
the comfort of the Resurrection

Cloud-puffball, torn tufts, tossed pillows | flaunt forth, then
   chevy on an air-
built thoroughfare: heaven-roysterers, in gay-gangs | they
   throng; they glitter in marches.
Down roughcast, down dazzling whitewash, | wherever an
   elm arches,
Shivelights and shadow tackle in long | lashes lace, lance and
   pair.
Delightfully the bright wind boisterous | ropes, wrestles,
   beats earth bare
Of yestertempest's creases; | in pool and rutpeel parches
Squandering ooze to squeezed | dough, crust, dust; stanches,
   starches
Squadroned masks and manmarks | treadmire toil there
Footfretted in it. Million-fuelèd, | nature's bonfire burns on.

---

[44] Hopkins, "The Autonomy of the Will," *Essays for T. H. Green, Esq.,
Unpublished Oxford Essays,* D10.

But quench her bonniest, dearest | to her, her clearest-selvèd spark
Man, how fast his firedint, | his mark on mind, is gone!
Both are in an unfathomable, all is in an enormous dark
Drowned. O pity and indig|nation! Manshape, that shone
Sheer off, disseveral, a star, | death blots black out; nor mark
Is any of him at all so stark
But vastness blurs and time | beats level. Enough! the Resurrection,
A heart's-clarion! Away grief's gasping, | joyless days, dejection.
Across my foundering deck shone
A beacon, an eternal beam. | Flesh fade, and mortal trash
Fall to the residuary worm; | world's wildfire, leave but ash:
In a flash, at a trumpet crash,
I am all at once what Christ is, | since he was what I am, and
This Jack, joke, poor potsherd, | patch, matchwood,
immortal diamond,
Is immortal diamond.

With the poem, "That Nature is a Heraclitean Fire and of the comfort of the Resurrection," we reach an antithesis as wide as that between Parmenides' Being and Non-Being. We have here, as Sr. Marcella Holloway says, Hopkins' most radical use of antithetical parallelism.[45] There is absolutely no modulation between the death that "blots black out" and "the Resurrection/ A heart's clarion!" The sharply divided diatonic and paratactic style betrays itself in the title. Both the Heraclitean vision of a consuming bonfire's endless strife and the turning of the tragedy into joy are true, though Hopkins' poem does nothing to reconcile them by causal or temporal explanations. Until the axis of the interjection "Enough!" all is flux: restless wind erases earth's landscape and humanity's footsteps; dark devours nature's "million-fuelèd" fire and the

[45] Sr. Marcella Holloway, "Hopkins' Theory of 'Antithetical Parallelism,' " p. 135.

spark of the human spirit. "Unmeaning night" appears to swallow all. Neither nature nor human life, so often opposed in earlier poems, can survive, much less retain their "mark" or inscape.

For Hopkins, who so treasured the distinctiveness and individuality of the human and natural worlds, this blurring vastness and extinction are the ultimate cruelty. Death seems to be the final and only stable condition, until it too succumbs at the pivotal caesura after the word "level." As Sr. Marcella notes, Hopkins rhymes the opposites, "dejection" and "Resurrection";[46] it was his intention with rhyme, as with every other form of parallelism, to let similarity in sound and form be joined to difference in meaning. The "beacon" of the first coda contrasts with the night that has gone before and overcomes the fading flesh and ashes that follow. It signals, as from a sinking, shipwrecked ship ("Across my foundering deck") to the second and final coda. This allusion to the "passion-plungèd giant risen" of *The Wreck of the Deutschland* brings Hopkins' mature poetic corpus full circle.

Now the poet sees himself to be "all at once what Christ is, since he was what I am," the ancient Athanasian formula that Christ became human in order that we might become like God. Never was there a copula that was more "the utterance and assertion" of Being than in Hopkins' final line, which performs an alchemical transformation of the "poor potsherd" into "immortal diamond." As elsewhere in his poetry, the perfect symmetry of this parallelism is used to connote ecstasy and wholeness—a complete vision accessible only to a self bowing to Being's utterance. The sheer iteration of the last four words is no tautology but expresses the faith that the miracle of Resurrection is here and now present, *in* this very "Jack, joke, poor potsherd" as well as beyond it. This last, most implausible, incongruous member of the series is turned by the final line into the true meaning of the whole. Then, the

[46] Ibid.

facets of that mirrored diamond retrospectively cast their brilliance over the whole poem.

The antitheses of Hopkins' poems, often widened to the outermost limits of the poem and unresolved, testify to his Heraclitean vision of the discord of all life and to his admission of the opposites in humanity. Though these antitheses may take up the poem's entire structure, however, they are not its final word. Neither is a Parmenidean monism. The final word is one of assent, given in contemplation, to both the dappledness and the Unchangeable, the earth's beauty and Christ's, death and Resurrection.

"The Ecstasy of Interest":
Contemplation as Parallelism's Praxis

*H*OPKINS WROTE parallelisms of resemblance and of antithesis into his poems to integrate and to disintegrate them, at times stretching their unity to the breaking point. As their unity recedes, the reader exercises an "energy of contemplation" to recapture it. This very experience of discovering a hidden wholeness amid apparent diversity and entropy was Hopkins' own experience in the contemplation of nature. His attentiveness to the most minute aspects of nature, its lucent green wheat, moonlight dropping on treetops like blue cobwebs, the sea's "walking wavelets edged with fine eyebrow crispings," is contemplation. And the awe and astonishment that accompany this contemplative act of vision are his "instress." Through its instress upon him, the world yielded up its inner beauty in a revelation of what he called its "inscape." Hopkins' inscape was in effect a religious experience in which things surrendered their deepest secret—God. In this sense, inscape can be compared to the *splendor formae* of medieval aesthetics, the mystics' "God shining out of every creature," and Heidegger's *apophainesthai*, the shining appearance of being. The surprises of the poem's parallelisms, where despite disorder unity discloses itself, and despite order antithesis remains, re-create in the poem the poet's contem-

plative instress of inscape. Contemplation is the poem's "par-
allelism of thought" and therefore the praxis, in effect the
reader response, of the poem.

Contemplation means stilling the inner voices of desire so
that the real beauty of the other can be seen. The contempla-
tive seer's self-forgetful attentiveness to the other begets an
indwelling of the other. Because it involves an uncluttered ap-
preciation of the existence of a thing,[1] contemplation effaces
even thought and feeling. Thus, in contrast to his contempo-
raries, many of whom were Romantics and symbolists who
presupposed that the poet's gift to his poetry was personal
passion, Hopkins provided his poems a very different kind of
ardor—the contemplative awe of instress. The inscape of his
vision differs from ordinary views of nature as perception of
Divine Reality within nature differs from positivistic appre-
hension. In Wordsworth, for example, the dialectic remains
between self and world, rarely achieving the self-transcen-
dence of the contemplative. He solves the problem of nature's
otherness at times by humanizing nature, at times by natural-
izing the self. Hopkins differs because, as a more contempla-
tive seer, he is willing to sacrifice the self, undergoing the
world's otherness and accepting it with a "yes." Insofar as pos-
sible, he has transposed the what of his contemplative seeing,
the inscape, and the how, the instress, into the contemplative
act of encountering the poem as its "parallelism of thought."

Although Hopkins did not define the phrase "parallelism of
thought," it can be connected with his many remarks on com-
parison and on the mind's synthesizing energies. Beauty,
Hopkins says, is "relation," and its apprehension is made by
"comparison" (*Journals*, pp. 80 and 95). Comparison is a
method that preserves the integrity and haecceitas of things
without dissolving them in a premature unity. With a wide
enough basis of comparison, "any two things, however un-

---

[1] See Gerald G. May, *Will and Spirit: A Contemplative Psychology* (San Fran-
cisco: Harper and Row, 1982), p. 25.

like, have something in common" (*Journals*, p. 104). In notes probably made at Newman's Oratory, he described the contemplative response necessary to art: "Art exacts this energy of contemplation . . . for even in the successive arts [like] music, for full enjoyment, the synthesis of the succession should give, unlock, the contemplative enjoyment of the unity of the whole" (*Sermons*, p. 126). Five years later, defining poetry and verse for his students at the Roehampton novitiate, he spoke of it as "speech framed for contemplation of the mind by the way of hearing or speech framed to be heard for its own sake and interest even over and above its interest of meaning" (*Journals*, p. 289). The inscape of speech that is created by repeating figures of sound and grammar must be "dwelt on."

In these formulations, Hopkins has not departed from his ideas on poetry written while an undergraduate at Oxford some eight years earlier. When he says figures of repeated sound and grammar must be "dwelt on," he is defining what he meant by "parallelism of thought" in the earlier essays. Hopkins' parallelism of thought, his dwelling on recurrent figures for their own sake over and above their interest of meaning, is accomplished by what he calls in his 1868 notes the mind's "abiding energy":

> The mind has two kinds of energy, a transitional kind, when one thought or sensation follows another, which is to reason, whether actively as in deliberation, criticism, or passively, so to call it, as in reading, etc.; (ii) an abiding kind for which I remember no name, in which the mind is absorbed (as far as that may be), taken up by, dwells upon, enjoys, a single thought: we may call it contemplation, . . . it is enough for the mind to repeat the same energy on the same matter. (*Journals*, pp. 125–26)

Hopkins meant his poetry to be read, then, not only with the "transitional energy" of reasoning, deliberation, and criticism, but above all with the mind's "abiding energy," that is, with contemplation. For the enjoyment of this abiding energy is characteristically contemplative, since contemplation was always seen as accompanied by delight. Further, repeating the "same energy on the same matter" is a mantra-like activity that stills the surface mind at the same time that it wakes up its deeper resources. The idea of being "taken up by" a single thought is confirmed by writers on contemplation who speak of a "communion" between knower and known, seer and seen.[2] In his several appositives for this experience, Hopkins sounds the keynotes of the contemplative tradition.

The term *contemplation* enjoyed currency in the nineteenth century both within the literature of spirituality and within literary criticism and aesthetics. Hopkins' thought was the beneficiary of both, especially after he undertook Jesuit training. Within the literature of spirituality, nearly all commentators sharply distinguish contemplation from meditation. Where meditation involves the use of deductive reason, imagination, and "affections" of the soul,[3] contemplation is regarded as the point of passage from self-effort to grace. Contemplation, even in Ignatius' system, is the goal of the meditative, discursive activity of the mind. For Hopkins, too, it is the goal. In spiritual notes from December 8, 1881, Hopkins sees contemplation as the "love" that crowns the "duty" of the first stages of the Ignatian spiritual journey (*Sermons*, p. 194).

In the literature of spirituality from Plato and Plotinus on, contemplation refers to that paradoxical "activity," where suddenly, but only after patient, resposeful attention, the object is "seen" as if for the first time. The contemplative comes before the object without the mental process of expecting, remembering, and especially desiring. In the place of desire and will, there is love and willingness. The contemplative has reached a place where there are no questions, where he is, as

[2] Underhill, *Mysticism*, p. 300.

[3] Louis Bouyer, *Introduction to Spirituality*, trans. Mary Perkins Ryan (Collegeville, Minn.: Liturgical Press, 1961), p. 69.

Eckhart put it, "living without a why."[4] At the center of Eckhart's mysticism is the notion of *abgeschiedenheit*, "detachment." In Eckhart's notion of abgeschiedenheit as amplified in his Sermon 2,[5] a person becomes virginal and detached through freedom from images. Rather than cluttering the mind even with sacred images and ideas of God, this person gives up inner ownership (*eigenschaft*) of all images, thereby cutting the self off from the world of creatures as it appears to self-will. Because such a world is really the negation of God, detachment is the negation of negation and the affirmation of God. The detached person's emptiness of creatures readies that person for receptivity to God. As one receives God, entering into God's life and activity, one receives God's creativity. For Eckhart, only this life in God is contact with the real and not with the delusions and projections born of attachments.

Correlative to the notion of detachment in Eckhart is that of *gelassenheit*, "releasement" or "letting be." Gelassenheit, from *lassen*, "to leave alone" or "to let be," is an attitude that unbinds the self from attachment to things and leaves things to be themselves rather than what the self would make of them. Thus, it frees both self and things. If detachment is an attitude regarding freedom of the self, gelassenheit is its counterpart with regard to things. Hopkins appropriated the concept of gelassenheit implicitly in his contemplative vision of nature and explicitly in the poem "To what serves Mortal Beauty?" where he asks: "What do then? How meet beauty?

---

[4] Meister Eckhart, *Meister Eckhart: The Essential Sermons, Commentaries, Treatises, and Defense*, trans. Edmund Colledge, O.S.A., and Bernard McGinn (New York: Paulist Press, 1981). Eckhart actually says, "If anyone went on for a thousand years asking of life: 'Why are you living?' life, if it could answer, would only say: 'I live so that I may live.' That is because life lives out of its own ground and springs from its own source, and so it lives without asking why it is itself living" (p. 184). God also has no "why." See the Introduction, pp. 60–61.

[5] *Meister Eckhart*, pp. 177–181.

Merely meet it; own,/ Home at heart, heaven's sweet gift, then leave,/ let that alone." To "own" heaven's sweet gift is paradoxically not to own it, not to be attached to or possessive of it, to be without eigenschaft, ownership of it. It is rather to "own" it as "heaven's sweet gift" in the sense of acknowledging or "stressing" it. This is the poem's task, Hopkins says in his Parmenides essay, for each word is a way of acknowledging Being (*Journals*, p. 129). Only then, because one's home is "at heart," will one's heart be at home, at peace, and one's serenity unbound. The beautiful, free from the desires and plans of the self, will be left just to be, which, as he says in "Ribblesdale," the earth "well dost."

Freed by detachment and letting be, contemplative seeing opens to the mystery of the object now made luminous as an aspect of the eternal. Remaining in all its physicality and concreteness, the tree, mountain, field, or flower reveals itself as redolent of Being. Like the contemplative seer, each rose is, as Angelus Silesius saw it, "living without a why,"[6] without an ulterior purpose other than being itself. Only the contemplative seer, capable of being surprised out of the complacency of ordinary seeing, appreciates the splendor of the simple and the hallowing of the everyday.

While it is the special gift of the mystic to know the many as one, the contemplative sees the one *in* the many, without effacing the individuality and plurality of things in an all-encompassing monism. Hopkins' contemplative vision stops short of mystical identification and union, probably because of his need for haecceitas. The whole of the Franciscan tradition that nourished Hopkins' beloved theologian, Duns Scotus ("who of all men most sways my spirits to peace"—"Duns Scotus's Oxford"), expressed delight in the unique particularity of things from Brothers Sun and Fire to Sister Water and

---

[6] "She blooms because she blooms, the rose does not ask why, nor does she preen herself to catch my eye." Angelus Silesius, *The Book of Angelus Silesius*, trans. Frederick Franck (Santa Fe, New Mexico: Bear and Co., 1985), p. 66.

Mother Earth of Francis' Canticle. Scotus' haecceitas is merely the scholastic version of a love of individual creatures that goes back to Francis himself. Hopkins reveres Scotus, for in his concept of haecceitas or this-ness he is "of realty the rarest-veinèd unraveller." For Hopkins, only the unique, un-repeatable being of each thing, not an abstraction from it, gets to the heart of reality. As Christopher Devlin points out (*Sermons*, pp. 293–294), Hopkins' spelling of haecceitas is *ecceitas*, a reminder of *ecce*, "behold" or "look." As his poem puts it, "These things, these things were here and but the beholder/ Wanting" ("Hurrahing in Harvest"). Like the Buddhist *tathagatha*, "suchness," haecceitas can be seen as a mysticism of or-dinary experience, a unique contemplative consciousness that recognizes and participates in the Being and truth of a thing but allows it just to be. Ecceitas is the "simple yes and is" of Being, found embodied in beings by the contemplative be-holder.

Hopkins appreciated the secret of being as the simple, ab-solute end or *telos* of nature and human beings, as his com-ment on the history of morals indicates: "The well known his-tory of morals shews more and more as we go back that a thing's being is sufficient reason why it sh[oul]d go on being" (Unpublished Oxford Notes, D6). In his spiritual notes he wrote that "the main stress or energy of the whole being . . . is its strain or tendency towards being" (*Sermons*, p. 137). And in his 1882 sonnet, "Ribblesdale," he commends the earth for its mere being: "Thou canst but be, but that thou well dost; strong/ Thy plea with him who dealt, nay does now deal,/ Thy lovely dale down thus and thus bids reel/ Thy river, and o'er gives all to rack or wrong." The "thus and thus" or just-so-ness of dale and river and earth, in its "living without a why," makes as strong a plea with the Creator as the heavens declaring the glory of God in Ps. 19. Hopkins' rhyming of the near opposites "strong" and "wrong," throwing considerable tension into the verse, subtly unites the Creator God ("him who dealt, nay does now deal") with the Destroyer, as does the biblical text he appended to the verse from Rom. 8:19–20: "For the creation waits with eager longing for the revealing of the sons of God; for the creation was subjected to futility, not of its own will but by the will of him who subjected it in hope."[7]

Hopkins' vision and contemplative spirit were nourished early by the philosopher most frequently mentioned in his undergraduate notes—Plato. Contemplation was for Plato both the means and the culmination of the life of the mind. Plato's *theoria*, Greek for contemplation, is the way not only to behold and understand but to participate and unite with the highest objects of knowledge. Vision then becomes union.[8] In the *Symposium*, as the soul ascends in contemplation of objects of beauty, from beauties of the body to those of the soul, the final vision of the Beautiful is not attained but bursts upon the soul.[9] One's life is only worth living, Diotima tells Socrates, "when he has attained this vision of the very soul of beauty."[10] Through contemplation of beauty's soul or form, the soul can even be assimilated to the divine.[11] As contemplation developed in the Eastern tradition of the Greek Fathers of the Church, *theoria* was seen to lead to *theosis*, the deification of the human being.

[7] Because he had already written such a strong antithesis between the polarities of the Godhead into much earlier poems like *The Wreck of the Deutschland*, I do not see this poem as exhibiting a darkened theology and pathetic fallacy as Daniel Harris in his recent study, *Inspirations Unbidden* (Berkeley: Univ. of California Press, 1982), chap. 1 passim, asserts. Notes written a few months before the composition of this poem state the condition for seeing all creation as God-informed and hardly exhibit a dark theology: "All things therefore are charged with love, are charged with God and *if we know how to touch them* give off sparks and take fire, yield drops and flow, ring and tell of him" (Notes on the "Contemplation for Obtaining Love," *Sermons*, p. 195, italics added).

[8] Andrew Louth, *The Origins of the Christian Mystical Tradition: From Plato to Denys* (Oxford: Clarendon Press, 1981), p. 3.

[9] Ibid., p. 13.

[10] Plato, *Symposium*, trans. Michael Joyce, in *Collected Dialogues*, 211a.

[11] Plato, *Theaetetus*, trans. F. M. Cornford, in *Collected Dialogues*, 176b.

The influence of Plato on Hopkins' understanding of con-
templation is undeniable. In an unpublished Oxford essay, on
the "Connection of Aristotle's metaphysics with his ethics,"
Hopkins took the opportunity to single out contemplation as
the "highest" and "fullest" activity of the human mind: "It has
been already implied what is the absolutely highest end of
man; it must be the fullest action of his mind—that is contem-
plation, and that on the purest attainable forms, namely what
is eternally and unchangeably true" (Unpublished Oxford Es-
say, D11, no. 4). The "purest attainable forms" became Hop-
kins' inscapes, their eternal truth the presence of Christ.

Hopkins employed a Platonic ladder of loves leading to
contemplation of true beauty in his poem, "To what serves
Mortal Beauty?" where he counsels: "Our law says: Love
what are | loves's worthiest, were all known;/ World's loveli-
est—men's selves. Self | flashes off frame and face. . . ./ Yea,
wish that though, wish all, | God's better beauty, grace."
Love, ascending from "mortal beauty" to beauty of soul
(self)[12] culminates in love of "God's better beauty," which,
when found in persons, is "grace." For Hopkins, grace is the
stress of Being in human life. As God's energy immanent in
human beings, "it is divine stress, holy spirit, and, as all is
done through Christ, Christ's spirit" (*Sermons*, p. 154). With
"God's better beauty" one surpasses Platonic conceptions, en-
tering into the circle of love of the Trinity, Christ and his
Spirit carrying one back to the Father God. This union is con-
templation's telos, the end toward which the stresses and con-
traries of existence move us.[13]

It was not only the literature of spirituality that explored the
nature of contemplation. The use of the word "contempla-
tive" was also prevalent in nineteenth-century aesthetics. In

---

[12] "Self," Hopkins says in his essay, "On Personality, Grace, and Free Will,"
"is the intrinsic oneness of a thing, which is prior to its being" (*Sermons*, p.
146).

[13] See the discussion of stress as both positive and negative in Part I of *The
Wreck of the Deutschland* in Chap. 2 of this study.

Germany, contemplation as an aesthetic exercise involved true seeing rather than seeing with desire. Schiller identifies it with our first act of reflection, one in which we cease to apprehend the world by desire but are rather freely related to it.[14] Once nature's power over human life is broken, calm ensues in our senses so that "time itself, the eternally moving, stands still while the dispersed rays of consciousness are gathered together, and *form*, an image of the infinite, is reflected upon the transient foundation."[15] This power to stop time, to gather the mind's scattered energies, and to see form, an "image of the infinite," was the contemplative power that Hopkins possessed.

Hegel, influenced by Schiller, likewise emphasizes the absence of desire in a contemplative relation to the work of art,[16] but he also maintains that a contemplative relation to things "has no interest in consuming them as particulars . . . but rather in becoming acquainted with them in their universality, in finding their inner being and law. . . . Therefore the theoretical interest lets the single things be."[17] For Hegel artistic contemplation differs from the theoretical interest of science in "cherishing interest for the object as an individual existence."[18] What we see in Hegel are several keynotes of Hopkins' contemplative aesthetic. In discovering inscape in nature, Hopkins found the "inner being and law" of things, though he did not thereby discard the sensuous particulars of the existence for the essence. Inscape as haecceitas by its nature individuates, makes unique, once and for all.

Within the English tradition, contemplation held a prominent place in the aesthetics of John Ruskin, a critic whose in-

---

[14] Schiller, *On the Aesthetic Education of Man*, p. 120. Schiller says, "Contemplation thrusts its object into the distance, thereby turning it into its true and inalienable possession and thus securing it from passion."

[15] Ibid.

[16] Hegel, "Lectures on Aesthetics," in *On Art, Religion, Philosophy*, p. 65.

[17] Ibid.

[18] Ibid., p. 66.

fluence on Hopkins we explored in Chapter 1. The "theoretic" or contemplative attitude (from θεωρία) in Ruskin is to be distinguished from a merely sensual or "aesthetic" one by the marks of gratitude, joyfulness, and reverence.[19] *Theoria*, he says, is "the full comprehension and contemplation of the Beautiful as a gift of God."[20] (Cf. "heaven's sweet gift" in Hopkins' poem above.) Even the pleasures of scents, such as Mary's spikenard or the myrrh of the *Song of Solomon*, when received "with reference to God's glory," become theoretic. For Ruskin, contemplative means the ability to perceive the divine in the natural, both "in what is harsh and fearful as well as in what is kind."[21] Christian *theoria*, says Ruskin, is "able to find evidence of [God] still where all seems forgetful of him, and to turn that into a witness of his working which was meant to obscure it."[22]

Although in his letters[23] Hopkins was ambivalent toward Ruskin the critic, Ruskin's emphasis on theoretic seeing in art must have left a deep impression on the young Hopkins. Hopkins' own practice in *The Wreck of the Deutschland* at the beginning of his career as a mature poet and the "terrible sonnets" at the end is to search for the divine even in the "harsh and fearful" storms of outer and inner life and to "turn that into a witness of [its] working" by stressing what he has been instressed by.

Moreover, another man whom Hopkins admired and emulated transposed the notion of contemplation from the exclusive domain of spirituality to that of poetry. That man was

[19] Ruskin, *Modern Painters*, 2:15.

[20] Ibid.

[21] Ibid., 2:17. There is not space to lay out the details of Ruskin's vast aesthetics. Suffice it to say that the "theoretic" contrasts with the imagination, which is itself divided into imagination associative, penetrative, and contemplative. This contrast with imagination may have contributed to Hopkins' bypassing of it.

[22] Ibid.

[23] *Further Letters* (September 6, 1863), p. 204. "A perfect critic is very rare, I know. Ruskin often goes astray."

John Henry Newman. Although Hopkins did not agree with many of the poetic theories expressed in Newman's 1828 essay, "Poetry, with Reference to Aristotle's Poetics,"[24] he was in sympathy with Newman's declaration that "poetry has in modern times . . . taken the place of the deep contemplative spirit of the early Church" and that "poetry, then, is our mysticism."[25] Newman, however, justifies even the poet's obscurity because the poet's habits of mind lead to contemplation rather than to communication, but Hopkins, with his emphasis on the poem's bidding, cannot follow in this dichotomy. For Hopkins, contemplation issues in communication, both with God and with the presumed reader.

With Ruskin's and Newman's application of contemplation to art as model, Hopkins too made the transposition. By increasing the parallelisms of his poetry, he has actually privileged the contemplative response to the poem "over and above its interest of meaning." His poems have been written with a kind of kenosis of discursive reason so that the mind can "abide" or dwell in them, making the linear meaning secondary. His frequent use of parataxis, simple coordinate conjunctions that support the parallelism of his poems, necessitates this kenosis of intellect. For, just as kenosis or self-emptying is the distinguishing mark of Christ's life and character for Hopkins,[26] so it is the underlying principle of both his life and

[24] John Henry Newman, *Essays Critical and Historical*, vol. 1, 2d ed. (London: Basil Montagu Pickering, 1872), pp. 2–25. Newman undertakes a Romantic revision of Aristotle's emphasis on craftsmanship in poetry.

[25] Ibid., pp. 290–291. In his *Grammar of Assent*, Newman concluded that "After all, man is *not* a reasoning animal; he is a seeing, feeling, contemplating, acting animal" (New York: Image Books, 1955), p. 90. It should also be mentioned that Coventry Patmore, Hopkins' correspondent and fellow poet, wrote of attention in his *Religio Poetae* that it is the "capacity for looking steadily at realities" and that it is the "result of patient listening and of the hardly acquired habit of suspending *active thought*" (London: George Bell and Son, 1893), pp. 32–36. Patmore and Hopkins discussed contemplation during their last visit together.

[26] He writes to Bridges in 1883: "This mind [Paul] says, was in Christ Je-

art. Hopkins wrote into much of his poetry a kind of "no" to self, a suppression of his own reasoning that enabled a more total "yes" or assent to what he saw. This kenosis was essential to his own contemplative vision of nature and therefore to the transmission of that vision in his poems. The two most important elements of Hopkins' contemplative vision and contemplative poetry are, then, kenosis and assent.

Contemplation, as abiding energy, is the response appropriate to the parallelism, just as parallelism is the poetic phenomenon appropriate to the contemplative response. Parallelism is the beginning, but only in seed-form, of a mysticism; for a pluralist such as Hopkins, it is the only unity possible until the eschaton. Parallelisms elevate or "pitch" the verse toward "the idea of holiness," departing from the prosaic and profane. And, as monks chanting the psalms through the centuries learned, parallelisms, with their mantra-like repetitions, slow the verse so that the reader can move into what it expresses. Hopkins deliberately designed his poems with their manifold parallelisms of sound and sense to beget parallelism of thought, that is, contemplation. The chiming of auditory and syntactic parallelisms heard throughout the poems is like the faint ringing of a bell summoning to prayer and contemplation, calling out a deeper, stiller response of the reader otherwise prepared to dominate the poem with intellect, memory, and desire. Because parallelism communicates what is nondiscursive—sameness in difference and difference in sameness, the pattern or inscape glimpsed by our deepest in-

sus—he means as man: being in the form of God—that is, finding, as in the first instant of his incarnation he did, his human nature informed by the godhead—he thought it nevertheless no snatching-matter for him to be equal with God, but annihilated himself, taking the form of servant. . . . It is this holding of himself back, and not snatching at the truest and highest good, the good that was his right, nay his possession from a past eternity in his other nature, his own being and self, which seems to me the root of all his holiness and the imitation of this the root of all moral good in other men." *Letters to Bridges*, p. 175.

tuition of reality—discursive reason alone is incapable of responding to it.

But it is important to note that parallelism does communicate, and that contemplation offers not only an ineffable but a noetic response. Hopkins makes this point in his 1873 notes titled "Poetry and Verse,"[27] where he defines poetry as: "speech framed for contemplation of the mind . . . even over and above its interest of meaning. Some matter and meaning is essential to it but only as an element necessary to support and employ the shape which is contemplated for its own sake" (*Journals*, p. 289). By the time of writing these notes, Hopkins has completely subordinated the discursive element of poetry to the contemplative. The shape is to be contemplated "for its own sake," not for its meaning. In Hopkins' more total disavowal here of meaning in art, we might be tempted to see him as something of a "proto-structuralist" or extreme formalist. It is as if he would abandon truth in art along with meaning. Those contemporary structuralists,[28] however, who see in him an abandonment of the referential and conative functions of art in an attempt to align him with structuralist principles are mistaken; rather, the contemplative response to the poem, which Hopkins clearly wants, brings about its own kind of *truth*, but not truth in the sense of discrete, isolable statement. Hopkins had said in his earliest essay, "On the Signs of Health and Decay in the Arts," that "Truth and Beauty are the ends of Art" and that the truer the "comparison of the representation in Art with the memory of the true thing . . . the more pleasure is perceived, thus fulfilling the condition of the principle of parallelism" (*Journals*, pp. 74–75).

[27] Again, they are undated, but they were probably compiled while he was teaching rhetoric from 1873 to 1874 at Manresa House, Roehampton.

[28] See Jacob Korg, "Hopkins' Linguistic Deviations," *PMLA* 92 (1977): 977–996. Korg actually says poetry for Hopkins "is mainly a matter of formal considerations, unconnected with either praise or imitation." Although he greatly qualifies that statement throughout his essay, he clearly wishes to see Hopkins as anticipating the modern conception of language as an autonomous system.

Hopkins' aesthetics goes beyond itself into metaphysics, that is, he wanted truth as well as beauty from art. Yet that truth was not one of propositional statement. The "truth" of the work of art consists of its penultimate comparisons, set into the poem in the form of parallelisms, and perceived by the reader in a recollective, contemplative act of "comparison of the representation in Art with the memory of the true thing. . . . The more intellectual, less physical, the spell of contemplation," he says, "the more complex must be the object, the more close and elaborate must be the comparison the mind has to keep making between the whole and the parts, the parts and the whole" (*Journals*, p. 126). Yet, even these dualistic comparisons yield ultimately to a unity—the unity achieved in the reader's own being by his contemplative, kenotic reading. Not only the comparison made by parallelisms of resemblance but the tensive antitheses and their "and yet's" ultimately give way to the final "and yet"—there is unity. It is that unity with which the poem began, the poet's prepossession, which has retired behind the multiplicity of clouds, leaves, waves, each with its insoluble integrity. This sense of unity is recovered not only within the reader but in the union effected between poem and reader, and between reader and "the true thing."

Thus, the parallelism begun in the poem, the dynamic that creates comparison, is extended outward beyond the poem, becoming a hermeneutical principle, Hopkins' "principle of parallelism."[29] "This kind of beauty," he says, is "extrinsic and

[29] Hopkins' emphasis on bidding is like Hans-Georg Gadamer's. Gadamer makes application the fundamental problem of his hermeneutics: "In the course of our reflections we have come to see that understanding always involves something like the application of the text to be understood to the present situation of the interpreter. Thus we are forced to go, as it were, one stage beyond romantic hermeneutics, by regarding not only understanding and interpretation, but also application as comprising one unified process." Gadamer derives his hermeneutics of application from legal and theological hermeneutics. Thus, "a religious proclamation is not there to be understood as a merely historical document, but to be taken in a way in which it exercises its

is implied in the spectator" (*Journals*, p. 75). The fundamental parallelism in Hopkins' poetics is between the instress and awe of the poet (his "prepossession" or "flush"), recovered in the poem (its "definition" or "utterance"), and the instress of the poem on us (its "application" or "extension"). The passive and active roles of the poet are then transferred to the reader through the poem. As he described the reader's task in his 1868 notes: "The further in anything, as a work of art, the organisation is carried out, the deeper the form penetrates, the prepossession flushes the matter, the more effort will be required in apprehension, the more power of comparison, the more capacity for receiving that synthesis of (either successive or spatially distinct) impressions which gives us the unity with the prepossession conveyed by it" (*Journals*, p. 126). This passage juxtaposes the active "power of comparison" with the passive "capacity for receiving," a juxtaposition characteristic of Hopkins' view of contemplation as active-passive.

As opposed to this view of the poetry as contemplative, recent studies of Hopkins have associated his poetic method either with the method of Ignatian meditation or with the poetics of the Tractarian movement, which, as we will see, Hopkins considered meditative. Some critics reason that since he was a Jesuit throughout the period of his mature work, he should be writing poetry that resembles the Ignatian method of meditation. Ignatian meditation involves imaginative reconstruction of the "composition of place" of the event or object contemplated, sometimes accompanied by application of the five senses, an intellectual or moral analysis, and a final act of faith or address to God in the colloquy. While contemplation on the one hand effaces discursive reason and imagination, meditation encourages them. When meditation assumes a literary structure, as it did in the seventeenth century, "the meditation-writer develops a habit of extending through sym-

saving effect." See *Truth and Method* (New York: The Seabury Press, 1975), pp. 274–278.

bolism and moral commentary, the imaginative reference of the matter in hand."[30] Symbolism and imagination, however, play very little role in Hopkins' poetry of realism. When moral commentary appears, as in "God's Grandeur," it follows naturally the "simple yes and is" of direct, realistic statement.

Louis Martz, in his *Poetry of Meditation*,[31] was the first to see Hopkins' poetry as meditative, and David Downes, in his book on Hopkins, subtitled *A Study of His Ignatian Spirit*, states that "it can hardly be denied that methodical meditative patterns influenced his poetry."[32] While I do not wish to deny or discount the Ignatian influence entirely, I believe Hopkins' own descriptions of poetry as contemplation should be given more weight before this label of "meditative" is applied. As Martz, Downes, Andreach, and others see it, the meditative structure of Hopkins' poems involves composition of place by memory or imagination, analysis by intellect, and the application of affections by the will in the colloquy. It is possible to take one of Hopkins' poems and with some modification (severe modification in many instances) make this order fit. Downes tells us, for example, that the windhover is an "intense imaginative image"[33] and that Hopkins' poem "Spelt from Sibyl's Leaves" is central to the tradition of meditative poetry. First of all, the construal of "The Windhover" as "imaginative," while it supports Downes' meditative theory, for the imagination is essential to meditation, ignores Hopkins' own distrust of the imagination. Speaking of mythology

---

[30] Harold Fisch, *Jerusalem and Albion* (New York: Schocken Books, 1964), p. 50.

[31] Louis L. Martz, *The Poetry of Meditation* (New Haven: Yale Univ. Press, 1962).

[32] David A. Downes, *Gerard Manley Hopkins: A Study of His Ignatian Spirit* (New York: Bookman Assoc., 1959), p. 166. Robert J. Andreach's *Studies in Structure: The Stages of the Spiritual Life in Four Modern Authors* (New York: Fordham Univ. Press, 1964) also maintains that the meditative technique underlies Hopkins' poems.

[33] Downes, *Ignatian Spirit*, p. 156.

to Dixon, he says, "For myself literally words would fail me to express the loathing and horror with which I think of it and of man setting up the work of his own hands, of that hand within the mind the imagination, for God Almighty who made heaven and earth."[34] In unpublished lecture notes on the Nicomachean Ethics (Unpublished Oxford Notes, G1), he comments on φαντασία: "It is the power which images things to us, differing from αἰσθήσεως in being active, not passive, and as being possibly wrong while αἴσθησις is always right." In this last comment, we can sense the reasoning behind Hopkins' distrust of the imagination. When the imagination is in the service of desire, it can lead to distortion, untruth, unreality, in short to "want of earnest."

A meditative construal of "The Windhover" further fails to acknowledge the immediacy and freshness of a visual image that is "caught this morning." In contemplation, we are invited to the sacrament of the present moment, not to the memories or imaginings of meditation. As Hopkins states in his unpublished notes, "You cannot undo the past but you can negative it" (Unpublished Oxford Notes, D8). In contemplation one "negatives" past desires and expectations while turning with freshness and purity of heart (Hopkins' phrase is "chastity of mind") to the present.

Further, to find composition of place and a colloquy in a poem such as "Spelt from Sibyl's Leaves," which seems to be about the meaninglessness of a world where there are only abstracts that are "earthless, equal, attuneable"—that is, arbitrary, abstract, and neutral rather than definite and earthy— seems to strain the imagination far too much. Hopkins' point in this poem is that, caught in our musings, steeped in self, we do not see earth's dapple. The particularity of contemplative vision gets wound on two mental, dualistic spools, where "thoughts against thoughts in groans grind."

Andreach, who states that "the meditative method begins

---

[34] *Correspondence*, p. 146.

to shape [Hopkins'] poems" toward the end of the early period,[35] that is before Hopkins entered the Roman Catholic Church or the Jesuit order, passes over the entire middle period, when Hopkins was a Jesuit, in his attempt to apply the meditative method to the poems.

I do not see a conscious, deliberate attempt on Hopkins' part to construct meditatively structured poems, nor do I think the mature poems from *The Wreck of the Deutschland* on are best opened up by the imposition of this structure as their inscape. Oddly enough, some early, pre-Jesuit poems, like "Nondum" and "A Soliloquy of One of the Spies Left in the Wilderness," do seem like actual meditations, built on internal soliloquies rather than direct confrontation with the world. In "Nondum" the speaker reasons:

> God, though to Thee our psalm we raise
> No answering voice comes from the skies;
> To Thee the trembling sinner prays
> But no forgiving voice replies;
> Our prayer seems lost in desert ways,
> Our hymn in the vast silence dies.

This poem, which shows the doubt that plagued Hopkins before his conversion, is a kind of reverse of the cosmological argument. Headed by the epigraph, "Verily Thou art a God that hidest Thyself" (Isa. 35:15), it argues to the absence of God from the silence of creation, although it ends with a prayer to this hidden God. "A Soliloquy of One of the Spies" comes closer than later poems to creating a composition of place:

[35] Andreach, *Studies in Structure*, pp. 231–237. I believe Andreach finds a very inappropriate category for the poems of the middle period when he says they correspond to the first stage, that is the purgative stage, of the spiritual life (p. 35). He himself confesses that he may be liable to the charge of "temporarily distorting" these works. I do not believe that Hopkins had the three stages of purgation, illumination, and union in mind when he wrote poems like "God's Grandeur" and "The Starlight Night."

Your hands have borne the tent-poles: on you plod:
The trumpet waxes loud: tired are your feet.
Come by the flesh-pots: you shall sit unshod
And have your fill of meat;
And bring your offerings to a grateful god,
And fear no iron rod.

Indeed, early poems like "A Vision of the Mermaids" have been called "Keatsian" because of their play of imagination and the lushness of their images. Before his conversion, Hopkins had not yet effaced imagination and reasoning. Thus, these early poems might be considered "meditative" in the sense of being discursive and imaginative, but the later poems, from the reopening of his poetic canon in 1875, are more appropriately considered contemplative than meditative.

It seems clear that Hopkins understood the crucial difference between meditation and contemplation, not only in the 1868 notes on the mind's two energies, but in notes on the *Spiritual Exercises* written during his year of tertianship in the Jesuit order in 1881. As commentary on the Second Week of the Exercises, Hopkins supplies "Notes on Contemplation" where he discusses this difference in these terms:

Henceforward all the Exercises have these 3 preludes. And all are called Contemplations, with two exceptions only, those on the Two Standards and the Three Couples, which he calls Meditations; otherwise he uses that word no more. See p. 154, where he implies that the Mysteries of Christ's life may be meditated *or* contemplated. The first Week is the one in which he makes use of Meditations.—Nevertheless the word 'meditando' occurs pp. 82, 85.

'Ut pie meditari licet'—This is the conclusion, he means to say, to which pious *reasoning* will lead us, . . . 'Meditari' refers to reasoning. (*Sermons*, p. 173; emphases are Hopkins')

Hopkins' understanding of meditation as *reasoning* in these notes reiterates the distinction he had made in undergraduate days between transitional energy as reasoning and abiding energy as contemplation. Further, he seems concerned here to show that meditation plays a subordinate or at least preliminary role in Ignatius' *Exercises.* "All are called Contemplations, with two exceptions only," he says; and then, "The first week is the one in which he makes use of Meditations." This concern may well stem from the fact that in the history of spirituality meditation is the activity of beginners. The goal of meditation, even in the Ignatian system, is contemplation; all the Ignatian meditations are intended to prepare for contemplation. As Louis Bouyer states in his *Introduction to Spirituality*: "Meditation, laborious by nature, is the activity of beginners in the spiritual life, or of those who have not yet progressed very far in it. But normally, one ought to attain a phase of spiritual progress in which meditation no longer adds anything, or even becomes psychologically impossible to carry out. Then, it would seem, contemplation will flower of its own accord."[36] By 1881 when Hopkins is writing his commentary on the *Spiritual Exercises*, he had had more than twelve years' exposure to them. In his early poetry and in his journals, he had long since passed through a meditative phase and was now what the spirituality books call a "proficient," someone practiced in contemplation. When he comments that "The only class of people St. Ignatius contemplates as making the Exercises . . . are in the Purgative Way and penitents at any rate now" (*Sermons*, p. 205) he expresses the belief that the *Exercises* are for beginners, those not yet embarked on the ways of illumination and union characteristic of contemplation.

Further, the preference for contemplation that he goes on to demonstrate in the Ignatian commentary as well as in the ear-

---

[36] Bouyer, *Spirituality*, pp. 68–77. See the discussion on p. 69 of St. Teresa's difficulties with meditation.

lier 1868 notes, is evidence of a natural tendency and perhaps of a reaction against the shackling, regressive effects of meditation. For, as Bouyer sees it, meditation, in "calling up a paroxysm of sensible impressions superimposed on what seems like an aggravated ratiocination in order that the will may finally be galvanized thereby," causes the subject to be self-absorbed and results in a "gradual fading and thinning out of the religious object."[37] The real dangers, according to Bouyer, are not only that "a curious concentration on the human subject and his behavior becomes more and more absorbing," but that there is no compensation by "an abundant and living objectivity."[38] As meditation becomes more psychological, its themes contract. Both the loss of contact with "an abundant and living objectivity" and the "Romantic" absorption in the self's reasoning and imaginings were naturally abhorrent to Hopkins. By the year 1888, writing his retreat notes in Ireland, he has given up the practice of meditation because of entering on "that course of loathing and hopelessness which I so often felt before" (*Sermons*, p. 262). For one "in earnest with reality," preoccupation with self and excessive introspection seemed his curse, not his salvation.

Hopkins exercises his preference for contemplation throughout his spiritual notes. He says of "consideration," a synonym for contemplation:

"Considerando . . an . . an . . quam . . quam" etc.—Not that the exercitant, if he has not been over the ground, will make much of it, but that, even by the realising—I mean more as we speak of realising a sum, a fortune—his ignorance or the small knowledge he has, he may reach the reality of the facts; something as to have been on pilgrimage to Jerusalem in the dark would be more full of

[37] Ibid., pp. 70 and 72. As Bouyer sees it, the meditative method is in part a cultural phenomenon appearing during the baroque period when the awareness of self was just emerging.

[38] Ibid., p. 72.

devotion than to see it in the best panorama. (*Sermons*, p. 173)

Hopkins, who *has* been over the ground of the *Exercises*, connects contemplation to the realizing of ignorance, a notion much akin to that of "kenosis of intellect," which describes his poetry. Like Socrates, who sought the knowledge of his own ignorance, or like John of the Cross, who advised, "In order to arrive at knowing everything, Desire to know nothing,"[39] Hopkins counsels the dark ignorance and kenosis of contemplation rather than the reasoning of meditation as the way to "reach the reality of the facts." Full knowledge comes not from exacerbating the intellect but from letting it be and passing beyond it into the "dark" of a devotional way.

Because contemplation has usually been seen as abstractive and interior, following the tradition of Plotinus and Augustine, a contemplation of nature has seemed a contradiction. Yet according to Evelyn Underhill, both the contemplation of nature and the contemplation of spirit are possible.[40] The contemplation of nature, she says, like the contemplation of spirit, requires a "stilling of that surface-mind" as its price, a slowing down of our "feverish mental time" that results in "a heightened significance, an intensified existence in the thing at which you look" and in an "answering current." These descriptions enlighten us as to the experiences of inscape and instress that lie behind Hopkins' use of the terms. Underhill's phenomenological description matches those given not only by mystics but by psychological experimenters as well. "The contemplative," she says, "is contented to absorb and be absorbed: and by this humble access he attains to a plane of

[39] St. John of the Cross, *Ascent of Mount Carmel*, trans. E. Allison Peers (New York: Image Books, 1958), p. 156.
[40] Underhill, *Mysticism*, p. 302. Underhill continually uses Hopkins' words, "innocence of eye," "flame out like shining from shook foil," and others to explain contemplation.

knowledge which no intellectual process can come near."[41] Hans Urs von Balthasar, too, in his writings on prayer, says that contemplation does not have to mean abstracting from all relation with the world.[42] William Johnston, an interpreter of both Zen and Christian mysticism, points out that in Zen there is a deliberate policy of keeping the eyes open and remaining close to the environment, which he associates with a "return to the market-place" that is compatible with the highest stages of imageless, nonconceptual contemplation.[43] And St. Teresa is most famous for her incarnational thrust at the height of contemplation.

Hopkins' comments on the three points of Ignatius' contemplation on the Nativity, in employing the Augustinian trinity of memory, understanding, and will, further describe the contemplative act:

> On the contemplating Persons, Words and Actions—
> These three points belong to the three powers, memory,
> understanding, and will. Memory is the name for that
> faculty which towards present things is Simple Appre-
> hension and, when it is question of the concrete only,
> γνῶσις, ἐπίγνωσις, the faculty of Identification; towards
> past things is Memory proper; and towards things future
> or things unknown or imaginary is Imagination. When
> continued or kept on the strain the act of this faculty is
> attention, advertence, heed, the being *ware*, and its habit,
> knowledge, the being *aware*. Towards God it gives rise to
> *reverence*, it is the sense of the *presence* of God. (*Sermons*,
> p. 174)

Hopkins' description of contemplation here is consistent with traditional definitions of contemplation as the "prayer of lov-

[41] Ibid.

[42] Hans Urs von Balthasar, *Prayer*, trans. A. V. Littledale (New York: Paulist Press Deus Books, 1967), p. 30.

[43] William Johnston, *Silent Music: The Science of Meditation* (San Francisco: Harper and Row, 1976), p. 87.

ing attention" or prayer of "simple regard."[44] Significantly, Hopkins chooses the Platonic memory, the least inventive faculty, as means of access to things. Hopkins' insightful rendering of a simple apprehension "continued or kept on the strain" and his string of appositives—"attention, advertence, heed, the being ware"—indicate the depth of his understanding of such an activity. Such simple apprehension echoes the "simple yes and is," the Parmenidean affirmation of Being of his Parmenides essay; it also echoes the "pitch" of simple positiveness or simple being of his spiritual notes. It is the "sense of the *presence* of God," not a manipulation of reality by conscious intellect, but an opening of reality to the patient, "ware" seer. Understanding issues from this faculty of attention in the form of "admiration, which issues in praise" (*Sermons*, p. 174). Admiration is itself the wide-open wonderment that we see on every page of Hopkins' journals and in his poems. It is inseparable from the act of praise. We have seen Hopkins make this relation between simple apprehension, understanding, and praise once before, in *The Wreck of the Deutschland*: "For I greet him the days I meet him, and bless when/ I understand." This meeting and encounter with God, though ineffable and therefore beyond knowledge, issues in understanding and in blessing or praise. Hopkins' apprehension of God ends not in an apophatic denial of reality but in the cataphatic speech of praise.

Ignatius too emphasizes the practical aspect of the contemplation of the Nativity by asking the exercitant to make himself "a poor little unworthy serving-boy, watching them, contemplating them, and ministering to them in their need, as if I was there present."[45] Yet, as this quotation implies, Ignatius' orientation is toward service, not toward the act of praise. When Hopkins adds in his commentary that "all voluntary ex-

---

[44] A. Allen Brockington, *Mysticism and Poetry* (London: Chapman and Hall, 1934), p. 137. Brockington discusses Hopkins' "askesis for poetry" and examines several of his poems.

[45] Ignatius, *Spiritual Exercises*, p. 71.

ercise of faculties is . . . practical; it is not mere speculation, whatever its name" (*Sermons*, pp. 174–175), he is pointing to understanding and praise as the praxis of the poem: he is pointing therefore to contemplation. Hopkins made his poems with their blessings of understanding the praxis of his own contemplation; the poems, in turn, generate contemplation in the reader.

Hopkins's final comment in this series of "Notes on Contemplation" is a revealing one, for it reestablishes the distinction between meditation and contemplation that may have blurred in his trinitarian division. He says, " 'Meditando . . . circumstantias earum'/ inferring what they must have been, 'contemplando'/ observing what they are" (*Sermons*, p. 175). He makes a sharp division, even an antithesis, between "what must have been" and "what they are." Contemplation takes place in the present, not in the reconstructed past. In this orientation to the present, there is contact with the reality of the facts, not with the inferences of the mind. The key word here is "inferring," a word from Newman's *Grammar of Assent*. Before turning to that work and to the poetics of the Tractarian movement, it may be well to make one more remark about meditation and contemplation.

As stated at the outset, the influence of Ignatius on Hopkins' poetry should not be completely discounted. Although Hopkins' thoughts about poetry cohere over the course of his adult life from Oxford to Manresa,[46] and his poetic practice draws its life from those thoughts, still Ignatius does exert a positive influence on Hopkins. For, as Hugo Rahner in his study, *Ignatius the Theologian*, states, Ignatius' theology was primarily

---

[46] Anthony Bischoff, himself a Jesuit, supports this view when he says "It is more his early studies at Oxford than his later Jesuit training that explain the basic criteria he followed in criticism." "Gerard Manley Hopkins as Literary Critic" (Ph.D. diss., Yale University, 1952), p. 142. Bischoff even states that it was only *after* he was a priest deeply familiar with the writings of mystics like John of the Cross, Marie Lataste, and Gertrude that he drew greater strength from the *Exercises* (p. 130).

a "theology of visibility."[47] And, as the *Dictionnaire de Spiritualité* puts it, "L'apport original d'Ignace de Loyola se résume dans la formule: chercher Dieu en tout et en tous. L'adage thérésien serait plutôt: chercher Dieu en vous, au plus intime de votre âme."[48] Ignatian spirituality begins at the level of the concrete in an outward turn to the world that would have been very compatible with Hopkins' instincts. The point of Ignatius' "application of the senses," however, is to produce a progressive internalizing and spiritualizing of taste, touch, sight, hearing, and smell.[49] Consider, for example, Ignatius' famous "meditation on hell," later satirized in Joyce's *A Portrait of the Artist as a Young Man*:

> To see in imagination the great fires, and the souls
>   enveloped, as it were, in bodies of fire.
> To hear the wailing, the screaming, cries, and blas-
>   phemies against Christ our Lord and all His saints.
> To smell the smoke, the brimstone, the corruption,
>   and rottenness.
> To taste bitter things, as tears, sadness, and remorse
>   ("the worm") of conscience.
> With the sense of touch to feel how the flames surround
>   and burn souls.[50]

In Ignatius' meditative method, the senses are to be redirected inward so that the "theology of visibility" becomes in effect a theology of imagination focused on a restricted number of events from salvation history and the life of Christ. The ultimate effect of this method was a romanticizing and psychologizing that was not compatible with Hopkins' earnestness with reality. He had accomplished the spiritualizing of the

[47] Hugo Rahner, *Ignatius the Theologian*, trans. Michael Barry (New York: Herder and Herder, 1968), p. 234.

[48] *Dictionnaire de Spiritualité*, Marcel Viller, S.J., F. Cavallero, and M. Olphe-Galliard, S.J. (Paris: Beauchesne et Ses Fils, 1949), p. 2030.

[49] See the discussion in Rahner's *Ignatius the Theologian*, pp. 184–187.

[50] Ignatius, *Spiritual Exercises*, p. 59.

senses himself not by turning them inward but by a selfless, kenotic seeing that opened up a revelation of the world's inner beauty—its inscape. It was to the interiority of other things that he wished to arrive, not to his own interiority. His experience of inscape should not, therefore, be literalized as if it involved only an external seeing of patterns and designs. To see the grandeur of God flaming out from matter is already an epiphanic, revelatory seeing—a contemplation.

In concluding our assessment of the Ignatian influence on Hopkins, we can say that Ignatius' injunction to seek God in all things, his "theology of visibility," not only reinforced Hopkins' sacramental sensibility but inspired such exuberant statements as, "All things therefore are charged with love, are charged with God and if we know how to touch them give off sparks and take fire, yield drops and flow, ring and tell of him" ("Notes on the Contemplation for Obtaining Love," *Sermons*, p. 195). In this statement there is evidence of a positive application of the senses not to mental images but to the contemplation of nature itself. We merely "touch" or apprehend, and nature does the rest—gives off sparks and yields drops of God as it rings and tells of him. Here in essence is the *instress* of Hopkins' inscape. No mere static designs open up to the beholder who knows "how to touch" but the experiencing of God's dynamism and ἐνέργεια. Ignatian theology encouraged Hopkins' experience of inscape, but Ignatius' method of meditation, as it calcified into the only acceptable method for both beginners and advanced,[51] to a great extent restricted it.

I would conjecture that the "terrible sonnets," written in the last four years of Hopkins' life, with their almost total absorption in the self and their loss of contact with nature, have suffered the worst effects of the Ignatian method. Hopkins admits that as he takes up the practice of meditation again in his retreat of 1888, his fear of madness returns. "I could therefore do no more than repeat *Justus es, Domine, et rectum judicium*

---

[51] See Robert W. Gleason, S.J.'s "Introduction," *Spiritual Exercises*, where Gleason questions the efficacy of the *Exercises* for the advanced (p. 26).

tuum and the like" (*Sermons*, p. 262). Certainly, the circumstances of Hopkins' isolation in Dublin, his duties of correcting countless examination papers, and his naturally despondent nature contributed enormously to the "self-drawing" nature of these poems, but his descent into his "winter world" was, I believe, in part abetted in these last years by the emphasis on self-observation and examination of conscience essential to the *Exercises*.

Another source of influence on Hopkins has been claimed in recent years. That is the influence stemming from what remained of the Tractarian Movement at Oxford. The story of his association with members of this movement—his confessions to Pusey and Liddon, his membership in the High Church Hexameron Society, and his reception into the Roman Catholic Church by Newman—has been well told in the first chapter of Alison Sulloway's *Gerard Manley Hopkins and the Victorian Temper*, and I will not repeat it here. What has been contended in the recent publication of G. B. Tennyson's *Victorian Devotional Poetry: The Tractarian Mode* is that Hopkins derived his ideas about poetry from the poetics of this movement. I believe this argument is misleading, and even though Tennyson greatly qualifies it, I still find it largely mistaken.

The tenets of the Tractarian poetic creed are Romantic ones. In Newman's early essay on poetry, "Poetry, with Reference to Aristotelian Poetics," he gives a very non-Aristotelian reading of Aristotle: "Greek drama," he says, "is modelled on no scientific principles" but is "a pure recreation of the imagination."[52] For Newman, as for the other Tractarians, the art of poetry is really "a free and unfettered effusion of genius."[53] "The art of composition," Newman concludes, "is merely accessory to the poetical talent."[54] As Tennyson sees it in interpreting Tractarian poetics, the concern for craft was felt by the

---

[52] Newman, *Essays Critical and Historical*, pp. 3–4.
[53] Ibid., p. 7.
[54] Ibid., p. 24.

Tractarians to be "indecorous."[55] This subordination of technique to feeling we can consider a major tenet of Tractarian poetics.

The corollary to that tenet is that poetry is the expression of intense inner feeling. No one exemplifies this emphasis more in his poetics than John Keble. In his *Lectures on Poetry*, Keble sees poetry as the absolutely necessary spigot for the flood of emotions threatening to overcome the poet who represses them. Poetry is medicine for the restless, overburdened soul. Paradoxically accompanying this nearly Freudian view of poetry as release from maddening passions is his equally felt belief that poetry must be "controlled by a tone of modest, religious reserve."[56] This apparent opposition between catharsis and restraint in the self-revelation of the poet derives from the Tractarian Movement's adoption of the allegorical method of the Alexandrian Fathers.[57] Origen and Clement saw God's self-revelation as spirit covered by the veil of the letter, both in the book of nature and in the scriptures. In God's self-utterance, there were both restraint and revelation. This veiled revelation became for Newman, Keble, and the other Tractarians the doctrines of reserve and analogy. Keble, coupling such qualities of poetic speech as "fervent yet sober," finds his model in the Hebrew prophet who "speaking to or of the true God, is all dignity and calmness."[58] Hebrew poetry therefore manages to combine spontaneity and order, passion and restraint.

Keble, much influenced by his predecessor in the Chair of Professor of Poetry, Robert Lowth, finds the perfect exem-

[55] G. B. Tennyson, *Victorian Devotional Poetry: The Tractarian Mode* (Cambridge, Mass.: Harvard Univ. Press, 1981), p. 41.

[56] John Keble, *Lectures on Poetry, 1832–1841*, trans. Edward Kershaw Francis. 2 vols. (Oxford: Oxford Univ. Press, 1912), 2:482.

[57] See Harold L. Weatherby, *Cardinal Newman in His Age* (Nashville: Vanderbilt Univ. Press, 1973), chap. 5.

[58] John Keble, *Occasional Papers and Reviews* (Oxford: Oxford Univ. Press, 1877), p. 91; quoted in Tennyson, *Victorian Devotional Poetry*, p. 30.

plum for his theories of poetry in the sacred poetry of the He-
brews. The irony in this choice of a paradigm is that the Trac-
tarians, by adopting the Romantic tenet of an overriding of
form by emotion, cannot be wholly faithful to Hebrew po-
etry. Newman, perhaps more consistently, chose the poetry
of Scott, Coleridge, and Wordsworth as his paradigm in the
Apologia, seeing in Wordsworth the characteristic of "philo-
sophical meditation" and in Scott a return to the Middle
Ages.[59] By taking his point of departure from the Romantic
poets, Newman sought to revitalize a dry, cerebral Church
with the living springs of emotion. His ultimate goal, as Ten-
nyson sees it, was to make the Church once again poetical.[60]

Tractarian poetics, Romantic in origin and in assumptions,
could hold little appeal for Hopkins. Newman's denigration
of form, Keble's insistence on poetry's relief from violent
emotions, and even the dualistic, two-storied universe im-
plicit in doctrines of analogy and allegory had no place in
Hopkins' poetics. In contrast to Newman, Hopkins insists
that "to recognize the form you are employing and to mean it
is everything."[61] In contrast to Keble, although Hopkins
chooses Hebrew poetic form as paradigmatic for poetry, he is
strongly critical of the Romantic ethos. He disdains even in
music all "subjective rot," providing a headnote to his poem,
"Henry Purcell," which says, "whereas other musicians have
given utterance to the *moods* of man's mind, he has, beyond
that, uttered in notes the very make and species of man"
(*Poems*, p. 80; emphasis added). He disdains the "self-drawing
web" of Swinburne, who either "does not see nature at all or
else he overlays the landscape with such phantasmata, second-
ary images, and what-not of a delirious-tremendous imagi-
nation that the result is a kind of bloody broth. . . . At any

[59] John Henry Newman, *Apologia pro Vita Sua*, ed. David J. De Laura (New
York: W. W. Norton and Co., 1968), p. 84.
[60] Tennyson, *Victorian Devotional Poetry*, p. 211.
[61] *Letters to Bridges*, p. 156.

rate there is no picture."[62] Of Keats he says, "his verse is at every turn abandoning itself to an unmanly and enervating luxury," and he "lived in mythology and fairyland the life of a dreamer."[63]

Hopkins' most pressing indictment of Romanticism may in fact be his most subtle, for it is hidden behind a survey of the various schools of Romanticism made for Dixon. Keats' school, which chose "medieval keepings" or settings, were "great realists and observers of nature" while the Lake poets "were faithful but not rich observers of nature," and Byron's school had "the most untrustworthy and barbarous eye for nature."[64] In the midst of this literary panorama, he says in passing, "The Lake School expires in Keble and Faber and Cardinal Newman." Clearly, then, he connects the Tractarians, Keble and Newman, with the Lake School of Wordsworth. Hopkins' remarks about Wordsworth are equally revealing. He contrasts Dixon's "directness" to Wordsworth's "works of reflection, they are self-conscious, and less spontaneous."[65] The Tractarians, along with each school of Romantic poets, have been judged according to the same criterion: realism. And the Tractarian poets, like their Romantic predecessors, are seen as "faithful but not rich observers of nature." Because Hopkins was critical of the Romantics, and because he associated the Tractarian poets with them, I do not think "we can now take it as established that Hopkins was both a Tractarian and a Tractarian poet."[66] While Hopkins was certainly a Tractarian in religion, he was by no means a Tractarian poet or even in sympathy with its poetics.

Hopkins' relationship to Newman is therefore at best ambivalent. What he seemed to have learned from Newman was to hold on to his originality despite any pressure he might

---

[62] Ibid., p. 202.
[63] *Further Letters*, p. 386.
[64] *Correspondence*, pp. 98–99.
[65] Ibid., p. 57.
[66] Tennyson, *Victorian Devotional Poetry*, p. 204.

have felt to adopt the Tractarian position wholesale. For New-
man had said originality "is in thought what strength of mind
is in action" and he had once defined poetry as "originality
energizing in the world of beauty."[67] But the originality Hop-
kins learned from his mentor ironically distanced him from
Newman. It may well be that by the time Hopkins came up
to Oxford nearly twenty years after Newman's conversion
and withdrawal, Newman had already won many battles for
him. Thanks largely to Newman, Hopkins came into a
Church that was already poetical and that was beginning to
take cognizance of the "whole person," the human being as
heart as well as mind. Hopkins could take such issues for
granted and be allowed his originality.

Hopkins' comments about Newman show a cautious, even
qualified, respect. Writing from Stonyhurst in 1873 to his
friend, Edward Bond, he tells of reading the *Grammar of As-
sent*: "It is perhaps heavy reading. The justice and candour and
gravity and rightness of mind is what is so beautiful in all he
writes but what dissatisfies me (in point of style) is a narrow
circle of instance and quotation . . . and a want, I think a real
want, of brilliancy (which foolish people think every scribbler
possesses, but it is no such thing)."[68] He makes a similar re-
mark about Newman's style to Patmore in 1887, saying that
it excludes "the belonging technic, the belonging rhetoric, the
own proper eloquence of written prose."[69] What is lacking in
Newman's writing, he goes on, is the oratorical *contentio*, the
strain of address, which builds continuity. Unlike Burke, an
"orator in form," Newman writes from "the language of con-
versation, of common life."[70] In this last phrase, we detect
again the association of Newman with Wordsworth. As he
says in this letter to Patmore, "The beauty, the eloquence, of

---

[67] Newman, *Essays Critical and Historical*, p. 20.
[68] *Further Letters*, p. 58.
[69] Ibid., p. 380.
[70] Ibid.

good prose cannot come wholly from the thought."[71] Hopkins' incarnational aesthetic of a unity of form and content, spirit and matter, is as applicable in prose as in poetry. Style and thought are intimately tied. In fact, Hopkins looked at style more than at thought—again a more contemplative than meditative approach—to learn the inscape of the man. What he says to Bridges to explain his sonnet on Henry Purcell applies to Newman as well: "while he is aiming only at impressing me his hearer with the meaning in hand I am looking out meanwhile for his specific, his individual markings and mottlings, 'the sakes of him.' "[72] By refusing a distinctive style, and adopting instead a Wordsworthian language of common life, Newman leaves behind a style without "individual markings and mottlings," in effect, then, without inscape.

Despite Hopkins' reservations about Newman's prose style, however, we find him writing to Newman in 1883 requesting to do a commentary on his *Grammar of Assent*. Hopkins must have written twice trying to persuade him, for two replies, both refusals, from Newman survive. Newman writes on February 27, 1883, that it is a "complimentary proposal"—"But I cannot accept it, because I do not feel the need of it, and I could not, as a matter of conscience, allow you to undertake a work which I could not but consider at once onerous and unnecessary."[73] If his work is worthwhile, he adds, it will survive, and if worthless, "a comment, however brilliant, will not do more than gain for it a short galvanic life, which has no charms for me." Hopkins must have tried again in April of that year, suggesting an analogy to commentaries on Aristotle that made Newman "blush purple."[74] So, like many other projects that Hopkins proposed during this period, this one was abandoned, and no commentary was written. Yet, I believe Hopkins' persistence in seeking permission to write on

[71] Ibid.
[72] *Letters to Bridges*, p. 170.
[73] *Further Letters*, p. 412.
[74] Ibid.

the *Grammar of Assent* does show a resonance with the thought of Newman in this work.

The basic distinction that shapes the philosophy of Newman's *Grammar* is that between real and notional apprehension or real and notional assent. "According as language expresses things external to us, or our own thoughts, so is apprehension real or notional," says Newman.[75] We can immediately discern the great appeal for Hopkins in this distinction. He made his primary encounters over the course of his life with "things external" rather than with his own thoughts. As he wrote to Dixon, "the world is full of things and events, phenomena of all sorts, that go without notice, go unwitnessed."[76] The very word "real" that Newman uses here would be applauded by one "in earnest with reality," one whose judgments of others' poetry were made on the standard of realism. Moreover, when Newman explains that "Singular nouns come from experience, common from abstraction,"[77] we can see how consonant this is with the poet of inscape and haecceitas. Likewise, the poet of instress would find much to agree with in Newman's description of objects of sight being able "to awaken the mind, take possession of it, inspire it, act through it, with an energy and variousness."[78] The concomitant of this real apprehension of things is real assent, which moves the person, inciting him or her to action, as notional apprehension and assent cannot.[79] Hopkins knew real assent in the form of instress, as he knew real apprehension in the form of inscape.

Although Hopkins could not follow Newman into his Ro-

---

[75] Newman, *Grammar*, p. 37.

[76] *Correspondence*, p. 7.

[77] Newman, *Grammar*, p. 38.

[78] Ibid., p. 49.

[79] Ibid., pp. 76–87. Hopkins may have had some difficulty accepting the idea of real assent to images impressed on the mind, but he would, I think, have agreed with the first part of this statement, "In its notional assents as well as in its inferences, the mind contemplates its own creations instead of things; in real, it is directed toward things, represented by the impressions which they have left on the imagination" (p. 76).

mantic conceptions of poetry, Newman's *Grammar*, because it so reinforced Hopkins' native and original instincts, left its stamp on his thought and even provided it with a philosophical framework. We have seen traces of it in his poetry; for example, in the lines, "What none would have known of it, only the heart, being hard at bay" from stanza 7 of *The Wreck of the Deutschland*; the "Heart, you round/ me right" of "Spelt from Sibyl's Leaves"; and "what looks, what lips yet gave you a/ Rapturous love's greeting of realer, of rounder replies?" of "Hurrahing in Harvest," there is evoked an implicit distinction between real apprehension and something less than that.[80] The fact that Newman's real apprehension is of things and experiences would have forcefully affirmed Hopkins' way of seeing the world. Then, too, Newman's real assent, which seems to follow on real apprehension, was equally essential to the poet who wrote, two years after he read the *Grammar*, "I did say yes" in stanza 2 of *The Wreck*. This kind of apprehension and assent lies behind so much of Hopkins' experience and so much of his poetry.

Returning to Hopkins' "Notes on Contemplation" in his commentary on the *Spiritual Exercises*, I would venture to say that Hopkins is interpreting Ignatius with the philosophical framework of the *Grammar of Assent* in mind. Thus, when he says, " 'Meditando . . . circumstantias earum'/ inferring what they must have been, 'contemplando' / observing what they are," he is implicitly associating meditation's "inferring" with notional apprehension, apprehension of the mind's own creations, and contemplation's "observing" with real apprehension. For Newman makes notional apprehension depend on inferences.[81] " 'Meditari,' " Hopkins says, "refers to *reason-*

---

[80] See Michael D. Moore, "Newman and the Motif of Intellectual Pain in Hopkins' 'Terrible Sonnets,' " for a discussion of the influence of Newman's sermons and devotional writings on the terrible sonnets. *Mosaic* 12 (1979): 29–46.

[81] "An act of Inference includes in its object the dependence of its thesis upon its premises, that is, upon a relation, which is an abstraction; but an act

ing." When Hopkins speaks of "realising . . . his ignorance" that he may "reach the reality of the facts," he is echoing Newman, who said in the *Grammar* that the purpose of meditation on the Gospels "is to realize them; to make the facts which they relate stand out before our minds as objects."[82] Finally, when Hopkins speaks of memory as the faculty of simple apprehension toward present things and toward the concrete, he is using but modifying the language of the *Grammar*. Newman had said in fact, "Memory consists in a present imagination of things that are past," and "inference . . . does not reach as far as the facts," while "Belief, on the other hand, [is] concerned with things concrete."[83] Hopkins' "memory" is not a "present imagination," though, but a real apprehension—devoid of inferences and abstractions—of the present, concrete thing.

Now, all this has led us to see once again that Hopkins is not trying to be a meditative poet, and that even when he offers his trinity of memory, understanding, and will, he is interpreting it in a way radically different from that of the meditative and interior *compositio loci*, intellection, and colloquy. Newman gave him a vocabulary for understanding apprehension as apprehension of the external thing itself rather than of notions or mental abstractions. Hopkins' word, "simple," also found in his "simple yes and is," effaces reasoning in that act of apprehension. We should recall that Hopkins' phrase, "simple yes and is," implying assent and apprehension, was written while he was teaching, and Newman was writing his *Grammar of Assent*, at the Edgbaston Oratory in 1868.

On the basis of Hopkins' reading of Ignatius through Newman, I would like to propose a different model for understanding his poems from that of the meditative poem. On this view, Hopkins' poems are poems of contemplation, poems of

---

of Assent rests wholly on the thesis as its object, and the reality of the thesis is almost a condition of its 'unconditionality.' " *Grammar*, pp. 51–52.

[82] Ibid., p. 79.

[83] Ibid., pp. 38–39 and 87.

"attendere, advertere, et contemplari," of simple attention and real apprehension "kept on the strain" followed only then by understanding. Hopkins makes quite a point of insisting on the predominance of simple apprehension by saying: "When the first faculty just does its office and falls back, barely naming what it apprehends, it scarcely gives birth to the second but when it keeps on the strain ('attendere, advertere, et contemplari') it cannot but continuously beget [the understanding.] This faculty [the understanding] not identifies but verifies; takes the measure of things, brings word of them; is called λόγος and reason" (*Sermons*, p. 174). In the act of attending, which can mean "to be present at," "to wait upon or minister to," as well as "to observe with care and consideration," the understanding does not prevail. When the understanding does arise from this simple attention, it "brings word of" things, a deliberate reference to λόγος, which for Hopkins is also the Logos, Christ. Although no programmatic structure can be proposed for contemplation, because it is characterized not by the self's activity but by its receptivity, this passage from simple apprehension or attention to understanding and Logos may approximate the act of contemplation in Hopkins.

Indeed, when we look at Hopkins' poems, especially the sonnets of his middle period, we do see such a movement. In "The Windhover," "The Starlight Night," "Spring," "The Sea and the Skylark," "Pied Beauty," "Hurrahing in Harvest," and "As kingfishers catch fire," the octave exhibits such attention "kept on the strain," followed, sometimes literally, by Logos, the Christ who is Word of things. Hopkins said in one of his sermons that whereas Christ is one, the Holy Spirit "delights in multitude" (*Sermons*, p. 98). There is movement in the poems, then, from the Holy Spirit's multitude to Christ's unity, from the Heraclitean many to the Parmenidean one, from being to logos, and from beauty to truth. From the kestrel's aerial antics we pass to the chevalier's "fire," from dappled skies, rose-moles, and finches' wings to beauty "past change," from circle-citadels and elves'-eyes to the spouse

Christ, from thrush's eggs and glassy pear leaves to maid's child, Christ, from barbarous "stooks" to Christ's world-wielding shoulder, and from ring of stone and bell to act of Christ. From out of the lovely-asunder, barbarous multitude, the "reality of the facts" silently contemplated, emerges their Logos. The sestet of these poems, then, both parallels the simple apprehension and affirmation given in the octave and breaks forth from them, going one better, sometimes in a near antithesis to the octave.

From another point of view, the octave of these poems represents Christ's and the poet's sacrifice of a reconciling unity. Christ, in his kenosis and self-sacrifice, sacrifices even the unity of the Incarnation, leaving the Holy Spirit, the "spirit of multitude," brooding over the bent world. In this sense, the octaves of the poems move from Christ's silence, a kenosis of reasoning and understanding, to the Holy Spirit's eloquence as the sestets begin to "ring and tell" of this Christ. The kenosis involved in simple apprehension then leads to real assent—to admiration and to praise.

On this reading of the poems, the parallelisms of resemblance, the many phonetic and grammatical recurrences, are the verbal instruments of contemplation, the aids to that abiding energy that gathers, unifies, and dwells in the poem's dispersals as it keeps the mind "on the strain." These parallelisms belong to the centripetal or radial energy of the poem that combats and counterpoints the centrifugal energy. They are that secret Heraclitean rhythm, not imposed relentlessly by the mind, but disclosed amid the plethora of forms. No poet who writes so much sheer iteration into his poems, as Hopkins increasingly did, can be concerned merely with their manifest sense. Hopkins' almost incantatory figures of repetition bring us closer to a state approaching trance (*Journals*, p. 126) as they still the mind's "transitional" energies. Like the refrains of a litany or hymn, parallelisms of resemblance elevate the poem toward unity as they cause a slowing down or lingering so that the mind can "repeat the same energy on the same matter" (*Journals*, p. 126). They even frustrate the linear, ratiocinative working of the mind. The reader, like the poet, dwells in and enjoys what is seen rather than using it as grist for the mental mill. What occurs is "the ecstasy of interest" (Hopkins' phrase in another context), an interest totally outside oneself (*ecs-stasis*) because the mind is "absorbed" and "taken up by," borne out and carried over by what it beholds. What occurs is instress from the parallelisms that form the inscape of the poem. Parallelisms of resemblance, as unexpected as parallelisms of antithesis, surprise the reader, shaking the reader out of complacency and into something more like awe. The dynamics begun within the poem, where pairs of words and phrases instress one another prospectively and retrospectively, both fulfilling and correcting one another, are carried outward to the reader. The reader experiences both broken and met expectations, both askesis of self and contemplative assent to the poem. The "bidding" of the reader to contemplation is explicit in the diction ("look," "pray," "bid") but implicit in the form: it is in the parallelisms of grammar and of sound that shine with a "brilliancy" and life of their own, independent of and sometimes counterpointing the poem's matter. These parallelisms initiate the reader into a "parallelism of thought," into contemplation.

Juxtaposed to the sprung or counterpointed rhythm of the poems, a Heraclitean or entropic force that "will flame out," the parallelisms of resemblance "gather to a greatness," becoming the unifying force of the poems. Explaining his technique of musical composition in one of his last letters to Bridges, Hopkins says he had "reached the point where art calls for loosing, not for lacing,"[84] and surely in his poetry the sprung rhythm performs the "loosing" function, while the parallelism does the "lacing." As Hopkins says in his lecture notes, "Rhythm and Other Structural Parts of Rhetoric—Verse," "It almost seems as if the rhythm were disappearing

[84] *Letters to Bridges*, p. 305.

and repetition of figure given only by the
nals, p. 278). The sprung rhythm of Hopkins
his tendency toward a deconstruction and dem
of form, while parallelism has a reconstructive e

The other deconstructive, loosing tendency in H
etry is parallelism of antithesis. The symmetry of
parallelisms of resemblance is broken up and counterp
by antitheses that keep the mind "poised" between the o
sites, but "on the quiver." As Hopkins remarked to Bridges
on his music, "in a really organic tune the second or third
strain or both tend to be good counterpoint . . . to the first."[85]
If parallelisms of resemblance testify to Hopkins' vision of the
inscapes or harmonies in all being, parallelisms of antithesis
testify to his equally persistent vision of the counterpointing
and discord of all life. Hopkins' sympathy with Heraclitus
finds expression, then, in his counterpointing of traditional
rhythms, his sprung rhythm, and his parallelisms of antithe-
sis. Many Hopkins' poems, with the kenosis of spirit given
through the parataxis and simple apprehension, leave the body
of the poem with its antitheses, like the body of Christ in its
agon. Yet, insofar as antitheses seem to have the last word in
poems like "Pied Beauty" and "That Nature is a Heraclitean
Fire," to that extent are we enjoined to greater exercise of the
mind to recover the poem's unity. We are enjoined to contem-
plation.

[85] Ibid., p. 278.

"And But the Beholder":
Contemplation in Hopkins' Poetry

*C*ONTEMPLATION AS A MODE of response to nature afforded Hopkins the moment of recovery of the unity nearly lost to Heraclitean flux. In the same way, the "energy of contemplation" as a response to his poems was intended to resolve into the unity of paradox the "wider antithesis" left unresolved at the end of many of Hopkins' poems. Here is the recuperative moment of Hopkins' aesthetics, the moment when the unity that has receded into the framework of the poem, and has been pointed to by the parallelisms, becomes once again attainable. The poems invite a return, however, no longer to Parmenidean unity of thought and being but to the union effected in contemplation. Contemplative union holds the Heraclitean moment of differences in tension, avoiding the monistic unity of Parmenides. Like parallelism, where difference mounts itself on the foundation of likeness, contemplation embodies paradox. The union achieved in contemplation, therefore, not only expresses a fundamental duality but is essentially a form of love that respects but transcends even Heraclitean antithesis and Scotist haecceitas.

Hopkins' poetry of inscape and instress, structured by parallelisms, is contemplative and invites a contemplative response. Contemplation becomes dialogue with the mystery and silence that lie behind the poems. In the poems of Hopkins' middle period, contemplation is illumination, joyfully lighting up each particular of nature in its true meaning—Christ—and its true direction, the ongoing transformation into Christ of all things. But even the "terrible sonnets" of his arid Dublin years can be called contemplative, though theirs is a dark contemplation. (In one sense, all contemplation is dark, for it is a passing beyond the discursive mind.) Even here the darkening of the ordinary mind turns out to be the luminosity of deeper faith. Contemplation in these sonnets turns from outer to inner, from bright to dark, mirroring the last stage of the contemplative life that is often described as one of progress in darkness.[1] In these penultimate sonnets, a powerful re-vision takes place in the nature of Hopkins' vision. From being extroverted and outward-seeing, his vision becomes introverted; from being cataphatic and affirmative, it becomes apophatic and negative; and from espousing masculine values it begins to take on more feminine dimensions. Hopkins' nearly final poem, "That Nature is a Heraclitean Fire," powerfully reconciles the opposites of darkness and light, death and resurrection, in the radiant image of the diamond retrieved from all that darkness.

Hopkins' continuing preference for contemplation rendered the poetry of his middle period iconic rather than discursive, producing a poetry of presence rather than of reflection and absence. The contemplative structure of his poetry—the sacralizing and elevating effect brought about by its parallelisms—deepens its sense of mystery and "idea of holiness."[2] The mystery evoked in these poems through contemplation is

[1] Two writers in the history of contemplation for whom this final stage is especially evident are Gregory of Nyssa in the *Life of Moses* and Bonaventure in his *Itinerarium Mentis Ad Deum* (The Mind's Journey to God). For both, the height of contemplation is a darkness because it involves the extinguishing of ordinary means of perception. Hopkins' darkness, though, while involving much mystery, also involves excruciating mental anguish.

[2] *Further Letters* (September 24, 1883), p. 309.

the cosmic presence of Christ in matter, the Real Presence extended to the whole world. Even if antitheses rend the poem like the body of Christ, one is not left in dualistic tension but is carried forward to a final unity of antitheses. The explicit movement toward the poem's inscape, Christ, at the end of many of Hopkins' poems becomes a movement toward the Incarnation's union of the opposites of human and divine, matter and spirit. Beyond that movement within the poem, there is movement toward the instress of Christ's Spirit, the Holy Spirit of communication and love (*Sermons*, p. 195). There is instress of inscape. The stress of the Holy Spirit makes possible *transformation* into the mystery of Christ seen within matter. Each poem is sacrament, then, not only in the sense of embodying spirit in matter, but in its efficacy of changing the seer. Stanley Fish has made us aware that great poetry achieves the conversion of the reader, that it "persuades by *changing* the mind into an instrument congruent with the reality it would perceive."[3] Hopkins' poems aim to effect the transubstantiation of all matter and the transformation of the reader into the sacrament of Christ.

Much of the presentational, iconic poetry of Hopkins' middle period reenacts the moment of contemplative wonderment of his own vision while "bidding" the reader to this fuller, deeper vision of the heart. It disallows the reader's chewing up of images in meditative rumination, but insists rather on the inviolable being of each object contemplated. The windhover, starlit sky, "glossy peartree leaves," "silk-sack clouds," and "bugle blue eggs" are to be *seen* by heart and eyes in wordless, adoring love. Hopkins' contemplative way of being related to the world and bidding to contemplation energize most of the poems of his middle period. In "God's Grandeur," unlike Moses, who takes off his shoes to stand on holy ground and contemplate God, our feet are "shod" in an

---

[3] Stanley Fish, *Self-Consuming Artifacts* (Berkeley: Univ. of California Press, 1972), p. 19.

exclusively utilitarian, commercial mode. The E
tion between human beings and soil, Adam and
been severed. Through contemplation's wakeful
ever, human beings can recover nature's "dearest fr
In "The Starlight Night," Hopkins bids the reader
with this fresh vision. With this vision, "Thrush's egg
little low heavens" ("Spring"), just as Blake could see he n
in a wildflower. In both "Spring" and "The Sea and the Sky-
lark," contemplation recovers Eden, "that cheer and charm of
earth's past prime" in the midst of sin and squalor. As the verb
"caught" in the first line attests, Hopkins' vision of the wind-
hover is made possible through contemplative receptivity.
And in "Pied Beauty," the patient contemplative seer, alert to
the beauty of every least thing, praises God even for the trout's
rose-moles.

   Everywhere throughout these poems it is evident that true
seeing, a "seeing" that is really grasping and being grasped by
the heart of Reality, was a passion for Hopkins. What this
seeing yields is insight that the world is charged with God,
that as he says in "God's Grandeur": "It will flame out,
like shining from shook foil;/ It gathers to a greatness, like
the ooze of oil/ Crushed." To Hopkins' contemplative eye,
the world becomes theophany. Both the expansive motion, the
unfolding of God in nature, and the integrative motion, the
enfolding of all things into God (in Nicholas of Cusa's terms
the *explicatio* and the *complicatio*), become transparent to the
contemplative seer. Even dark events somehow betray the
hand of God. Hopkins' recognition in this poem of the horror
impending in human existence ("And though the last lights
off the black West went") parallels with the deeper insight that
"morning, at the brown brink eastward springs—." Resurrec-
tion follows on and is embedded in crucifixion as springs in
winters and morning in "last lights." The change to the sin-
gular "morning" implies a more universal dawn. The contem-
plative's loving gaze performs a kind of blessing of even trivial
or ugly things, beheld and appreciated not by human values

but by God's. Somehow the contemplative, like the four-teenth-century mystic, Julian of Norwich, for whom the hazelnut is "all that is made,"[4] or like Coleridge's Mariner who blesses the water-snakes, knows that the full mystery of Being is concealed in each small thing's life. Hopkins' vision from *The Wreck of the Deutschland* through the poems of the middle period encompasses and transcends ontological horror. It is the vision of the contemplative who sees beyond and even in the pain and contradiction of existence the redeeming hand of God.

Hopkins' metaphysics of art, his vision of the Logos at the heart of reality, sets him apart from other poets of his age. Christ, the ultimate reference or truth of the poems of the middle period, is his "earnest" or warrant of reality. This truth must be more than subjective piety, for "the denying all objectivity to truth and to metaphysics . . . destroys earnestness in life" ("Plato's Philosophy," Unpublished Oxford Notes, D8). With his goal that of "passing through stage after stage, at last arriving at nature's self"[5] he is revealed as a contemplative rather than a meditative or Romantic poet. His is not a poetry of imagination or of discourse or of feeling. Neither Romantic feeling nor Victorian ideas, whether of politics, science, or religion, overrun Hopkins' poetry. Clear seeing, the innocence of eye of the contemplative, overcame what for him were sabotages of the poetic act. Missing in his work are the soliloquies and prosaic wanderings of a Tennyson, the philosophizings of a Wordsworth, and the emotional laments of a Yeats.

In conveying to the reader his theophanic vision, Hopkins deliberately chooses an art of embodiment of the prepossession, an incarnational aesthetics. For "works of art of course like words utter the idea and in representing real things con-

[4] *Julian of Norwich, Showings*, trans. Edmund College, O.S.A., and James Walsh, S.J. (New York: Paulist Press, 1978), pp. 130 and 183.
[5] *Further Letters* (July 10, 1863), p. 201.

vey the prepossession with more or less success," he says in
his 1868 notes (*Journals*, p. 126). The reference to the real is
essential to Hopkins' earnestness with reality, for "The saner
moreover is the act of contemplation as contemplating that
which really is expressed in the object" (ibid.). He rejects the
temptation of his day, the Romantic one, which conveyed the
prepossession by the "least organic," "most suggestive" way.
This way was the art of the sublime, where the idea relates
negatively to the real, nearly canceling it out in allegorical
fashion. Hopkins consistently avoids the mode of the sublime,
choosing the comparison of two or more things together over
the suggestive comparison of finite with infinite (*Journals*, p.
74). In the suggestive mode, "the prepossession and the defi-
nition, uttering, are distinguished and unwound, which is the
less sane attitude" (*Journals*, p. 126). This attitude's lack of san-
ity derives from the predominance of the poet's feeling or
thought. Hopkins needs to reject this Romantic and ulti-
mately solipsistic view, for, while the prepossession unwound
from its object might represent a triumph of spirit over mat-
ter, it would leave the reader incapable of "contemplating that
which really is expressed in the object" (ibid.). Ironically, sees
Hopkins, this preference for the "disengaged and uncondi-
tioned" prepossession is often found with "an intellectual at-
traction for very sharp and pure dialectic or, in other matter,
hard and telling art-forms" (ibid.). What begins as a Romantic
exaltation of feeling over nature and the work of art can end
as mere didacticism unless the subjective moment is subjected
to the humbling of the real. Romanticism, the safeguarding of
emotion, ends as its opposite, rationalism.

Hopkins' poem, "The Blessed Virgin compared to the Air
we Breathe," illustrates his move away from the Romantic
sublime of allegory and into an incarnational and contempla-
tive vision of the real. In this poem, Hopkins takes medieval
allegory and transforms it not only into symbol but especially
into realistic metaphor; he makes the heavenly, remote Mary
of allegory as available as the most common but vital of sub-

stances—air. His metaphor deliberately creates immanence, that which is always and everywhere appearing, yet never appears in the sense of a world-transcending apparition. Hopkins' contemplative vision does not read off from the literal and historical an abstract, spiritual significance in the manner of the allegorist or emblematist, but delves deep within the material until its pattern, still fully embodied, appears. Mary remains the maiden of Nazareth who "Gave God's infinity/ Dwindled to infancy/ Welcome in womb and breast/ Birth, milk, and all the rest." Mary, the homely, practical nursing mother, *is* the air, a mystical conflation of ordinary with extraordinary. Hopkins distinguishes his Mary from the "deemèd" and "dreamèd" goddesses of Romantic literature by making her "Merely a woman," who "yet" is a sacrament of God's presence, her task being to "Let all God's glory through." But unlike the Jewish Shekinah, the feminine radiance of God's glory in the world, Hopkins' Mary is embodied. The appositions and other parallelisms, like strings of beads, fill out and enrich this poem's aura of physical abundance. Internal repetitions, rhymes, and alliterations help weave the "wild web" of mercy interconnecting disparate images, like Mary's mantle cast over the "guilty globe," for as Hopkins said in a sermon, "she is in fact *the universal mother*; however unlike her children [Mary] loves them all" (*Sermons*, p. 29).

Mary's humanity also functions in this poem to mediate the terrible, unmediated presence of a God whom one cannot see and live. In Poem 65, a sonnet of desolation, Hopkins calls on her again to mediate what he knows must be God-inflicted anguish. As mediatrix, she is in Bernard of Clairvaux's words, "the one through whom we have received thy mercy, O God, she is the one through whom we, too, have welcomed the Lord Jesus into our homes."[6] Hopkins quotes Bernard's " 'All

---

[6] Quoted in Jaroslav Pelikan, *The Growth of Medieval Theology, The Christian Tradition*, 4 vols. (Chicago: The Univ. of Chicago Press, 1978), 3:167.

grace given through Mary' " and comments, "this is mystery. Like blue sky, which for all its richness of colour does not stain the sunlight" (*Sermons*, p. 29).

The historical moment, "Of her flesh he took flesh," transmuted into allegory by the Middle Ages—"Not flesh but spirit now"—can become again a this-worldly affair, causing "New Nazareths" and "New Bethlems," the conception and birth of Christ in our lives. In this way, Hopkins' poem parallels a twelfth-century development in the exegesis of Scripture, where allegory, the external edifice erected above the text and beyond this life, became tropology, an account of the soul in this world. This birth of Christ in the soul, a major theme of Meister Eckhart's Rhineland mysticism, makes Christ an ever-present reality rather than an other-worldly hope. Because Hopkins wanted not allegorical analogy dependent on a two-story universe, like the Tractarians, but identity between heaven and earth, a sacramental, inscaped vision, he collides the two terms of his metaphor in the final prayer: "Be thou then, O thou dear/ Mother, my atmosphere." Unlike the Tractarians with their doctrine of correspondences, Hopkins eschewed allegory, turning to the living and actual—for him the locus of repeated incarnations and redemptions. Unlike the Tractarians with their doctrine of Reserve, Hopkins has a God remarkably manifest. It is "but the beholder/ Wanting."

Two poems of Hopkins' middle period illustrate further the contemplative quality of his poetry and distinguish him from his Romantic and Tractarian precursors. In "Hurrahing in Harvest," with contemplative attention "kept on the strain," he masses images of summer's end, haystacks ("stooks") and "silk-sack clouds," with the question "has wilder, wilful-wavier/ meal-drift moulded ever and melted across skies?" The question is in effect an exclamation of wonder and delight. The very wildness and willfulness of the clouds, their moulding and melting, being and not-being, instress the seer with the beauty of their barbarousness. Juxtaposed to this profligate scene, the poet gives a kind of prescription of contemplative seeing:

> I walk, I lift up, I lift up heart, eyes,
> Down all that glory in the heavens to glean our Saviour;
> And, éyes, heárt, what looks, what lips yet gave you a
> Rapturous love's greeting of realer, of rounder replies?

Beginning in utter, childlike simplicity ("I walk"), as simple as Zen, the poet adds his next gesture by incremental repetition, "I lift up," making it seem a movement of the whole body and the whole self. Then, daringly repeating the phrase, he makes it transitive, its object the heart and eyes. The effect of this line is that it moves from the diffuse openness of "I walk" to the centered, focused alertness of "I lift up heart, eyes." Gerald May, a modern interpreter of contemplative psychology, tells us that contemplation involves both an open awareness and a focused, sharpened attention.[7] As we recall, Hopkins himself spoke of "attention, advertence, heed, the being *ware*, and its habit, knowledge, the being *aware*" (*Sermons*, p. 174). In contemplation, a feminine, open awareness combines with masculine attention. This line also plays with the traditional definition of prayer as "a lifting up of the heart and mind to God," for, indeed, such vision, wherever and whenever it occurs, is prayer, as Hopkins recognizes elsewhere: "It is not only prayer that gives God glory but work. Smiting on an anvil, sawing a beam, whitewashing a wall, driving horses. . . . To lift up the hands in prayer gives God glory, but a man with a dungfork in his hand, a woman with a sloppail, give him glory too. He is so great that all things give him glory if you mean they should" (*Sermons*, pp. 240– 241).

The effect of the first word of the second line, "Down," is dramatic and unexpected, contrasting sharply with the re-

---

[7] May, *Will and Spirit*, pp. 46–47. We might even consider these the feminine and masculine poles of the experience.

peated "up" of the first line. "Downing" that glory means taking it in with open receptivity. With this word, ascent suddenly becomes descent to the heart of matter where Christ is found. As in "Pied Beauty" and "The Blessed Virgin" the movement of this poem does not leave one in a Platonic heaven of forms but reveals the transcendent as immanent. Just as Hopkins submitted his ideals of beauty and truth to the real, making it the vehicle of the ideal, so too he submitted spirit to matter, trusting that its stress might the more "flame out" from matter's density. What is needed to apprehend the presence of spirit is contemplative seeing.

Contemplative vision requires a seeing with the eyes of the heart ("heart, eyes" . . . "éyes, heárt") to glean and harvest Christ from barbarous beauty. Hopkins couples "heart" and "eyes" in several poems to differentiate this way of seeing from that of the scientific observer, "who knows how." Several critics have observed the prominence of the heart in Hopkins' poetry without noting that the essential quality of the heart for Hopkins is its ability to see. "The heart," Hopkins says in meditation notes from 1884, "is what rises towards good, shrinks from evil, *recognising the good or the evil first by some eye of its own*" (*Sermons*, p. 257; italics added). With the chiastic repetition of these instruments of true seeing, the poem completes a hermeneutic circle, beginning and ending in the heart where the vision of Christ embeds itself by being beheld and held.

The prominence of the heart in this poem is emphasized in an earlier draft titled "Heart's Hurrahing in Harvest" (*Poems*, p. 269). Unlike the Romantics, Hopkins did not see the heart as the seat of emotions so much as that within us that not only possesses vision but most "sympathises with and expresses in itself what goes on within the soul" (*Sermons*, p. 103).[8] His is

---

[8] Hopkins defends the doctrine of the Sacred Heart throughout this sermon, seeing the heart as "the truth of nature" and the Sacred Heart of Christ as his "most perfect character." He has derived his defense of the Sacred Heart in part from his reading of one of its first proponents, St. Gertrude the Great

a more biblical notion of the heart as the center of personality. Compared to the soulfulness of a response that is "heart-whole" (ibid.), the superficial sensuality of "looks" and "lips" is clearly unable to evoke the instress of a "Rapturous love's greeting of realer, of rounder replies." Rapturous love (from Latin *raptus*, "to be lifted up") belongs to that "ecstasy of interest," that "stem of stress between us and Being," that lifts one above oneself, so that what began as active seeking ("I lift up") ends as being taken up by and into the vision. Contemplation involves both a deep intuitive knowing ("realer" and "rounder") and a participation in what is known.

The poem continues:

And the azurous hung hills are his world-wielding shoulder
Majestic—as a stallion stalwart, very-violet-sweet!—
These things, these things were here and but the beholder
Wanting; which two when they once meet,
The heart rears wings bold and bolder
And hurls for him, O half hurls earth for him off under his
    feet.

The sestet addresses the reason why "Rapturous love's greeting(s)," the instresses of the heart's contemplative vision, do not occur more often: "These things, these things were here and but the beholder/ Wanting." Hopkins wants us to hear in the word "beholder" the New Testament injunction to "behold," to look with self-prostrating awe and delight. But the beholder is "Wanting" in the several senses of being missing, of lacking those qualities ("heart, eyes") that can respond, of being too filled with self-interested desires, and of living in an unspecified, indeterminate longing.[9] In the antithetical

---

of Helfta, whose *Legatus Divinae Pietatis* [ed. P. Doyere, 4 vols., *Sources Chré-tiennes* (Paris: Sources Chrétiennes, 1968)] embodies a heart-centered mystical experience of Christ as a consuming fire that burns away her sins and unites even her unlikeness to himself.

  [9] Hopkins distinguishes wanting from wishing in early notes: "A wish is particular; craving, longing, or want may be general. . . . We say for instance There is a want of something, I cannot tell what it is, and we have longings

expression, "which two when they once meet," a sense of union and of an I-Thou encounter is conveyed between the beholder and "these things," between knower and known. Contemplation by its nature moves the beholder beyond self. Whenever this vision is attained, mere antithesis is overcome, and the possibility of union exists.

The many parallelisms of structure in "Hurrahing in Harvest"—for example, alliteration of "r" in the last line of the second quatrain, and parallelisms of expression such as parallel phrases and word repetition—engender in this poem a parallelism of thought. The whole poem is shaped by parallelism, from the level of sound to the level of ideas. The poem's parallelism of thought operates through the abiding energy of contemplation where the mind "is absorbed, taken up by, dwells upon, enjoys, a single thought" (*Journals*, pp. 125–126). The single thought or harvest of the whole poem, the means of return to Parmenidean unity from Heraclitean barbarousness, is Christ, who is the glory of the heavens, the "azurous hung hills," the "stallion stalwart," and, in the final transformation of the poem, the "heart"—now become itself the stallion Christ hurling the earth off under its feet. The beholder, assenting in radical self-effacement to the vision, is transformed by it into Christ. The "heart in hiding" of "The Windhover," now "rapturous," becomes the windhover, rearing its own wings to take flight. What began as receptive *theoria* empowers the contemplative to put on the freedom and strength of Christ. The poem ends then with that union and transformation into Christ that is the end of contemplative seeing.

This notion of a transformation into Christ, implicit in

---

and cravings—children especially do, and we do in seeing a pathetic landscape or hearing such music—which we do not know what will satisfy: the pain is in fact in not knowing what to wish." Unpublished Oxford Notes, D10. Applying this idea of the vagueness and intransitiveness of wanting, we can see Hopkins' poetic line as a statement of humankind's inability to find satisfying objects of desire and, conversely, to achieve the desirelessness of contemplation.

"Hurrahing in Harvest," becomes explicit in "As kingfishers catch fire."

As kingfishers catch fire, dragonflies draw flame;
    'As tumbled over rim in roundy wells
      Stones ring; like each tucked string tells, each hung bell's
Bow swung finds tongue to fling out broad its name;
Each mortal thing does one thing and the same:
    Deals out that being indoors each one dwells;
    Selves—goes itself; *myself* it speaks and spells,
Crying *What I do is me: for that I came.*

Through its series of parallel images, this poem conveys the meaning of contemplative selfhood. An apparently passive receptivity, the feminine side of the contemplative nature, explodes by the end of the octave in action, its masculine side. The entire first half of this poem's octave consists of a series of tightly paralleled similes from first the animate and then the inanimate worlds of nature. Both similes of the first line, parallel to each other in form and meaning, involve an active receptivity of fire. The kingfisher's irridescent radiance is not his own possession but is caught, just as the fiery dragonfly draws its flame from elsewhere (and as the speaker has "caught" the image of the falcon in "The Windhover"). Hopkins does not say from where, but perhaps both nature's million-fueled bonfire and the "fire that breaks from [Christ]" fires these creatures.

While the verbs in the first line are active, in each of the similes that follows, a passive past participle precedes the object, qualifying it with a prior action still somehow resident in the object. Stones have been "tumbled," string "tucked," bells "hung," and their bows "swung." In each case, the actor remains unnamed and unspelled. In each case too, the object resonates with the action—whether of tumbling, tucking, hanging, or swinging—though the hand of the mover has disappeared. It is this receptivity that enables the hung bell's swung bow to find "tongue to fling out broad its name."

Commentators on this poem, while stressing the action each element accomplishes, often fail to note this empowering receptivity. The defining mark of each thing is its receptivity to the unnamed mover. Although the second half of the octave with its universal sweep explodes with the action each mortal thing does as it spells itself, the first half, with its eye on the particulars, has given us ample opportunity to see that these actions are not autonomous but received.

It is the graced "being indoors," like "The Candle Indoors" 's "Come you indoors, come home; your fading fire/ Mend first and vital candle in close heart's vault" that must be expressed and dealt out. In fact, selving only occurs when one deals out "that being indoors," for the self, says Hopkins, "consist[s] of a centre *and* a surrounding area or circumference" and "in the relation [they] bear to one another" (*Sermons*, p. 127). And his 1888 retreat notes state that a person's moral good consists in both being good and doing good and that "Neither of these will do by itself" (*Sermons*, p. 261). Hopkins recognized the possibility of disjunction when he wrote: "the outer life must not indeed contradict the forces within but can only rudely register them and will become less and less their adequate expression" (Unpublished Oxford Notes, D10). Increasingly, in his own life, he was to experience this disjunction in his "winter world" of Dublin and consequently to turn to the "forces within."

This disjunction and unselving cannot occur, however, with any of the natural things mentioned in the octave, for each thing naturally and spontaneously deals out its inmost being. Neither bird nor insect nor stone nor bell thinks to dissemble, probably because of its intimate atunement to the source of its fire or its tumbler and tucker. Grace, carrying "the creature to or towards the end of its being" (*Sermons*, p. 154), operates throughout all levels of creation. Each thing proclaims, and we are meant to hear a shout of all creation, "*What I do is me: for that I came.*" Each thing "selves" in its doing, the natural issue of its being. The distant echoes in this line of Christ's, "I have come that they may have life and have it more abundantly" (John 10:10), prepare us for the subject of the sestet. For Christ's more abundant life is the resonance "tucked" into "the just man."

> Í say more: the just man justices;
>   Keeps gráce: thát keeps all his goings graces;
> Acts in God's eye what in God's eye he is—
>   Chríst—for Christ plays in ten thousand places,
> Lovely in limbs, and lovely in eyes not his
>   To the Father through the features of men's faces.

Parallelism in the poem creates convergences: the receptivity of dragonfly and kingfisher to fire *is* the human being's receptivity to grace, the fire of Christ and the Holy Spirit. The ultimate parallelism is created between this poem about receptivity and the reader's own receptivity first to the poem and then to the graces of life. As in many of Hopkins' sonnets, the sestet parallels the octave by going one better, "Í say more." But here the human speaker, with the stress on "Í," unlike the earth "with no tongue to plead, no heart to feel" ("Ribblesdale"), "finds tongue." What the human being can do that says more than all creation silently spelling and selving itself, is to act Christ, the grace received and kept by the just person. Christ is the tumbler, tucker, and "fire" "a billion/ Times told lovelier, more dangerous." The sestet parallels the octave by assuming the element of receptivity in human life and pointing to the only kind of person who can say with the rest of creation, *"What I do is me: for that I came."* This is the just person whose "being indoors" and consequent act are "justicing." Recalling Hopkins' family motto, *Esse quam videri*, we can say that the just person is concerned to be rather than to appear. By verbalizing the noun "justices," Hopkins implies that the just one's justice is both that person's essence and existence; the union of the two in one word captures the unity between inner and outer. The hearer of this line, and Hopkins preferred his poetry to be heard, catches a pun, hearing instead "the just

man just *ises*." As Lao Tzu saw it, the way to do is to be. The just one "just," only, but also equally and fairly, deals out what that person really is.

In this poem, Hopkins has gone to the heart of the contemplative program, for the contemplative person is required to discard a false self or ego for the true self that she or he just is. The justice of one's nature consists in this meting out of the truth of one's being. The second line of the sestet reveals the source of the person's "keeps" or "sakes" or individuality as grace. Behind the humble "just" of the just person lies the exalted "I Am" of God, for human "isness" is God's.[10] Grace constitutes the justice of the just person, as Paul wrote of just men that "they are justified by his grace as a gift" (Rom. 3:24). The just man's receptivity to grace "keeps all his goings graces," so that his acts, like the kingfisher's, become graceful. Everything that follows the colon that splits the second line is therefore an outpouring from the inner spring or well of grace.

In the next line Hopkins offers yet another parallel verb, "Acts," that gains vigor by its first place in the revised version (*Poems*, p. 281). This man's "freedom of pitch," his graced, gifted being, empowers him to find "freedom of play" (*Sermons*, p. 149). What he acts is no mere performance but his true inner being. The rest of the line ("in God's eye what in God's eye he is") echoes with its perfect symmetry the integrity between inner and outer of the just man's being. God, giver of grace, is the subject of seeing and being oneself. Wrought with sheer iteration, this line creates a heightened emotion that prepares for the one-word appositive, Christ. Like "Í" and "gráce," "Chríst" is also stressed. Inchoately, these elements fuse, as they do explicitly in the exuberant last lines of the poem. The "play" of Christ Hopkins knew "is no play but truth; That is Christ *being me* and me being Christ" (*Sermons*, p. 154). Christ's play in the just man's being is re-

[10] *Meister Eckhart*, Sermon 6, pp. 185–189.

created in the poem's play between beauty and justice and truth. It echoes the play of Wisdom before God and among humankind in Prov. 8:22–30: "I was daily his delight rejoicing before him always, rejoicing in his inhabited world and delighting in the sons of men."

In all the movements of this poem there is self-diffusion: in the involuntary radiance of kingfisher and dragonfly, the continued ringing of tumbled stones and hung bells, and finally in the just person who, in "justicing himself out," becomes Christ. Moreover, behind all these movements stands God's act of self-giving in Christ and Christ's kenosis of self not only once in history but now "in ten thousand places." Christ has created through "freedom of play" his own "freedom of field" (*Sermons*, p. 149) ten-thousand-fold. Yet, this outward-going procession and self-diffusion of Christ from God and of the human being from Christ is reversed in the poem's final line by the return "To the Father." Christ is both the beginning and end of creation in its return to its ultimate source, the Father who "fathers-forth" ("Pied Beauty"). Christ in this poem has two essential meanings, then: he is the mirroring and shining forth of God in human beings and other creatures, and he is the *esse ad Patrem*, being toward the Father.

The contemplative, aware of God's unfolding and outflowing in creation, seeks to be transformed into Christ and thus drawn up in the return to the Father. Hopkins expresses these two movements of Christ in explaining the feast of Corpus Christi to Bridges: "Christ went forth from the bosom of the Father as the Lamb of God and eucharistic victim to die upon the altar of the cross for the world's ransom; then rising returned leading the procession of the flock redeemed."[11] Both movements, that of being from God and that of existing toward God, are brought together in the sestet's axis, Christ, the idea in God's mind preexisting creation and the transform-

---

[11] *Letters to Bridges*, p. 149.

ing goal of that creation.[12] Transformation into Christ is the way back to the Father. As "Hurrahing in Harvest" and "As kingfishers catch fire" show, Hopkins was much impressed by an Ephesians theology of the human being transformed into Christ and of an eternal destiny "in Christ" (*Sermons*, p. 196). In his spiritual writings, he quotes in Greek and interprets a passage from the Letter to the Ephesians (Eph. 3:16–19), on which he comments, "This πλήρωμα τοῦ θεοῦ is the burl of being in Christ, and for every man there is his own burl of being, which are all 'by lays' or 'byfalls' of Christ's and of one another's" (*Sermons*, p. 156). He sees no contradiction between the haecceitas of individual being and its completion in Christ. Thus, the just person can say *"What I do is me"* and at the same time "Act Christ."

The end or goal of contemplative vision in Hopkins is, then, union with and transformation into Christ. One's true identity is hidden "in God's eye," and in God's self-mirroring it is revealed as Christ. The steady reflection on and of Christ (as in "Hope holds to Christ the mind's own mirror out"; Poem 151) turns the contemplative seer whose vision penetrates the mystery into a further mirror of the object beheld. "We become what we behold; we behold what we are," as the fourteenth-century Flemish mystic, Ruysbroeck, declared.[13] The contemplative learns the secret expressed by Paul: "And

[12] Marie Lataste, the religious writer to whom Christopher Devlin, in his edition of Hopkins' *Sermons*, devotes an Appendix because of Hopkins' extended quotations from her writings, speaks of these two movements in a person's religious life: "that of his being, created by God, towards existence, and that of his existing being towards God . . . by these two movements man, if he so desire, will infallibly return to God. I say *if he so desire*, because man can change the direction of his movement." *Sermons*, pp. 289 and 327. Although Hopkins encountered Marie Lataste's writing in his retreat of 1878 and his "kingfishers" poem possibly dates from 1877, he found in this peasant girl's works confirmation of the underthought of this poem.

[13] John Ruysbroeck, *The Spiritual Espousals*, trans. Edmund College (London: Faber and Faber, 1952), p. 309. Ruysbroeck concisely defines the contemplative life: "In this simple seeing we are one spirit with God."

we all, with unveiled faces, beholding the glory of the Lord, are being changed into his likeness from one degree of glory to another; for this comes from the Lord who is the Spirit" (2 Cor. 3:18). This intimate connection between knowing and being, first iterated in Hopkins' Parmenides essay, translates to seeing and becoming in the poems. One not only gazes upon but becomes Christ ("Hurrahing in Harvest," "As king-fishers catch fire," "The Starlight Night," and "That Nature is a Heraclitean Fire").

And the enabler in this process of transformation is the Holy Spirit, who makes the one into many and the many into one. In his sermon for the Fourth Sunday after Easter Hopkins points to the Holy Spirit's work of making Christs:

> Christ was himself but one and lived and died but once; but the Holy Ghost makes of every Christian another Christ, an AfterChrist; lives a million lives in every age; is the courage of the martyrs, the wisdom of the doctors, the purity of the virgins; is breathed into each at baptism . . .; passes like a restless breath from heart to heart and is the spirit and the life of all the Church: what the soul is to the human body that, St. Austin says, the Holy Ghost is to the Church Catholic, Christ's body mystical. (*Sermons*, p. 100)

It is the Holy Spirit as spirit of multitude that enables Christ who is one to live in "ten thousand places," effecting the paradox of unity in diversity.

Hopkins envisions not only the individual but the whole world transformed into Christ, as he makes clear in his notes on the final section of Ignatius' *Spiritual Exercises*, the "Contemplation for Obtaining Love": "Suppose God shewed us in a vision the whole world inclosed first in a drop of water, allowing everything to be seen in its native colours; then the same in a drop of Christ's blood, by which everything whatever was turned scarlet, keeping nevertheless mounted in the scarlet its own colour too" (*Sermons*, p. 194).[14] Hopkins' "scarlet" vision differs from the monist vision of Parmenides or of the American transcendentalists, for example, not only because it preserves the "eachness" or haecceitas of everything rather than burying it in the All-Soul, but also because it views God's presence most often under the sign of the Crucifixion.

The cross, embodiment and archetypal symbol of antithesis, afforded the final transformation into Christ of Hopkins' life and art. In the "terrible sonnets" Hopkins achieves identification with Christ even as the light of Christ as God's self-mirroring becomes extinguished in darkness. Hopkins' cross, made up of the antitheses he had almost courted in early and middle years of speculation, became the reality of his life and the substance of the group of poems of his last years (1885–1889) now referred to as the "terrible sonnets." In spiritual notes made during a week-long retreat in September 1883, he even prayed for this cross: "In meditating on the Crucifixion I saw how my asking to be raised to a higher degree of grace was asking also to be lifted on a higher cross" (*Sermons*, p. 254). Hopkins' great interests in both Parmenidean and Heraclitean poles of experience were bound to come into collision. The symbol that best signifies the crossing of the horizontal plane of Heraclitean multiplicity by the vertical plane of Parmenidean sameness is the cross, at once a symbol of antithesis and of the hidden seed of love overcoming antithesis. The word of unity spoken so resolutely at the origin of Hopkins' doctrine of poetics can be reclaimed in this symbol of the op-

---

[14] Hopkins' transformed cosmos can be compared with any number of passages from his fellow Jesuit, the mystic, Teilhard de Chardin. Chardin sees the world in just this way when he says, "When all the things around me, while preserving their own individual contours, their own special savours, nevertheless appear to me as animated by a single secret spirit . . . then I shall know that I am approaching that central point where the heart of the world is caught in the descending radiance of the heart of God." *Hymn of the Universe*, trans. Gerald Vann, O.P. (New York: Harper and Row, 1965), pp. 35–36.

posites returning to alignment with each other and thus to wholeness. In his poetry, Hopkins had appeared to reject Parmenidean unity for Heraclitean fecundity. Yet in his outer life, his routine of university scholar among the Irish Jesuits, a stultifying Parmenidean monotony, devoid of surprises, prevailed. The dynamism of Heraclitean change was reserved for nature, not for his own inner and outer life. Hopkins had so long effaced himself in the service of one or the other external task—teaching, preaching, or even the writing of poetry in response to the beckoning of some superior—that he had neglected the union of his own opposites.

As we saw in Chapter 3, Hopkins viewed the world, himself, and even Christ as antithesis. He praised antithesis as a formal device in poetry because it reflected ontological truth. Hopkins, "strung by duty, strained to beauty," finds himself split by his antitheses, attempting to meet the conflicting demands of body and soul. The Jesuit religious order, with its ideals of service and obedience, as well as his own ascetic nature had exercised him in meeting the demands of duty. Yet, his poetic self could not quite give up its ideal of a beauty revelatory of truth. Hopkins' split was between elective and affective wills, between law and gospel, between duty and love. In his notes on the "Contemplation for Obtaining Love" that conclude the *Spiritual Exercises*, Hopkins recognizes that in the Foundation of the *Exercises* "there is no mention of love; everything is of bounden duty, the duty of a servant: here [in 'Contemplatio'] everything is of love, the love and duty of a grateful friend, —And it serves as a foundation for the rest of life" (*Sermons*, p. 194).

Hopkins sensed that love alone could heal the split, unite the affective and elective wills, and make him a whole person. Love represented the heart's wholeness rather than the dualisms of the mind's "thoughts against thoughts." Love, in its freedom and spontaneity, would transform the demands of duty as the joy of contemplation transcends the work of meditation. In a sermon from 1880 he had said, "*Duty is love.* What a shame to set duty off against love" (*Sermons*, p. 53). But in these notes from the Feast of the Immaculate Conception of Mary, December 8, 1881, Hopkins' preference for love as the "foundation for the rest of life" overcomes the Victorian equation of duty with love and implies the reawakening of his need for unity in himself and in his world.

While adhering to the one-sidedness of duty, he had unwittingly shrunk "reality" to the compass of its exterior forms. As far as his poems were concerned, his own inner reality went without a beholder. Having disdained throughout his life the "subjective rot" of the Romantic and sentimental that overlays the real with the "what-not of a delirium-tremendous imagination,"[15] he found that his own inner barren landscape now forced his earnestness with its reality. That Hopkins sensed the need to turn inward is clear in his fragment from this period, "The times are nightfall," where after briefly surveying the "world undone" he states, "Or what is else. There is your world within. There rid the dragons, root out there the sin" (Poem 150). Throughout his retreat notes from these years he resolves to make the particular examination of conscience (*Sermons*, pp. 256–257, 262), focusing on his inwardness. And in these last sonnets, he moves, however unwillingly ("they came like inspirations unbidden and against my will," he told Bridges[16]) to confront and contemplate the subjective realm of reality. Contemplation here becomes dark and inward-turning, resembling at times the *makyo* or nightmare state on the way to Buddhist *satori*. Although the "terrible sonnets" may seem a kind of self-contracted reflex response to pain, it is in them that Hopkins becomes contemplative of his own inner being and enfolds his own darkness in the reality that is Christ. In Christ as paradoxical union of opposites, antithesis reaches the breaking point so that in the final sonnets of his life, "That Nature is a Heraclitean Fire," "St. Alphonsus

---

[15] *Letters to Bridges*, p. 202.
[16] Ibid., p. 221.

Rodriguez," and "To R. B.," antithesis is transcended in paradox.

The "terrible sonnets" form the itinerary of his night-journey of labyrinthine descent down the perilous cliffs of his mind into the inner darkness where the "immortal diamond" could be mined. The images of darkness that form a motif in the "terrible sonnets"—God's "darksome" eyes, "That night, that year/ Of now done darkness," "dark heaven's baffling ban," "the fell of dark," and "blind/ Eyes in their dark"—testify to Hopkins' frustrated but determined will to see in the dark. The condition of darkness posed the greatest challenge to his contemplative impulse. Indeed, he almost invited this condition in his 1881 spiritual notes where he remarks that "to have been on pilgrimage to Jerusalem in the dark would be more full of devotion than to see it in the best panorama" (*Sermons*, p. 173). Hopkins' dark pilgrimage to Jerusalem leads, like Christ's, to the cross and its final surrender.

Far from being a failure of the artistic impulse or of the religious quest, these sonnets represent a courageous attempt to chart an inscape of the depths. The poet of inscape must now seek the Christ of fields, stars, faces, and "barbarous beauty" in his own darkness, even in the dark side of his shadow personality. And yet, at the end of this tortuous journey of self-examination, lies the paradox of the "terrible crystal," the lapis lazuli, the immortal diamond, Christ. In the dark of the terrible sonnets, however, there is little gleam from that Light.

Hopkins' longing for the light is expressed in spiritual notes of these years where he writes, "It is as if one were dazzled by a spark or star in the dark, seeing it but not seeing by it: we want a light shed on our way and a happiness spread over our life" (*Sermons*, p. 262). There is in this statement some sense of the paradox that darkness will itself reveal new light. Such an insight would not be unprecedented in the history of contemplation. Many mystics testify to the paradox of a darkness that is really the drawing near of God. In Pseudo-Dionysius, it is the "dazzling obscurity . . . outshining all brilliance with the intensity of [its] darkness" that enlightens a person.[17] The "apophatic" way goes beyond the cataphatic way of seeing God in divine energy, manifestation, and Logos, to "seeing" God in the absolute darkness of divine incomprehensibility. Throughout the tradition of writers like Gregory of Nyssa, Augustine, and of course John of the Cross, darkness is actually the culmination of a theology of light. Yet, in this ultimate darkness, seeing is not seeing, knowing is unknowing.[18] It is this not seeing and unknowing, along with a deep yearning for God, that Hopkins' "terrible sonnets" largely express. In the *via negativa* of the "terrible sonnets," even God's Logos, Christ, is subsumed in the darkness of the Godhead. Before this, Hopkins' God had been creative, God's silence eloquent ("Elected Silence"), and God's earth fruitful. The essence of God was one with and manifest in the divine energy and utterance. Now, the God so supremely manifest during Hopkins' middle period is silent, hidden, and unknowable.

In this dark type of contemplation Hopkins is, in his own words, "realising . . . his ignorance" to reach "the reality of the facts" (*Sermons*, p. 173). On the Feast of Epiphany of his last year he realizes that the star seen by the Magi may not have been visible to ordinary observers but only to those who practiced their art of seeing (*Sermons*, pp. 264–265). Like the Magi following the star, Hopkins is drawn on a journey through darkness, guided only by the star in the dark and by his own contemplative "art of seeing." Ordinary ways of seeing must be abandoned. The elusive diamond-star at the center of Hopkins' dark being, connected to his flammable "matchwood" self by the great maker of paradox, the copula "Is," could be seen only in dark contemplation.

Like Christ and Buddha and many saints who had fierce encounters with their own demons to arrive at new vision,

[17] *Dionysius the Areopagite: On the Divine Names and the Mystical Theology*, trans. C. E. Rolt (New York: Macmillan, 1966), p. 191.
[18] Louth, *Origins of the Christian Mystical Tradition*, p. 88.

Hopkins had to experience the abysmal darkness of his own being. Through this experience Hopkins' poetry turns from "cataphatic," that is, revealing, speaking, and affirming the presence of God in creation, to "apophatic," moving away from speech and affirmation of God toward a remotive, negative way. Now Hopkins can only affirm the absence of God and the terror and pain of a life without God. Still, there is affirmation, and in that sense the rhythm of negation and affirmation, apophatic and cataphatic, silence and poetry is restored.

Hopkins' darkness and terror were presaged in a poem some interpreters see as a prelude to the "terrible sonnets." In "Spelt from Sibyl's Leaves" Sibyl, in classical literature a guide to the underworld, is a guide to the psyche of the age and correlatively to Hopkins' psychic underworld. Her oracles spell the enclosure of earth's "dapple" and of the self in an encompassing, neutralizing darkness. I read this poem not as a description of apocalypse in the physical world but as a foreboding of solipsism in any self losing vitalizing contact with the world and left to its own abstractions, particularly its divisive, dualistic, antithetical ones. As Hopkins knew, both the Enlightenment's confidence in the power of reason and Romanticism's confidence in the power of imagination to define reality could leave one with such abstractions rather than with the real. The oracle signals not so much a Last Judgment in an eschatological sense but ongoing mental judgments of Romantic feeling and Victorian thinking. To a "self ín self steepèd and páshed—qúite" the earth's being is unbound, disconnected, and atomized. The bonding of spiritual connection through contemplation's "ecstasy of interest" can no longer be achieved. The self, in crossing the river of forgetfulness like Virgil led by the Sibyl, is "Disremembering" its connectedness to earth and the things of earth. The act of remembrance, and even more of Platonic recollection, would join the self to its eternal origins. But without this remembrance the self remains unrelated to anything, and the world becomes atomistic, "dísmémbering."

Only the heart retains the vision that experiences this condition as a loss. The heart recognizes the coming of darkness for the alienated self: "Heart, you round me right/ With: Our évening is over us, óur night whélms, whélms ánd will end us." The heart, always an instrument of seeing for Hopkins (*Sermons*, p. 257), continues to see even in darkness. What it sees are the unreal, shadowy qualities of an evening that is "earthless, equal, attuneable," arbitrary and free to be shaped at will, eclipsing earth's definite particularity and shading into an even more overwhelming night for the self. Even the heavens, their two main lights gone out, are "Fíre-féaturing," a phrase made ominous by what follows, perhaps in the sense of Heraclitus' "Fire [which] in its advance will catch all things by surprise and judge them." The stars, too, once a guarantee of the beauty of Christ, now threaten impending chaos. Hopkins' Sibyl prophesies that the suggestive, anthropocentric, Romantic tendency, unwound from its organic expression in the object (*Journals*, p. 126), is winning the day. Hopkins realized at this juncture in his life that for the benighted self, earth's dapple and its "once skéined . . . variety" would not appear.

The stressed first-person pronouns of the octave's last line ("Óur evening . . . óur night") draw the descriptions of the entire octave into the inner world. A parallel movement occurs in the sestet where even night is sucked into the cerebral combat of "thóughts agaínst thoughts." Both octave and sestet end, then, in the solipsism of inner darkness. What remains in the sestet is the nightmare vision of earth ("the beakleaved boughs dragonish"), the bad dreams of the Romantic, and an irreconcilable duality ("Now her áll in twó flocks, twó folds"), "the very sharp and pure dialectic" (*Journals*, p. 126) of the rationalist. This poem's "wider antithesis" cannot be reconciled. The world as it appears to the self "selfwrung, selfstrung," by way of the prevailing options of Romanticism and rationalism, becomes hideous, repellent, and ultimately inaccessible.

Was this poem a prophecy then of the inevitable consequences of Romantic feeling and Victorian orthodoxy, or was it a description of the state of Hopkins' own mind? Many scholars have seen primarily the latter, but it can be said that in aiming at the former it indirectly reveals the latter. If this poem unwittingly exposes the inner state of the speaker's mind, a mind where "thóughts agaínst thoughts in groans grind," it may represent a half-conscious rejection of the antitheses Hopkins had previously cultivated in his life and art. With "Spelt from Sibyl's Leaves," the introduction to the last phase of the poet's oeuvre, antithesis reaches the zenith, at which point he moves away from or possibly beyond it, without apparently offering a positive term of mediation. In rejecting the artificial winding up of life "áll on twó spools," he is sensing that mere dualism—between night and day, death and life, infinite and finite—is, as Kierkegaard said, "negative unity."[19] Caught in a dualism of body and soul, the human being is tossed back and forth between the extremes.

Yet, in spite of all the tensions and dualisms of "Spelt from Sibyl's Leaves," within this poem, hidden from the standpoint of the speaker, is the very means of overcoming dualistic alienation. Hopkins' speaker, in despairing a "selfwrung, selfstrung" state, unconsciously posits the terms of his redemption. The self having become a problem to itself initiates the therapy for its own renewal. For the self to which Hopkins must now attend can become not only negative unity but, as the psychologist Carl Jung puts it, "a union of opposites par excellence."[20] Having returned to a self whose problem is its antithetical nature ("thóughts agaínst thoughts in groans grind"), Hopkins can begin to let the opposites join in unity.

[19] Søren Kierkegaard, *The Sickness Unto Death*, ed. and trans. Howard V. Hong and Edna H. Hong (Princeton: Princeton Univ. Press, 1980), p. 13.

[20] C. G. Jung, *Psychology and Alchemy*, vol. 12, *The Collected Works of C. G. Jung*, trans. R.F.C. Hull (Princeton: Princeton Univ. Press, 1968), p. 19.

But for this to happen, transformation is necessary. To describe transformation, many including Jung have used the language of alchemy, whose goal was to discover the incorruptible stone, a symbol of the immortal self. Hopkins himself had toyed with the subject of alchemy in an early poem, "The Alchemist in the City," a poem whose first stanza could be seen as a paraphrase of "Spelt from Sibyl's Leaves." Hopkins' early alchemist is unsuccessful but by the end of the poem is left wanting to "pierce the yellow waxen light/ With free long looking," a contemplative gesture that could lead to alchemical transformation. In understanding the process of transformation, the comparative mythologist, Joseph Campbell, asserts that there must be "the beginning of a dissolution, moving toward the primal state of chaos where all pairs of opposites coalesce; and in the human psychological sphere it corresponds to the beginning of a regression."[21] From this standpoint, within the Heraclitean dissolution and the regression to solipsism prefigured in "Spelt from Sibyl's Leaves," lies the "Heraclitean Fire" 's "immortal diamond," the coalition of the self's oppositions and the means of the self's redemption.

The "terrible sonnets" chronicle in agonizingly slow motion the process, incomplete as it remained, of that self-healing. Before writing them, Hopkins' overcoming of the Romantic subjective through kenosis of self had won transcendence of self at the expense of fullness of reality. Through the dark contemplation of the "terrible sonnets," Hopkins encloses the inner world into the real. As unsettling as these sonnets can be to the unwary reader, they provided for Hopkins the therapeutic to his one-sided objectivism. In his own journey, they are the necessary return to the starting point of the hermeneutic circle. The self, bracketed for encounter with the world, must return to itself to heal its oppo-

[21] Joseph Campbell, *The Masks of God: Creative Mythology* (New York: The Viking Press, 1970), p. 282.

sites and take on the task of self-knowledge. All events in Hopkins' "winter world," the sheer tedium of grading countless examination papers, his disaffection for Irish politics, and his own melancholic state, conspired to create the conditions for this self-examination.

An aesthetic reading of the "terrible sonnets" establishes their contemplative character. In their parallelisms, their asyndeton, and their chiasms these sonnets display the urgency and impulsiveness of biblical style for a desperate man, trying to see in the dark. Throughout these poems, parallelism's abrupt, "diatonic" effects break in on the reader's complacency with the force of a revelation. Parallelism in these poems seems to increase with the growing intensity of religious emotion. As Hopkins again experiences "God's finger touching the very vein of personality" (*Sermons*, p. 158) in the sestet of "Carrion Comfort," parallelisms intensify. Parallel expressions ("lapped strength, stole joy, would laugh, cheer") convey mounting enthusiasm as the memory of his past religious experience returns in waves of emotion. His addresses to the Holy Spirit and to Mary in Poem 65 ("Comforter, where, where is your comforting?/ Mary, mother of us, where is your relief?") approach the perfect conformity of the Hebrew *parallelismus membrorum*, the parallelism of clauses. Christ in Poem 66 is named with a series of parallel but antithetical appositives: "And he my peace/ my parting, sword and strife," embodying his sense and now his experience of Christ as "rhetorical antithesis." As joy begins to "size" at the end of Poem 69, the verse becomes symmetrical in syntax and word repetitions: "At God knows when to God knows what." The enjambment and repetition of "let" in the first lines of this poem ("My own heart let me more have pity on; let/ Me live to my sad self forever kind,") call attention to the contemplative ethic of "letting be" he counsels in "To what serves Mortal Beauty?"

And, of course, forming the underthought of these poems and their "brilliancy, starriness" (*Journals*, p. 290) in the midst of blackest night are the rhymes, alliterations, and assonances that constitute what Hopkins had called parallelism of structure. In *The Wreck of the Deutschland*, we saw parallelisms hint at order and meaning behind an apparently chaotic world. Here too they give glimpses of that "spark or star in the dark" that the poet can see but not see by (*Sermons*, p. 262), even counterparting or giving the lie to these poems' overthoughts.[22] Thus, parallelism continues to function in the "terrible sonnets" as a guarantee of meaning.

Also serving the intensity of religious feeling in these poems is the condensed style of asyndeton. The asyndetic quality of much of this verse, its lack of connectives, makes it "more austere and pathetic," as Hopkins told Bridges it would.[23] Image follows image in breathless, spasmodic succession, creating an anvil-like battering and the thumping of an accelerated heartbeat. The almost total lack of connectives only increases the verse's sense of mystery and leaves the poet defenseless in the face of a seemingly demonic God. For example, in Poem 67:

> I am gall, I am heartburn. God's most deep decree
> Bitter would have me taste: my taste was me;
> Bones built in me, flesh filled, blood brimmed the curse.

But where connectives are used, they mirror brief moments of mitigation of the speaker's inner state. The paratactic connector at the end of Poem 68, "Patience fills/ His crisp combs, and that comes those ways we know," relaxes the verse. At other times, use of the connector protracts the verse, mirroring the poet's languishing. Such is the case in Poem 67, "And my lament/ Is cries countless," and "But where I say/ Hours I

---

[22] *Further Letters* (Letter to Baillie, January 14, 1883), pp. 252–253. This underthought, Hopkins tells Baillie, is chiefly conveyed by metaphors "and is often only half-realised by the poet himself . . . the underthought is commonly an echo or shadow of the overthought, something like canons and repetitions in music."

[23] *Letters to Bridges*, p. 70.

mean years," and in Poem 68, "And where is he who more
and more distills/ Delicious kindness?" In this last poem, the
verse loosens even as the speaker himself adopts the attitude
of patience. In all these instances, parataxis supplants reason-
able explanation with the simplicity of mystery. Only once,
in the sestet of "Carrion Comfort," does Hopkins say "why"
and pursue a more hypotactic course in his desperation to find
meaning in his suffering. Even there the "answer" is shrouded
in the deeper mystery of a union of identities born in combat
with God. Both asyndeton and parataxis contribute to the
feeling of awesomeness in the relationship with God.

Besides parallelism, another form, not altogether new to
Hopkins' verse-making, emerges in the "terrible sonnets."
This form is chiasmus. Where parallelism takes the form a b/a'
b', as Hopkins tells us in his 1873 lecture notes (*Journals*, p.
267), chiasmus's form is a b' a'. Chiasmus is a kind of re-
verse parallelism whose effect is more closural and fulfilled.
Where parallelism works to create mere likeness, chiasmus's
force is toward a unifying center. Where repetition at best cre-
ates tension, at worst tedium, chiasmus brings both conflict
and the paradoxical resolution of conflict. It is a curious fact
that a form often used by the mystics to express their paradox-
ical intuitions of unity should be found in poems of disinte-
gration. Clearly, these forms must make up part of that "half-
realised" underthought giving the lie to the manifest sense of
the poems. Chiastic structure is present in each stanza of Poem
66:

> To seem the stranger lies my lot, my life
> Among strangers. Father and mother dear,
> Brothers and sisters are in Christ not near
> And he my peace/my parting, sword and strife.
>
> England, whose honour O all my heart woos, wife
> To my creating thought, would neither hear
> Me, were I pleading, plead nor do I: I wear-
> y of idle a being but by where wars are rife.

I am in Ireland now; now I am at a thírd
Remove. Not but in all removes I can
Kind love both give and get. Only what word

Wisest my heart breeds dark heaven's baffling ban
Bars or hell's spell thwarts. This to hoard unheard,
Heard unheeded, leaves me a lonely began.

It is difficult to know how to account for these chiasms—in
the first and second lines, the seventh and eighth, the ninth,
and the last two lines—unless one posits a conscious or uncon-
scious aiming at integration and balance. Chiasms appear
again in Poem 67 ("And my lament/ Is cries countless, cries
like dead letters sent" and "Bitter would have me taste: my
taste was me;") and at the beginnings of Poems 68 and 69
("Patience, hard thing! the hard thing but to pray,/ But bid
for, Patience is! Patience who asks"—three interwoven
chiasms in two lines—and "My own heart let me more have
pity on; let/ Me live to my sad self hereafter kind"). The pres-
ence of these more centering structures may be a deeply in-
choate signal from that "eternal beam" that finally gains entry
to consciousness in "That Nature is a Heraclitean Fire."

Hopkins' "terrible sonnets" begin the process of self-heal-
ing by confronting and embracing the negative in himself.
While in "Spelt from Sibyl's Leaves" the self has been nearly
swallowed up by an internalized night, in "Carrion Comfort"
it is the self that considers swallowing a personified Despair.
Despair is here rejected as food for those already dead. Yet in
Hopkins' very personification of his despair, he establishes a
relation to it. The poet discovers he can wish, can call forth
the affective will. But just as he musters the purposefulness to
win the battle with his own demon, Despair, a greater battle,
one that almost "unmade" him, is recalled, this time not with
the acquiescence of the *Deutschland* but with final questioning
and horror. Yet, in a subtle way, this renewed unmaking and
its regression point to the alchemical transformation made
possible by laying oneself open to the divine. Whereas Hop-

kins had understood kenosis to involve annihilation and un-making, God would not allow so total a destruction of the self.

In exploring his inner world, Hopkins discovered the re-cesses of "no" still remaining in himself. He had celebrated the "simple yes and is" of all creation and given it and its Creator his full assent. In creation, he knew the paradoxical truth that the greatest immanence is the greatest transcendence, that Christ, the inscape of the Father's creation, brought the Holy Spirit, its transforming power or stress. But in himself there were still areas not opened to God's redeeming stress. His own immanence remained unaffirmed and unredeemed in its possibilities for transcendence. It is telling that in his comment on Ignatius' first-person statement that God dwells "in me, giving me being, life, sensation" Hopkins switches to the third person, "Christ as a solid in his member as a hollow or shell, both things being the image of God" (*Sermons*, p. 195). With the elimination of the first person and the change to ob-ject language goes loss of the personal appropriation of this truth.

Parallel to his "war within" ("St. Alphonsus Rodriquez") are both his own war with God and Job's. The second quatrain draws on the imagery of Job huddled on the dungheap "frantic to avoid" his tormentor God. Like Job, Hopkins saw many of the external supports of his world collapse, forcing him to confront God within. With his turn to the story of Job, Hop-kins universalizes his personal suffering and leaves us with the conclusion that at the heart of all suffering is the quarrel with God. But paradoxically, this face-to-face combat with God re-lieves him of the self-reflexive agony of "thóughts agaínst thoughts," giving him the most healing contact of all—with the otherness of God.

Conversely, it is only Job's relentless questions, insults, and doubts that bring him to the point where he can "see God with his own eyes" (Job 42:5), the end of every contemplative quest. The problem here is the need to see "with his own eyes," to be that self that has its own eyes. As C. S. Lewis put it in his novel *Till We Have Faces*, "How can they [the gods] meet us face to face till we have faces?"[24] Hopkins must be about the restoration of a self he had too readily denied. To that end, the five staccato questions of the sestet assert for the first time the rights of a self in relation to God. "Me?" at the beginning of the line almost negates the preceding alternative ("the hero whose heaven-handling flung me") and is reinforced by the "me" of the question that follows. Despite kenosis, Hopkins had still to accept his own haecceitas, his own taste of me (*Sermons*, p. 123). The speaker cannot properly meet God until he has entered and affirmed his own darkness.

The allusion to Jacob in the final line is appropriate, for like Job, the self-centered, cunning Jacob is a model of self-assertion. In his wrestling match with God (Gen. 32) Jacob receives a new name, signaling a new identity and a paradoxical renewal through divine combat. He also receives the gracious gift of seeing God face to face and yet surviving. In both Job's and Jacob's stories, self-preoccupation and the awful terror of struggle end in the calm of contemplative vision. In Hopkins' poem, the speaker has entered into the kind of struggle that can lead to that outcome though it remains latent possibility by the end of the poem.

The last words of the poem recall Jesus' anguished cry of God-forsakenness on the Cross: "My God, my God why hast thou forsaken me?" (Matt. 27:46). Before this poem, the self-annihilating poet had failed to encompass his own depths in the reality that is Christ. With Hopkins' Christed cry from within, that failure is remedied. Hopkins identifies with Christ at the moment of greatest despair, the abandonment by God. By entering into Christ's despair, he moves beyond that Despair rejected at the poem's beginning as only "carrion comfort" into a more healing and self-affirming one that, like Luther's and Kierkegaard's, is a gateway to grace.

Hopkins frames the sestet in terms of the progression in the

---

[24] C. S. Lewis, *Till We Have Faces* (Grand Rapids, Mich.: Eerdmans Publishing Co., 1960), p. 294.

spiritual life from purification, the clearing away of his "chaff," to illumination, when his heart "lapped strength," to a hint of that union with God, "is it each one?" made possible by the struggle with God. In the poem's underthoughts, there is hope of regeneration. As Michael Moore in his fine article, "Newman and the Motif of Intellectual Pain,"[25] has shown, Hopkins draws substantially from the language and imagery of Newman in this and other "terrible sonnets." Because of the submerged references to biblical figures whose crises end in reconciliation with God, the "half-realised" allusions to stages of the religious life, and the influence of Newman, his mentor in faith, I agree with Moore that the poet's outlook is "more hopeful than has been thought."[26] The "terrible sonnets" ' unmaking is in reality a healing and transformation of the self.

In Poem 65, Job's conflicting needs both to seek and to avoid God continue to form the paradigm for Hopkins' experience. Like Job, whose classic statement of his paradoxical faith was "Though he slay me yet will I trust him" (Job 13:15—Vulgate translation), Hopkins must seek comfort from his torturer. He must simultaneously pray "Comforter, where, where is your comforting?" and creep away for refuge from this whirlwind God. The God who created this anguish is the only one who can heal it. Parallelism in "No Worst" has the effect of equating the psychological torment of the mind's "cliffs of fall" with God's "age-old anvil." Ultimately, as Job knew, the true nature of mental anguish is God-forsakenness; yet, even God's absence and the ensuing darkness are forces hammering us to beaten gold on his anvil, working an alchemical transformation.

Moore suggests that words like "herds-long" and "steep" may have been drawn from Newman's sermon, "Neglect of

[25] Michael Moore, "Newman and the Motif of Intellectual Pain," pp. 29–46.
[26] Ibid., p. 42.

Divine Calls and Warnings," where Newman refers to the "herd of swine, falling headlong down the steep," an allusion to the New Testament cure of the Gerasene demoniac.[27] Hopkins himself comments on this miracle-story in his meditation notes from 1885, the year the poem was probably written: "The man did not kill himself," he says, "because the devils were not allowed to drive him to that" (*Sermons*, p. 259). If this poem conceals an almost secret reference to the demoniac's cure, and if Hopkins' comment is considered, then the ultimate ineffectuality of evil, even its being enfolded into the divine plan ("the devils were not allowed"), is part of this poem's meaning.

In "I wake and feel the fell of dark," darkness has become the palpable air of the poet's existence in place of the Blessed Mother's atmosphere. Ironically, the poet "wakes" to his inner world, a world of darkness. But even in darkness, he is contemplative: "with witness I speak this." The heart's visions, however, are now nightmares replacing the bright contemplations of earlier days and causing "heartburn." His own taste, which he had found "more distinctive than the taste of ale or alum" (*Sermons*, p. 123), is now "gall." His spirit is not open to the transforming Holy Spirit but his own "Selfyeast," creating a dull, soured dough. In the last nightmare vision of the poem he sees the damned in hell. Like Dante, he has moved into his own hell and acknowledged his own demons, a necessary yet temporary stage in the journey toward union with God. It is "God's most deep decree" (as in "not my will, but thine, be done," Luke 22:42) that the poet taste the bitter gall, Christ's drink on the cross, of self. Hopkins' identification with Christ does not alleviate personal suffering but can give it transcendent meaning.

In Poem 66, "To seem the stranger," increasing isolation from family and country only intensifies his deepest alienation—from "dark heaven"—and leaves him "a lonely began,"

---

[27] Ibid., pp. 41–42.

a person whose fresh starts are all in the past. Even Christ is "my peace/my parting, sword and strife," in the sense of that which divides him from familial ties (cf. Luke 12:51–53). The heart's wisest "word" (Christ) is banned by "dark heaven" or hell or both. Still, the heart hoards this word, keeps Christ, though it is "unheard" or "unheeded."

In representing the psychological, inward turn of Hopkins' life and poetry, the "terrible sonnets" perform a compensatory function in a poetic vision and corpus otherwise quite extroverted. Applying Carl Jung's theory on psychological types, one could describe Hopkins as extroverted, an outer-directed type for whom the object itself, not what is abstracted from it, has supreme value.[28] Although it may seem odd to consider such a reserved, often solitary poet as extroverted, Jung's description of the type seems relevant to Hopkins' behavior and to the psychology we may deduce from it: "his inner life is subordinated to external necessity, though not without a struggle; but it is always the objective determinant that wins in the end. . . . Not only people but things seize and rivet his attention."[29] The great poetry of Hopkins' Welsh years and beyond is rigorously objective and extroverted, looking outward to nature and other people. Even in his adherence to the demands of Jesuit spirituality, Hopkins was extroverted, sensing the divine in the world and in human beings, and conforming to the moral ideals of the order without a trace of reservation or rebellion. In fact, he chose a religious order whose highest virtue was obedience.[30] Through most of his life, the instress of inscape came from without. The "terrible sonnets," however, form a corrective to that pattern.

[28] Carl Jung, "Psychological Types," in *The Portable Jung*, ed. Joseph Campbell, trans. R.F.C. Hull (New York: Penguin Press, 1976), p. 179.

[29] Ibid., p. 183.

[30] See Ignatius' "Letter on Obedience" where he states that "with a true submission of our wills and abnegation of our judgments, those that serve God our Lord in this Society become outstanding." In *Powers of Imagining: Ignatius de Loyola*, trans. Antonio T. de Nicolas (Albany: State Univ. of New York Press, 1986), p. 303.

Along with his extroversion, Hopkins seems to have relied primarily on sensation rather than intuition as his characteristic way of taking in data from the objective world. The poems are full of visual, auditory, and other sensory experiences. Where intuition might discover the possibilities latent in actuality, sensation is content with the pure fact. Hopkins' distrust of imagination may have prevented greater reliance on intuition. His preference for sense experience over intuition seemed as deliberate as his extroverted over introverted direction. The consequence was his passion for reality. "No other human type," Jung tells us, "can equal the extroverted sensation type in realism."[31]

These explorations offer some explanation from a psychological standpoint of what happened to Hopkins from about 1885 to his death in 1889. From this standpoint, the poems generated during this period provide a counter-balance,[32] a theme Hopkins loved, to what went before. For during this period introversion overwhelms Hopkins' extroverted tendencies, while repressed intuitions begin to arise in place of outward sensation. Because intuition seeks out the possibilities of a situation, it is, according to Jung, "the auxiliary that automatically comes into play when no other function can find a way out of a hopelessly blocked situation."[33] Hopkins' lack of intuition as a dominant mode of experiencing the world may have accounted for a feeling of entrapment evident earlier in the poems such as "The Caged Skylark."[34]

The introverted, intuitive tendencies of these poems allow the poet to come face to face with his demons of despair, grief, and self-loathing, and in the process to begin to embrace even

---

[31] Jung, "Psychological Types," p. 217.

[32] *Correspondence*, p. 93.

[33] Jung, "Psychological Types," p. 222.

[34] See Donald Walhout's *Send My Roots Rain: A Study of Religious Experience in the Poetry of Gerard Manley Hopkins* (Athens: Ohio Univ. Press, 1981), chap. 2, a study of the phenomenology of "encagement" in Hopkins' religious experience.

these darkest aspects of the self. Hopkins is actually involved in an act of love of his greatest enemy—himself. Notes of self-acceptance are especially sounded in "Patience" and "My own heart let me more have pity on." Although these poems cannot be established to have been written at the end of the "terrible sonnets" series,[35] they still represent the self's gift of a reprieve from self-torment. And, oddly, as self-torment ends, so too does God's torment. In fact, God has been "patient," *suffering* the poet's agony himself. Both poems end looking toward not only a mastering but a merciful God, a God whose mastery and mercy are *both* acts of love. In them there is a breakthrough to the insight Hopkins had when he wrote on the "Contemplation for Obtaining Love," "all God gives or does for us He gives and does *in love*" (*Sermons*, p. 194). These poems tell us that the darkness of the "terrible sonnets" is lit, even if faintly, by God's smile (Poem 69). And God's honeycomb, the "crisp combs" (Poem 68) of the eucharistic feast, continues to feed the poet in his anguish.

In his recent study of Hopkins' "terrible sonnets," *Inspirations Unbidden*, Daniel Harris has pronounced these poems failures in that they no longer succeed in capturing the inscapes of nature and they "constitute failures in Ignatian meditation."[36] I agree with Harris that "Hopkins' deviation cannot be construed in aesthetic terms as a conscious effort at formal experimentation. . . . The deviation is chiefly theological, a sign of the extremity of Hopkins' crisis."[37] The presupposition of Harris' work, however, must be that Hopkins consciously intended to write structures of Ignatian meditation throughout his poetry and that he failed in that intention in writing the "terrible sonnets." No such express intention has been found in Hopkins' secular and spiritual writings. And no-

[35] See Harris, *Inspirations Unbidden*, chap. 1, on problems in dating and in sequencing the manuscripts.

[36] Ibid., chap. 2, "Nature and the Human Body: Altered Images," and chap. 3, "Ignatian Structure: Hopkins' Failures in Colloquy."

[37] Ibid., p. 80.

where does Hopkins state that he wished to end his poems with the colloquy that ends an Ignatian meditation. Harris particularly insists on these poems' failure to achieve colloquy: "the 'terrible sonnets,' lacking proper colloquy, were imperfect."[38] If, however, one applies Ignatius' own definition of colloquy—"thinking of what I should say to the three Divine Persons, or the eternal Word Incarnate, or to His Mother and our Lady, asking help according to the need that I feel within myself"[39]—these poems, even more than previous ones, embody direct and honest colloquies. In "Carrion Comfort," there is the question addressed to God the Father: "But ah, but O thou terrible, why wouldst thou rude on me/ Thy wring-world right foot rock?" In Poem 64, there are questions addressed to the Holy Spirit and to Mary: "Comforter, where, where is your comforting? / Mary, mother of us, where is your relief?" And, while colloquy is indirect in Poems 67–69, it is direct and sustained in Poem 74, which begins with Jeremiah's prayer, "Thou art indeed just, Lord, if I contend/ With thee; but sir, so what I plead is just." We should not expect Hopkins' colloquies to be pious and sentimental and to avoid the real issues. These poems could only have been failures if they had evaded coming to terms with Hopkins' inner truth. To continue to focus exclusively on external nature at a time of spiritual crisis would have constituted the real failure for Hopkins. That he proved willing to break with old patterns is a testimony to his courage, his honesty, and his earnestness with reality.

We have examined the "terrible sonnets" in aesthetic and psychological terms, but, to be true to the fullness of Hopkins' genius, it is necessary to see them theologically. For, whatever may be said to explain them in terms of structure or of the inner state of the poet's mind, these poems are about

[38] Ibid., p. 83.
[39] Ignatius, "Spiritual Exercises," in *Powers of Imagining*, trans. de Nicolas, p. 125.

God and about the poet's yearning for God. Hopkins' mature
work is dominated at beginning and end by poems describing
the intensity of his relationship with God. Such a relation es-
tablishes the framework of his nature poems.

The cross that Hopkins prays for and embraces in living
through the spiritual desolation of his last years symbolizes
not only antithesis between the crossed wills of God and hu-
man beings but also the love that bridges this infinite distance.
This love at the height of suffering is part of the great mystery
opened up by contemplation. Hopkins' continuing love for
God even in his pain makes of his cross a tree of life rather
than spiritual death. Simone Weil offers these insights into the
mystery of the cross: "This infinite distance between God and
God, this supreme tearing apart, this agony beyond all others,
this marvel of love, is the crucifixion. . . . Moreover, corre-
sponding to the infinite virtue of unification belonging to this
love, there is the infinite separation over which it triumphs,
which is the whole creation spread throughout the totality of
space and time, made of mechanically harsh matter interposed
between Christ and his Father."[40] Love, with its capacity to
unite the contraries of body and spirit, of self and world, of
world and God, is the great paradox, for in love there is both
union and separation. In early notes Hopkins had seen that
Plato pairs two such opposite things as dialectic and love and
that "love, like all affections or passions but more than the
rest, covers every unlike act, place, sight, sound or circum-
stance with one character" (Unpublished Oxford Notes,
D10), recognizing its capacity to overcome extreme differ-

---

[40] Simone Weil, *Waiting for God*, trans. Emma Craufurd. Intro. Leslie A.
Fiedler (New York: Harper Colophon Books, 1973), pp. 124 and 127. Com-
pare Hopkins' statement that "God's utterance of himself in himself is God
the Word, outside himself is this world. This world then is word, expression,
news of God. . . . The World, man, should after its own manner give God
being in return for the being he has given it or should give him back that being
he has given. This is done by the great sacrifice. To contribute then to that
sacrifice is the end for which man was made" (*Sermons*, p. 129).

ence.[41] Love is only possible when duality, not undifferentiated oneness, is preserved. Hopkins' Heraclitean moment of difference preserves this duality but does not resolve it. Love and the God of love, especially the Holy Spirit, is the great reconciler, and this love is attained, Hopkins and the Ignatian tradition knew, through contemplation. Hopkins' contemplation had brought him to identification with Christ in the cross's infinite separation and to its capacity for infinite healing—to love.

The "terrible sonnets" afforded Hopkins the possibility of sharing the fullness of union with Christ, even to the extent of the cross. Indeed, he spoke at this time of having his life "determined by the Incarnation down to most of the details of the day" (*Sermons*, p. 263). Christ, as incarnation of God in a human being, was both antithesis and reconciliation of antithesis. For Hopkins' theologian, Duns Scotus, the incarnation was not so much an atonement to an angry God but God's spontaneous act of love. In this life, however, Christ's sacrifice, the "Great Sacrifice" (*Sermons*, p. 197), prevails, just as antithesis prevails in Hopkins' poetry. Yet, both Christ's kenosis and the antitheses of Hopkins' poetry point beyond themselves to the paradox of reticent unity. Like Paul, Hopkins understood the great paradox of Christ's life—that God's "power is made perfect in weakness" (2 Cor. 12:9). He expresses this paradox of both Christ's and, implicitly, his own life in a letter to Canon Dixon: "Above all, Christ our Lord: his career was cut short and, whereas he would have wished to succeed by success—for it is insane to lay yourself out for failure . . . —nevertheless he was doomed to succeed by failure; his plans were baffled, his hopes dashed, and his work was done by being broken off undone."[42]

Hopkins in his own life may have appeared caught in the

[41] Compare Prov. 10:12, "Hatred stirs up strife/ but love covers all offenses."

[42] *Correspondence*, pp. 137–138.

dialectic of priestly and poetic vocations, of elective and affective wills, never quite reaching the point of living out a paradoxical existence. But Hopkins' movement toward the paradox of a truly religious and not merely dialectical vision of reality can be traced in the final poems. "That Nature is a Heraclitean Fire" is a poem of paradox as well as antithesis, for within the devouring fire of this poem the principle of redemption rises phoenix-like from the ashes. All the dark blotting out and threat of extinction of "Spelt from Sibyl's Leaves" are here, but now the true nature of destructiveness, the God-force at work within it, is revealed. In Hopkins' "Heraclitean Fire" the suffering of the "terrible sonnets" "falls, galls itself, and gashes gold-vermilion." But it has taken the mining motions of the "terrible sonnets" to unearth the "immortal diamond" from this "Jack, joke, poor potsherd." In his "immortal diamond," Hopkins has discovered an image that resonates throughout mystical literature, most notably in Teresa of Avila, who compares divinity to a very clear diamond symbolizing "how all things are seen in God and how He contains all things within Him."[43] Hopkins' "immortal diamond" therefore represents the breakthrough to the insight that all nature's million-fueled bonfire, along with his own pain and suffering, takes place within God.

The most important chiastic statement of Hopkins' poetry, unifying God and human beings in utter paradox, comes at the end of this poem: "I am all at once what Christ is,/ since he was what I am." Hopkins' subjective, first-person assertion represents a leap from his previously objective statements. *I* in my absurdity ("Jack, joke") and Job-like despair ("poor potsherd") am redeemed. Identification with Christ in his passion in the "terrible sonnets" sweeps this "poor Jackself" (Poem 69) into the Resurrection. If "Spelt from Sibyl's

[43] St. Teresa of Avila, *The Life of Saint Teresa*, trans. J. M. Cohen (Edinburgh: Penquin, 1957), pp. 309–310. Teresa uses the crystal castle as her primary image of God in the center of the self in her *Interior Castle*.

Leaves" represents the condition of a world where no one is in earnest with the reality of Christ and only opposition prevails, then "Heraclitean Fire" represents the quiet reconciling of those opposites effected by the Creator God at the heart of creation. Creation and Redemption emerge out of a desolation both cosmic and personal, revealing themselves inherent in the Sacrifice itself. Even fallen to an infinite distance, we find ourselves not unmade but newly created at the Creator's hands. The opposites, once wound in utter conflict "áll on twó spools," now "pair" (line 4). This nearly final poem in Hopkins' corpus wins through to a *coincidentia oppositorum*.

"That Nature is a Heraclitean Fire" restores balance between death and resurrection in the external world and creates an almost absurd union of opposites in Christ, healing the disrelations of "Spelt from Sibyl's Leaves." "St. Alphonsus Rodriguez" restores this balance in the inner world, healing the antitheses of the "terrible sonnets." Here the masculine virtues, the duty, courage, and discipline of the warrior, so prized by this follower of Ignatius, are complemented by the contemplative seeing and being, the more feminine virtues, of a saint who merely "Watched the door." Bereft of any usefulness in human terms, Alphonsus' life lays bare the contemplative value of being itself. The uselessness Hopkins could accept with his assent toward nature he now accepts in the self. The extroverted warrior and his duty have become the contemplative and his love. Antithesis between action and contemplation, masculine and feminine, becoming and being, reveals itself as polarity, opposites in relation, and ultimately as the union of those opposites. The "war within" issues in a calm conveyed even in the poem's untwisting of syntax and return to more parallelistic structure. Hopkins' final poem, "To R. B.," brings the fundamental male-female polarity into relation and therefore into potential union.

Thus, we see Hopkins at the end of his life envisioning that unity he had idealistically posited in his earliest Oxford essays. If he failed to achieve it in his life, it was not for lack of vision.

Contemplation, especially in the dark of the "terrible son-
nets," brings him not to the Parmenidean unity of monism but
to the threshold of a union of opposites in love. Nevertheless,
he had to enclose the negative as boldly as he did in the "ter-
rible sonnets" ' heart-wrenched prayers. In doing so, he indi-
rectly expresses the insight that these experiences too occupy
the unified sphere of God's love.

Christ is the model of effecting unity though being himself,
in Hopkins' phrase, "rhetorical antithesis." For as Hopkins
read in his Douay-Rheims version of Eph. 2:14–16: "For he is
our peace, who hath made both one . . . that he might make
the two in himself into one new man, making peace. And
might reconcile both to God in one body by the cross, killing
the enmities in himself." Whether Hopkins ever made "the
two in himself into one new man, making peace" is doubtful.
Yet, because he suffered those antitheses between idealism and
reality, between affective and elective wills, that "he too might
reconcile both to God in one body by the cross," we are im-
mensely the richer. For, as we encounter in contemplation the
antitheses he left us in his poems, our awareness of the reality
of crucifixion deepens, while their equally unexpected conver-
gences encourage the hope that Being draws-home to Being.

Bibliography

Works by Hopkins

The Poems of Gerard Manley Hopkins. Ed. W. H. Gardner and N. H. MacKenzie. 4th ed. London: Oxford Univ. Press, 1967.

The Journals and Papers of Gerard Manley Hopkins. Ed. Humphry House, completed by Graham Storey. London: Oxford Univ. Press, 1959.

The Letters of Gerard Manley Hopkins to Robert Bridges. Ed. Claude Colleer Abbott. London: Oxford Univ. Press, 1935.

The Correspondence of Gerard Manley Hopkins and Richard Watson Dixon. Ed. Claude Colleer Abbott. London: Oxford Univ. Press, 1935.

Further Letters of Gerard Manley Hopkins. Ed. Claude Colleer Abbott. 2d ed. London: Oxford Univ. Press, 1956.

The Sermons and Devotional Writings of Gerard Manley Hopkins. Ed. Christopher Devlin, S J. London: Oxford Univ. Press, 1959.

Unpublished Manuscripts, Hopkins' undergraduate Oxford essays and notes, are preserved at Campion Hall, Oxford University. Letters and numbers in parentheses following their citation in the text refer to the catalogue of these manuscripts listed in Appendix F of the *Journals.*

Books and Articles Consulted

Abrams, M. H. *The Mirror and the Lamp: Romantic Theory and the Critical Tradition.* New York: Oxford Univ. Press, 1958.

Albright, William Foxwell. *Yahweh and the Gods of Canaan*. New York: Doubleday and Co., 1968.

Alter, Robert. *The Art of Biblical Narrative*. New York: Basic Books, 1981.

Andreach, Robert J. *Studies in Structure: The Stages of the Spiritual Life in Four Modern Authors*. New York: Fordham Univ. Press, 1964.

Ap-Roberts, Ruth. "Old Testament Poetry: The Translatable Structure." *PMLA* 92 (1977): 987–1004.

Arnold, Matthew. *Isaiah of Jerusalem*, with an Introduction, Corrections, and Notes. London: Macmillan and Co., 1883.

———. *Literature and Dogma: An Essay Towards a Better Understanding of the Bible*. New York: Macmillan and Co., 1883.

Auerbach, Erich. *Mimesis: The Representation of Reality in Western Literature*. Trans. Willard R. Trask. Princeton: Princeton Univ. Press, 1953.

Baker, Aelred. "Parallelism: England's Contribution." *Catholic Biblical Quarterly* 35 (1973): 429–440.

Bender, Todd K. *Gerard Manley Hopkins: The Classical Background and Critical Reception of His Work*. Baltimore: Johns Hopkins Univ. Press, 1966.

Bischoff, Dolph Anthony. "Gerard Manley Hopkins as Literary Critic." Ph.D. diss., Yale University, 1952.

Blenkinsopp, J. "Ballad Style and Psalm Style in the Song of Deborah, A Discussion." *Biblia* 42 (1961): 61–76.

Bouyer, Louis. *Introduction to Spirituality*. Trans. Mary Perkins Ryan. Collegeville, Minn.: Liturgical Press, 1961.

Boyle, Robert R., S.J. "The Thought Structure of *The Wreck of the Deutschland*. "In *Immortal Diamond: Studies in Gerard Manley Hopkins*. Ed. Norman Weyand, S.J. New York: Sheed and Ward, 1949.

Brewer, R. F. *Orthometry: The Art of Versification and the Technicalities of Poetry*. Edinburgh: J. Grant, 1931.

Bridges, Robert. "Preface to Notes." *The Poems of Gerard Manley Hopkins*. 1st ed. London: Oxford Univ. Press, 1918.

Brockington, A. Allen. *Mysticism and Poetry*. London: Chapman and Hall, 1934.

Bruce, F. F. *The English Bible: A History of Translations*. London: Oxford Univ. Press, 1961.

Bump, Jerome. "Providence, 'The Wreck of the Deutschland,' and a New Hopkins Letter." *Renascence* 31 (Summer 1979): 195–204.

Chomsky, Noam. *Aspects of the Theory of Syntax.* Cambridge, Mass.: Harvard Univ. Press, 1965.

Christ, Carol T. *The Finer Optic: The Aesthetic of Particularity in Victorian Poetry.* New Haven: Yale Univ. Press, 1975.

Cochran, Leonard. "A World of Difference(s): Images of Instress in Hopkins' Poetry," *Hopkins Quarterly* 12 (October 1985–January 1986): 94–96.

Coleridge, Samuel Taylor. *Biographia Literaria.* 3 vols. 2d ed. London: William Pickering, 1847.

Cotter, James Finn. *Inscape: The Christology and Poetry of Gerard Manley Hopkins.* Pittsburgh: Univ. of Pittsburgh Press, 1972.

Coulson, John. *Religion and Imagination.* Oxford: Oxford Univ. Press, 1981.

Crossan, John Dominic. *The Dark Interval.* Niles, Ill.: Argus Communications, 1975.

Culley, Robert C. *Oral Formulaic Language in the Biblical Psalms.* Toronto: Univ. of Toronto Press, 1967.

Dallas, E. S. *Poetics: An Essay on Poetry.* London: Smith, Elder, 1852.

Davie, Donald. *Articulate Energy: An Inquiry into the Syntax of English Poetry.* London: Routledge and Paul, 1955.

DeLaura, David J. *Hebrew and Hellene in Victorian England.* Austin: Univ. of Texas Press, 1969.

De Man, Paul. *Interpretation: Theory and Practice.* Ed. Charles S. Singleton. Baltimore: Johns Hopkins Univ. Press, 1969.

Downes, David A. *Gerard Manley Hopkins: A Study of His Ignatian Spirit.* New York: Bookman Assoc., 1959.

Dunlap, Elizabeth. "Sound and Sense in 'Pied Beauty.'" *Hopkins Quarterly* 3 (April 1976): 35–38.

Duns Scotus on the Will and Morality. Selected and trans. with an Introduction by Allan B. Wolter, O.F.M. Washington, D.C.: Catholic Univ. of America Press, 1986.

Dyck, Joachim. *Athen und Jerusalem. Die Tradition der Argumentativen verknupfung von Bibel und Poesie im 17. und 18. Jahrhundert.* Munich: Beck, 1977.

Festugière, A. J. *Contemplation et Vie Contemplative selon Platon.* 3d ed. Paris: Librairie Philosophique J. Urin, 1967.

Fisch, Harold. *Jerusalem and Albion.* New York: Schocken Books, 1964.

Forbes, Rev. John. *The Symmetrical Structure of Scripture or the Principles of Scripture Parallelism Exemplified.* Edinburgh: T. and T. Clark, 1854.

Freedman, David Noel. "Psalm 29: A Structural Analysis." *Harvard Theological Review* 66 (1973): 237.

Frei, Hans W. *The Eclipse of Biblical Narrative.* New Haven: Yale Univ. Press, 1974.

Frye, Northrop. *Anatomy of Criticism.* Princeton: Princeton Univ. Press, 1957.

Gadamer, Hans-Georg, "Aesthetics and Hermeneutics." In *Philosophical Hermeneutics*, trans. David E. Linge. Berkeley: Univ. of California Press, 1976.

Gardner, W. H. *Gerard Manley Hopkins: A Study of Poetic Idiosyncrasy in Relation to Poetic Tradition.* 2 vols. New Haven: Yale Univ. Press, 1948.

Geller, Stephen A. *Parallelism in Early Biblical Poetry.* Harvard Semitic Monographs, ed. Frank M. Cross, Jr. Missoula, Mont.: Scholars Press, 1979.

Gerard Manley Hopkins by the Kenyon Critics [Contributions by Austin Warren, H. M. McLuhan, Harold Whitehall, Josephine Miles, Robert Lowell, Arthur Mizener, and F. R. Leavis]. London: D. Dobson, 1945.

Gevirtz, Stanley. *Patterns in the Early Poetry of Israel.* Studies in Ancient Oriental Civilization, No. 32. The Oriental Institute of the Univ. of Chicago. Chicago: Univ. of Chicago Press, 1963.

Gray, George Buchanan. *The Forms of Hebrew Poetry.* Prolegomenon by David Noel Freedman. Hoboken, N.J.: KTAV Publishing House, 1972.

————. *Isaiah.* 2 vols. Vol. 1. *International Critical Commentary*, Vol. 21. New York: Charles Scribner's Sons, 1912.

Gummere, Francis B. *A Handbook of Poetics.* Boston: Ginn, 1885.

Gunkel, Hermann. *What Remains of the Old Testament and Other Essays.* Trans. A. K. Dallas. London: G. Allen and Unwin, 1928.

Harries, Karsten. *The Meaning of Modern Art: A Philosophical Interpretation.* Evanston: Northwestern Univ. Press, 1968.

Harris, Daniel. *Inspirations Unbidden.* Berkeley: Univ. of California Press, 1982.

Hartman, Geoffrey. *Beyond Formalism: Literary Essays 1958–1970*. New Haven: Yale Univ. Press, 1970.

———, ed. *Hopkins: A Collection of Critical Essays*. Englewood Cliffs: Prentice-Hall, 1966.

———. *The Unmediated Vision*. New York: Harcourt, Brace, and World, 1966.

Heidegger, Martin. *Identity and Difference*. Trans. Joan Stambaugh. New York: Harper and Row, 1969.

Hegel, G.W.F. *On Art, Religion, Philosophy*. Ed. J. Glenn Gray. New York: Harper Torchbooks, 1970.

Herder, J. G. *The Spirit of Hebrew Poetry*. Trans. James Marsh. 2 vols. Burlington, Vt.: Edward Smith, 1833.

Heuser, Alan. *The Shaping Vision of Gerard Manley Hopkins*. New York: Oxford Univ. Press, 1958.

Holloway, Sister Marcella Marie. *The Prosodic Theory of Gerard Manley Hopkins*. Washington, D.C.: Catholic Univ. of America Press, 1947.

———. "Hopkins' Theory of 'Antithetical Parallelism.' " *Hopkins Quarterly* 1 (October 1974): 130–136.

Hunter, Jim. *Gerard Manley Hopkins*. London: Evans Bros., 1966.

Immortal Diamond: Studies in Gerard Manley Hopkins. Ed. Norman Weyand, S.J. New York: Sheed and Ward, 1949.

Inge, William Ralph. *The Philosophy of Plotinus*. Vol. 1. 3d ed. London: Longmans, Green, and Co., 1948.

Jakobson, Roman. "Grammatical Parallelism and Its Russian Facet." *Language* 42 (1966): 399–429.

———. "Linguistics and Poetics: A Closing Statement." In *Style in Language*, ed. Thomas A. Sebeok. Cambridge, Mass.: MIT Press, 1960.

———, and Morris Halle. *Fundamentals of Language*. The Hague: Mouton, 1971.

Johnston, William. *Silent Music: The Science of Meditation*. San Francisco: Harper and Row, 1976.

Keble, John. *Lectures on Poetry, 1832–1841*. Trans. Edward Kershaw Francis. 2 vols. Oxford: Oxford Univ. Press, 1912.

Kelly, Sidney. "Psalm 46: A Study in Imagery." *Journal of Biblical Literature* 89 (1970): 305–312.

Korg, Jacob. "Hopkins' Linguistic Deviations," *PMLA* 92 (1977): 977–996.

Kosmala, Hans. "Form and Structure in Ancient Hebrew Poetry." *Vetus Testamentum* 14 (1964): 423–445 and *Vetus Testamentum* 16 (1966): 152–180.

Kugel, James L. *The Idea of Biblical Poetry: Parallelism and Its History.* New Haven: Yale Univ. Press, 1981.

Kunkel, Francis L. "The Two Dominant Views of God in Modern Poetry." In *God in Contemporary Thought: A Philosophical Perspective,* ed. Sebastian A. Matczak. New York: Rose Sharon Press, 1977.

Kuper, Von Christoph. *Wälische Traditionen in der Dichtung von Gerard Manley Hopkins.* Bonn: Bouvier Verlag, 1973.

Lahey, G. F., S.J. *Gerard Manley Hopkins.* New York: Octagon Books, 1970.

Louth, Andrew. *The Origins of the Christian Mystical Tradition: From Plato to Denys.* Oxford: Clarendon Press, 1981.

Lowth, Robert. *Isaiah: A New Translation with a Preliminary Dissertation.* 10th ed. Boston: William Hilliard, 1834.

———. *Lectures on the Sacred Poetry of the Hebrews.* Trans. G. Gregory. 2 vols. London: J. Johnson, 1787.

Loyola, St. Ignatius. *The Spiritual Exercises of St. Ignatius.* Trans. Anthony Mottola. New York: Image Books, 1964.

———. *Powers of Imaginina.* Trans. Antonio T. de Nicolas. Albany: State Univ. of New York Press, 1986.

Ludwig, Hans-Werner. *Barbarous in Beauty: Studien zum Vers in Gerard Manley Hopkins' Sonetten.* Munich: W. Fink, 1972.

MacKenzie, Norman. "The Imperative Voice—An Unpublished Lecture by Hopkins." *Hopkins Quarterly* 2 (October 1975): 101–117.

———. *A Reader's Guide to Gerard Manley Hopkins.* Ithaca: Cornell Univ. Press, 1981.

Mariani, Paul L. *A Commentary on the Complete Poems of Gerard Manley Hopkins.* Ithaca: Cornell Univ. Press, 1970.

Maritain, Jacques. *Creative Intuition in Art and Poetry.* Cleveland: World Publishing Co., 1954.

Martin, Philip M. *Mastery and Mercy: A Study of Two Religious Poems.* London: Oxford Univ. Press, 1957.

Martz, Louis L. *The Poetry of Meditation.* New Haven: Yale Univ. Press, 1962.

May, Gerald G. *Will and Spirit: A Contemplative Psychology*. San Francisco: Harper and Row, 1982.

Miller, J. Hillis. *The Disappearance of God: Five Nineteenth-Century Writers*. Cambridge, Mass.: Harvard Univ. Press, 1976.

Moore, Michael D. "Newman and the Motif of Intellectual Pain in Hopkins' 'Terrible Sonnets,' " *Mosaic* 12 (1979): 29–46.

Mott, Marylou. *"Mined with a Motion": The Poetry of Gerard Manley Hopkins*. New Brunswick: Rutgers Univ. Press, 1984.

Moulton, Richard G. *The Literary Study of the Bible*. Boston: D. C. Heath, 1895.

New Catholic Encyclopedia. Prepared by an editorial staff at the Catholic Univ. of America. New York: McGraw-Hill, 1967–1979.

Newman, John Henry. *Essays Critical and Historical*. Vol. 1. 2d ed. London: Basil Montagu Pickering, 1872.

———. *Grammar of Assent*. New York: Image Books, 1955.

Newman, Louis I. *Parallelism in Amos*. Part 1 of *Studies in Biblical Parallelism*. Berkeley: Univ. of California Press, 1918.

Nowottny, Winifred. "Hopkins' Language of Prayer and Praise." *Hopkins Society Fourth Annual Lecture*. Univ. of London, March 5, 1973.

Ong, Walter J., S.J. *Hopkins, the Self, and God*. Toronto: Univ. of Toronto Press, 1986.

Pater, Walter. *Miscellaneous Studies*. London: Macmillan and Co., 1901.

Patmore, Coventry. "Essay on English Metrical Law." *Poems*. Vol. 2. London: George Bell and Son, 1886.

———. *Selected Poems of Coventry Patmore*. Ed. with an Introduction by Derek Patmore. London: Chatto and Windus, 1931.

Peters, W.A.M., S.J. *Gerard Manley Hopkins: A Critical Essay Towards the Understanding of His Poetry*. London: Oxford Univ. Press, 1948.

Pick, John. *Gerard Manley Hopkins: Priest and Poet*. 2d ed. New York: Oxford Univ. Press, 1966.

Plotinus. *Enneads*. Vol. 1. *On the Three Principal Hypostases*. A commentary with translation by Michael Atkinson. Oxford: Oxford Univ. Press, 1983.

Rahner, Hugo, S.J. *Ignatius the Theologian*. Trans. Michael Barry. New York: Herder and Herder, 1968.

Rahner, Hugo, S.J. *The Spirituality of St. Ignatius Loyola*. Trans. Francis John Smith, S.J. Westminster, Md.: Loyola Press, 1953.

Raine, Kathleen. "Hopkins: Nature and Human Nature." *Hopkins Society Third Annual Lecture*. Univ. of London, March 6, 1972. Reprinted by the Hopkins Society at the Stanbrook Abbey Press, Worcester.

Readings of the Wreck: Essays in Commemoration of the Centenary of G.M. Hopkins' The Wreck of the Deutschland. Ed. Peter Milward, S.J., and Raymond Schoder, S.J. Chicago: Loyola Univ. Press, 1976.

Ritz, Jean-Georges. *Le Poète Gérard Manley Hopkins, S.J.: L'Homme et Oeuvre poetique*. Paris: Didier, 1963.

Robertson, James. *The Poetry and the Religion of the Psalms*. Edinburgh: W. Blackwood and Sons, 1898.

Robinson, T. H. *The Poetry of the Old Testament*. London: Duckworth, 1947.

Roston, Murray. *Prophet and Poet: The Bible and the Growth of Romanticism*. Evanston: Northwestern Univ. Press, 1965.

Ruskin, John. *Modern Painters*. 5 vols. 2d ed. London: Smith, Elder, and Co., 1873; originally published 1843.

Sanders, Charles Richard. *Coleridge and the Broad Church Movement*. New York: Octagon Books, 1972.

Sands, P. C. *Literary Genius of the Old Testament*. Oxford: Oxford Univ. Press, 1926.

Schiller, Friedrich. *Naive and Sentimental Poetry and On the Sublime*. Trans. Julius A. Elias. New York: Frederick Ungar, 1966.

―――. *On the Aesthetic Education of Man*. Trans. Reginald Snell. New York: Frederick Ungar, 1965.

Schneidau, Herbert N. *Sacred Discontent: The Bible and Western Tradition*. Baton Rouge: Louisiana State Univ. Press, 1976.

Schneider, Elisabeth W. *The Dragon in the Gate: Studies in the Poetry of Gerard Manley Hopkins*. Berkeley: Univ. of California Press, 1968.

Schokel, Luis Alonso, S.J. *The Inspired Word*. Trans. Francis Martin, O.C.S.O. New York: Herder and Herder, 1965.

Simpson, D. C., ed. *The Psalmists*. Oxford: Oxford Univ. Press, 1926.

Smith, Barbara Herrnstein. *Poetic Closure: A Study of How Poems End.* Chicago: Univ. of Chicago Press, 1968.

Smith, George Adam. *The Early Poetry of Israel in its Physical and Social Origins.* London: Oxford Univ. Press, 1912.

Smith, Nathaniel B. *Figures of Repetition in the Old Provençal Lyric: A Study in the Style of the Troubadours.* Chapel Hill: Univ. of North Carolina Press, 1976.

Sprinker, Michael. *"A Counterpoint of Dissonance": The Aesthetics and Poetry of Gerard Manley Hopkins.* Baltimore: Johns Hopkins Univ. Press, 1980.

Sulloway, Alison G. *Gerard Manley Hopkins and the Victorian Temper.* London: Routledge and Kegan Paul, 1972.

————. "St. Ignatius Loyola and the Victorian Temper: Hopkins' Windhover as Symbol of 'Diabolic Gravity.' " *Hopkins Quarterly* 1 (April 1974): 43–51.

Tennyson, G. B. *Victorian Devotional Poetry: The Tractarian Mode.* Cambridge, Mass.: Harvard Univ. Press, 1981.

Thomas, Alfred, S.J. *Hopkins the Jesuit: The Years of Training.* London: Oxford Univ. Press, 1969.

Thompson, Paul. *William Butterfield Victorian Architect.* Cambridge, Mass.: MIT Press, 1971.

Underhill, Evelyn. *Mysticism.* New York: E. P. Dutton, 1961.

Von Balthasar, Hans Urs. *Prayer.* Trans. A. V. Littledale. New York: Paulist Press Deus Books, 1967.

Walhout, Donald. *Send My Roots Rain: A Study of Religious Experience in the Poetry of Gerard Manley Hopkins.* Athens: Ohio Univ. Press, 1981.

Walliser, Stephon. *That Nature is a Heraclitean Fire and of the Comfort of the Resurrection: A Case-Study in Gerard Manley Hopkins' Poetry.* The Cooper Monographs on English and American Language and Literature. Bern: Francke, 1977.

Warren, Alba H., Jr. *English Poetic Theory, 1825–1865.* Princeton: Princeton Univ. Press, 1950.

Weatherby, Harold L. *Cardinal Newman in His Age.* Nashville: Vanderbilt Univ. Press, 1973.

Wheelwright, Philip, ed. *The Presocratics.* New York: Odyssey Press, 1966.

Wimsatt, W. K. *The Prose Style of Samuel Johnson*. New Haven: Yale Univ. Press, 1941.

———. *The Verbal Icon*. Lexington: Univ. of Kentucky Press, 1954.

———. "Verbal Style: Logical and Counterlogical." *PMLA* 65 (1950): 5–20.

Wordsworth's Literary Criticism. Ed. Nowell C. Smith. London: Humphrey Milford, 1925.

Index

INDEX

nature, 8, 14, 17-19, 24, 28, 33, 55,
67, 78, 85-87, 89, 90, 96, 98, 105,
106, 108, 113, 115-117, 120, 123-
127, 129, 130, 133, 135, 138, 141,
151, 156, 158-160, 170, 171, 173,
174, 175, 182, 190, 206, 208-210,
212, 213
New Realism, 14
Newman, John Henry, 7, 76, 102,
115, 140, 154, 157-165, 204, 205;
Apologia, 159; *Grammar of Assent*,
154, 163; Newman's Edgbaston
Oratory, 7, 9, 131, 165
Newman, poetics: "Poetry, with
Reference to Aristotle's Poetics,"
140, 157
Nietzsche, Friedrich, 104
nominalism, 11

ode, 63
onomatopoeia, 5
ontology, 8, 10, 11, 13, 25, 29, 31,
54, 55, 107, 174, 190
Oriental style, 54
origin, 24, 26, 27, 34, 51, 73, 107,
109, 110, 189
Otto, Rudolf, 78; *The Idea of the
Holy*, 78
Oxford, 4, 7, 11-13, 16, 17, 42, 44,
47, 63, 102, 112, 124, 131, 134,
137, 154, 157, 161, 213

parallelism, 7, 8, 15, 16, 18, 19, 21,
23-29, 31, 35-40, 42-51, 54-69,
71, 73, 77, 78, 80-82, 84, 85, 87,
89, 92, 94, 96-98, 108, 109, 113,
114, 118, 119, 121-124, 126, 127,
129-131, 140-144, 167-171, 176,
181, 184, 198-200, 204; aesthetic,
98; and asymmetry, 31; and con-
templation, 64; and surprise, 30;
and the absolute, 15; antithetical,
46, 109; as inscape, 5, 8, 67, 98; as

instress, 31; as ontological princi-
ple, 54, 55; as order and disorder,
8; between poet and reader, 143,
144; cognitive, 98; in Hebrew po-
etry, 25, 26, 28, 36, 38, 47, 51,
109; in nature, 8, 18, 19, 55; of
antithesis, 89, 108, 169; of expres-
sion, 36, 43; of resemblance, 64,
108; of structure, 36, 43, 64; of
thought, 36, 63, 122, 130, 131,
168, 181; synonymous, 44; syn-
thetic, 46
parallelisms: of antithesis, 4, 29,
108, 168, 169; of resemblance, 4,
29, 64, 65, 108, 118, 129, 143,
167, 168, 169; of structure, 181; of
thought, 63, 64, 122, 130
parataxis, 28, 73, 74, 76, 110, 111,
140, 169, 200; paratactic struc-
ture, 83
Parmenides, 8-11, 14, 17, 18, 21,
24, 37, 75, 86, 88, 122, 126, 134,
153, 170, 188, 189
Parmenides essay, 122, 153, 188
Pater, Walter, 12, 13, 19, 23, 24, 27,
102
Patmore, Coventry, 16, 25, 39, 40,
86, 120, 161; "Essay on English
Metrical Law," 39
Pindar, 52
pitch, 75
Plato, 20; *Philebus*, 61; *Symposium*,
136; *Timaeus*, 20
Plato and Platonism, 9, 13, 14, 16,
20, 23, 24, 32, 60, 61, 100, 101-
103, 123, 132, 136, 137, 153, 174,
179, 194, 210
Plotinus, 60, 117, 132, 151
poetry: Hopkins' definition, 142
Pope, Alexander, 41
prayer, 153, 178
proportion, 23, 112; chronic kind
of, 23

·229·